THE PENGUI ~~~~~~ KRII READER

Mukunda Rao teaches English at Dr. Ambedkar Degree College, Bangalore. He is the author of *Confessions of a Sannyasi* (1988), *The Mahatma: A Novel* (1992), *The Death of an Activist* (1997), *Babasaheb Ambedkar: Trials with Truth* (2000), *Rama Revisited and Other Stories* (2002), *Chinnamani's World* (2003) and *The Other Side of Belief: Interpreting U.G. Krishnamurti* (2005). He lives with his wife and son in Bangalore. He can be contacted at mukunda53@gmail.com

The Penguin
U.G. Krishnamurti Reader

Edited by

MUKUNDA RAO

PENGUIN BOOKS

PENGUIN BOOKS
Published by the Penguin Group
Penguin Books India Pvt. Ltd, 11 Community Centre, Panchsheel Park, New Delhi
110 017, India
Penguin Group (USA) Inc., 375 Hudson Street, New York, New York 10014, USA
Penguin Group (Canada), 90 Eglinton Avenue East, Suite 700, Toronto, Ontario,
M4P 2Y3, Canada (a division of Pearson Penguin Canada Inc.)
Penguin Books Ltd, 80 Strand, London WC2R 0RL, England
Penguin Ireland, 25 St Stephen's Green, Dublin 2, Ireland (a division of Penguin
Books Ltd)
Penguin Group (Australia), 250 Camberwell Road, Camberwell, Victoria 3124,
Australia (a division of Pearson Australia Group Pty Ltd)
Penguin Group (NZ), 67 Apollo Drive, Rosedale, North Shore 0632, New Zealand
(a division of Pearson New Zealand Ltd)
Penguin Group (South Africa) (Pty) Ltd, 24 Sturdee Avenue, Rosebank, Johannesburg
2196, South Africa

Penguin Books Ltd, Registered Offices: 80 Strand, London WC2R 0RL, England

First published by Penguin Books India 2007

This anthology copyright © Penguin Books India 2007
Introduction copyright © Mukunda Rao 2007

All rights reserved
10 9 8 7 6 5 4 3 2 1

ISBN 9780143101024

Typeset in Bembo by Mantra Virtual Services, New Delhi
Printed at Repro India Ltd., Navi Mumbai

For

Valentine de Kerven

ACKNOWLEDGEMENTS

Over the past thirty-odd years several persons have worked selflessly and silently to record, transcribe and edit UG's conversations with people in different parts of the world. With his exceptional editorial skills and insights, JSRL Narayana Moorty has been the philosopher-guide in this great endeavour. Personally, I am deeply indebted to him. Also, I am indebted to K. Chandrasekhar and Dr Mundra for their continuous encouragement and support, and to Rodney Arms, Terry Newland, Ellen J. Chrystal, Mahesh Bhatt, Frank Noronha, Julie Thayer, Louis Brawley, Shanta Kelkar and Nagaraj, from whose works/books on UG I have drawn inspiration and borrowed freely and immensely to compose this book. My grateful thanks also to everyone at Penguin India, especially Ravi Singh and Paromita Mohanchandra, for their excellent work in producing the book so well.

CONTENTS

PREFACE

U.G. Krishnamurti, lovingly called UG by his friends and admirers all over the world, died on 22 March 2007, at 2.30 p.m., at the villa of friends, in Vallecrosia, Italy. A few days before the end, his long-time friend, the noted Indian filmmaker, Mahesh Bhatt, had asked, 'How should we dispose of your body?' In the same vein as he had spoken about death and the body over the years, UG replied, 'Life and death cannot be separated. When the breathing stops and what you call clinical death takes place, the body breaks itself into its constituent elements and that provides the basis for the continuity of life. So, nothing here is lost. In that sense there is no birth and no death for the body. The body is immortal.'

Seven weeks earlier, UG had fallen and this was the second such occurrence in two years. Although he did not suffer a fracture, he did not want such an incident to occur again which would make him further dependent on his friends. He refused medical or other external intervention. He decided to let his body take its own natural course. He was confined to a couch, surrounded by friends, and his consumption of food and water became infrequent and then ceased altogether. UG did not show the slightest signs of worry or fear about death or concern for his body even at the end of his life.

Mahesh Bhatt, along with the two American friends, Larry and Susan Morris, cremated the body in Vallecrosia. There was no chanting from the sacred texts, no death ceremony or funeral rites. Ten days before the end came, the large number of friends who had come from all over the world to see him had been advised by UG to return to where they lived. He had simply said, 'Thank you all. It's time to go.'

INTRODUCTION

The Search, the 'Calamity' and the Birth of a New Human Being: A Life Sketch Of U.G. Krishnamurti

◈══◉   ◉══◈

Two months before the completion of his forty-ninth year, UG and Valentine happened to be in Paris. J. Krishnamurti was also there, giving his public talks. One evening, friends suggested that they go and listen to JK's talk. Since the majority, including Valentine, was in favour of the idea, UG relented and joined them. But when they got there, and realized that they had to pay two francs each to get in, UG thought it was ridiculous to pay money to listen to a talk however profound or spiritual. Instead, he suggested, 'Let's do something foolish. Let's go to Casino de Paris.'

And to Casino de Paris they went. What happened to UG at the casino may sound stranger than fiction. Sitting with his friends and among the fun-lovers watching the cabaret, UG says: 'I didn't know whether the dancer was dancing on the stage or I was doing the dancing. There was a peculiar kind of movement inside of me. There was no division there. There was nobody who was looking at the dancer.' Eventually, after his thymus gland was fully activated, this was to become his everyday 'normal' experience; for instance, while travelling in a car, he would feel the oncoming car or any vehicle as if passing through his body.

A week after this experience, one night in a hotel room in Geneva, he had a dream. He saw himself bitten by a cobra and die instantly. He saw his body being carried on a bamboo stretcher and placed on a funeral pyre at some nameless cremation ground. And as the pyre and his own body went up in flames, he was awakened.

It was a prelude to his 'clinical death' on his forty-ninth birthday, and the beginning of the most incredible bodily changes and experiences that would catapult him into a state that is difficult to understand within the framework of our hitherto known mystical or enlightenment traditions. His experiences were not the blissful or transcendental experiences most mystics speak of, but a 'physical torture' triggered by an explosion of energy in his body that eventually left him in what he calls the 'natural state'.

For seven days, UG's body underwent tremendous changes. The whole chemistry of the body, including the five senses, was transformed. His eyes stopped blinking; his skin turned soft; and when he rubbed any part of his body with his palm it produced a sort of ash. He developed a female breast on his left-hand side. His senses started functioning independently and at their peak of sensitivity. And the thymus gland which, according to doctors is active throughout childhood and then becomes dormant at puberty, was reactivated. All the thoughts of man from time immemorial, all experiences, whether good or bad, blissful or miserable, terrific or terrible, mystical or commonplace, experienced by humanity from primordial times (the whole 'collective consciousness') were flushed out of his system, and on the seventh day, he 'died' but only to be reborn in 'undivided consciousness'. It was a terrific journey and a sudden great leap into the primordial state untouched by thought.

UG insists that this is not the state of a self-realized or god-realized man. It is not the 'Satori' of Zen Buddhism nor 'Brahmanubhava' of the Upanishads. It is neither 'emptiness' nor 'void'. It is simply a state of 'non-experience', but the inevitable sensations are still functioning. The reactivation of the thymus gland seems to enable him to 'feel' these sensations without translating or interpreting them as good or bad, for the interpreter, the self, 'I' doesn't exist.

UG says, 'People call me an "enlightened man"—I detest that term—they can't find any other word to describe the way I am functioning. At the same time, I point out that there is no such thing as enlightenment at all. I say that because all my life I've searched and wanted to be an enlightened man, and I discovered that there is no such thing as enlightenment at all, and so the question whether a particular person is enlightened or not doesn't arise....There is no power outside of man. Man has created God out of fear. So the problem is fear and not God.'

Further, he says, 'I am not a saviour of mankind. I am not in the holy business. I am only interested in describing this state (the natural state), in clearing away the occultation and mystification in which those people in the business have shrouded the whole thing. Maybe I can convince you not to waste a lot of time and energy looking for a state which does not exist except in your imagination.'

With his long, flowing silver-grey hair, deep-set eyes, Buddha-like long ears showing through his thinning hair, and fair complexion, UG looked a strange pigeon from another world. Speaking in non-technical language in a simple conversational style, informal and intimate, at times abusive, serene or explosive, his hands rising and moving in striking mudras, he carried the 'authority' of one who had literally seen it all.

★

Uppaluri Gopala Krishnamurti was born on 9 July 1918 in Masulipatnam, a small town in the state of Andhra Pradesh. His mother, who died seven days after he was born, is believed to have told her father, T.G. Krishnamurti, that her son was born with a high spiritual destiny. T.G. Krishnamurti was a prosperous lawyer and quite an influential person in the town of Gudivada. Taking his daughter's prophecy seriously, he gave up his lucrative career to bring up his grandson. He was a great believer in the theosophical movement and contributed huge sums of money for its various activities. The walls of his house were adorned with pictures of theosophical leaders, including one of Jiddu Krishnamurti, who was then looked upon as the 'World Teacher'. But this theosophist was also a firm believer in the Hindu Brahmincal tradition. He was a 'mixed-up man' in the words of UG. And so UG grew up in a peculiar milieu of both theosophy and Hindu religious beliefs and practices. Hindu gurus visited the house frequently and chanting and reading from the scriptures were held on a regular basis. There were days when readings from the Upanishads, Panchadasi, Naishkarmya Siddhi and other such religious texts would start in the early morning hours and go on until late in the evening. By the age of eight, UG knew some of these texts by heart.

With all this religious practice and exposure to theosophy at quite an early age, UG grew to be a passionate yet rebellious character. Brilliant and sensitive as he was, he could see through the games the elders played. They spoke of high ideals and principles, but their lives were in direct contradiction to what they spoke. One day, he saw his grandfather rush out of his meditation room in fury and thrash a two-year-old child because she was crying. The supposedly deeply religious grandfather's behaviour was quite upsetting to the young boy. Once, when he was hardly five years old, his grandfather, infuriated by his misbehaviour, had hit him with a belt. Livid with anger, the boy had grabbed the belt from his grandfather and hit him back, shouting, 'Who do you think you are? How can you beat me?' The grandfather never again dared to raise his hand against the boy.

A sense of disgust with religious rituals came early to UG. This happened when he was fourteen, during the death anniversary of his mother. He was in a rage at the hypocrisy of the priests who performed the rituals. He was expected to fast the whole day, as were also the Brahmin priests who performed the death memorial rituals. After a while into the chanting of mantras and rituals, UG saw a couple of priests get up and go out. Out of curiosity he followed them and noticed the priests, who were also expected to fast, sneak into a restaurant. Rushing back home, UG removed his sacred thread and threw it away, then went and announced to his grandfather that he was leaving home and needed some money.

'You are a minor. You cannot have the money,' replied the grandfather harshly.

'I don't want your money. I want my mother's money,' demanded the grandson.

'If you go on this way, I'll disown you,' the old man tried to scare the little boy.

The little boy, whose mind had grown much beyond the boys of his age, said coolly, 'You don't own me. So how can you disown me?'

If UG was difficult for his grandparents to handle, he was kind and affectionate to his school friends and servants at home. As a boy he detested the caste discrimination practised at home. He observed that the domestic workers, who came from the lower caste, were fed with the leftovers of the food cooked the previous day. When his protest against such a practice had no effect on his grandmother, he went and sat with the workers one mealtime and insisted upon being served the same cold food. He was also quite sensitive to the problems of those of his school friends who came from poor families. With the pocket money he received or the money he occasionally stole from his grandfather, he would pay their tuition fees, and at times, even buy them school textbooks and shoes.

Perhaps the grandparents put up with his eccentricities because they knew he was precocious and believed that he was destined for higher things. In fact, UG says that he used to be constantly reminded about his great spiritual destiny by his grandfather. It is quite possible that UG also took his mother's prediction quite seriously and looked upon himself as a great guru in the making.

When he was about fourteen years of age, a well-known Sankaracharya of the famous Sivaganga Math visited T.G. Krishnamurti's house. The young boy was quite fascinated by the pomp and glory that surrounded the pontiff, and the great reverence he commanded from his disciples and admirers. He decided he wanted to be like the pontiff when he grew up. He was ready to throw away all his little desires, quit his studies, bid goodbye to his grandparents and follow in the footsteps of the pontiff, and hopefully become the head of the famous Math. He even dared to express his wish to join the pontiff. The pontiff only smiled and politely turned down his request. He was too young for the hard life of a sannyasi, and leaving home at his tender age would only cause unnecessary unhappiness to his grandparents, he said. However, he gave UG a Shiva mantra. UG took the pontiff's advice seriously and chanted the mantra 3000 times everyday for the next seven years. Keen on achieving spiritual success and greatness, the boy chanted the mantra anywhere and everywhere, even in his classroom while the teacher chugged on with the lessons. What spiritual benefit the chanting had on him is not known, but it certainly did affect his studies and in the final exams of his SSLC, he failed in the Telugu language paper.

UG's grandmother, Durgamma, played as important a role as the grandfather in his upbringing, although she remains on the margins of UG's story. She was a woman of strong feelings, and made no secret of her likes and dislikes. She was illiterate, but a virtual repository of mythical stories and native intelligence. Giving an instance of it, UG says that it was from her he learnt the original or the etymological meaning of the concept of *maya* and other such Hindu concepts. But as a boy, it seems that he often used to be quite irritated and angry with her. He never called her 'grandma'. The more she pleaded with him to at least once call her 'Ammamma-Grandma', the more stubborn he would become and even refuse to speak to her. Exasperated, once she is believed to have said that he had 'the heart of a butcher'. True enough, one day he got so irritated with her begging and cajoling that he screamed at her, letting fly a string of abusive words in English he had picked up at school. A stunned grandfather later sighed thus with relief: 'Thank god she doesn't understand English!'

In the story of UG, it is the grandfather who stands out as an imposing, formidable figure, who had to be demolished and reduced to nothing. But, in point of fact, he was a man of great strength and determination. If he had not taken his daughter's prediction seriously, if he had not loved his grandson, he couldn't have abandoned his lucrative career and devoted himself to the upbringing of this little maverick. He threw open his house to holy people not merely for his own satisfaction or spiritual pleasure, but because he must have believed that an early exposure to things spiritual would have a positive effect on the boy. Further, he not only took UG along with him every time he visited the Theosophical Society at Adyar, he also took young UG to various holy places, ashrams and centres of learning in India. He was a wealthy man all right, but he was no miser and spent generously on his grandson. It was surely because of his encouragement and support that for seven summers, and a few more times in between, UG could travel to the Himalayas to learn classical yoga from the famous guru Swami Sivananda of Rishikesh. Ultimately the old man's efforts might not have led to the result he expected. That is a different matter. But, in hindsight, one can say that he did play an important role in the life of his grandson, in providing him with the necessary financial support and social security so that the young UG could pursue his interests without any encumbrance.

★

It is not through the study of religious texts, nor through contemplation, but through a series of 'shocks' that UG, as a young man, developed disgust for rituals and philosophies, and decided to strike out on his own and find things out for himself. The words or teachings of the religious masters he had met, including those of his grandfather, did not correspond with their actions. Their beliefs and philosophies did not operate in their lives. They all spoke well, but theirs were all empty words. Still, the boy wanted to test the validity or otherwise of these ideas and beliefs before rejecting them. He had to find out, to use UG's own words, 'by myself and for myself, if there was anything to these teachings.' Talking about that period and his own search and struggles, UG says quite candidly: 'I did not know how to go about, I did not know then that wanting to be free of everything was also a want, a desire.'

After UG completed his schooling in Gudivada, he moved to Madras so that he could pursue his higher studies without any bother. By then UG had developed a fairly cordial relationship with Arundale and Jinarajadasa, the then president and vice-president of the Theosophical Society, and had no difficulty in finding a place to live in the headquarters of the Theosophical Society. He lived there until his marriage in 1944.

UG took up a BA Honours course in philosophy and psychology at Madras University. But the study of the various philosophical systems and of Freud, Jung and Adler made very little impression on him. In fact, it didn't seem to have much bearing on the way he experienced life, or on the way he was 'functioning'. 'Where is this mind these chaps have been talking about?' he asked himself. One day, he asked his psychology teacher, 'We are talking about the mind all the time. Do you know for yourself what the mind is? All the stuff I know about the mind is from these books of Freud, Jung, Adler and so on that I have studied. Apart from these descriptions and definitions that are there in the books, do you know anything about the mind?' It was an extraordinary and original question from a boy hardly twenty years old. The professor was naturally taken aback and perhaps a little intimidated too; nevertheless, he is reported to have advised UG to take his exams and just write the answers he had been taught if he wanted a degree. 'At least he was honest,' recalls UG.

It was during this three-year degree course at the university that UG made several trips to Sivananda's ashram at Rishikesh, both to learn yoga and to perform his *tapas* in the caves there. There were several caves in Rishikesh. Spiritual seekers or *sadhaka*s would live in these caves to perform rigorous penance for years. UG had a little cave to himself, where, sitting cross-legged, he would meditate, at times, for ten to seventeen hours at a stretch. At that time, young though he was, UG experimented with his body by going without food or water for several days, pushing the body to the limits of its endurance. Once, he even tried to live on grass. This was the time he also came upon certain mystical states. These mystical experiences came and went, says UG, but deep within him there was no transformation; they did not touch the core of his being. It was indeed a period of great learning, excitement, and frustration too.

By then UG was in his twenties, a period of extreme restlessness and change. The study of philosophy and psychology had only added to his confusion and he had quit the university in great frustration. The training in yoga had left him high and dry. He had found that Swami Sivananda (eating hot pickles behind closed doors) was no different from several other yogis he had met. To make matters worse he became aware that he was in no way different from the others either. He had meditated and performed penance to no avail. He had come upon several mystical states, but to his horror he found himself still caught up in conflict, in greed. He found himself burning with anger all the time. And sex remained a nagging problem. UG's own description of his situation at the time is telling. 'I arrived at a point, when I was twenty-one, where I felt very strongly that all teachers—Buddha, Jesus, Sri Ramakrishna, everybody—kidded themselves, deluded themselves and deluded everybody. This, you see, could not be the thing at all—where is the state that these people talk about and describe? That description seems to have no relation to me, to the way I am functioning. Everybody says "Don't get angry"—I am angry all the time. I am full of brutal activities inside, so that is false. What these people are telling me I should be is something false, and because it is false it will falsify me. I don't want to live the life of a false person. I am greedy, and non-greed is what they are talking about. There is something wrong somewhere. This greed is something real, something natural to me; what they are talking about is unnatural. So, something is wrong somewhere. But I am not ready to change myself, to falsify myself, for the sake of being in a state of non-greed; my greed is a reality to me... I lived in the midst of people who talked of these things everlastingly—everybody was false, I can tell you. So, somehow, what you call "existentialist nausea" (I didn't use those words at the time, but now I happen to know these terms), revulsion against everything sacred and everything holy, crept into my system and threw everything out: No more slokas, no more religion, no more practices—there isn't anything there; but what is here is something natural. I am a brute, I am a monster, I am full of violence—this is reality. I am full of desire. Desirelessness, non-greed, non-anger—those things have no meaning to me; they are false, and they are not only false, they are falsifying me. So I said to myself I'm finished with the whole business.'

UG did not 'shop' around much, but, though briefly, he did shop around seriously. He was not only frustrated with swamijis such as Sivananda Saraswati, he was disgusted with himself too. His own sadhana and mystical experiences had led him nowhere. There seemed truly no way out and he became 'sceptical of everything, heretical to my boots'. Studying UG's cynical state of mind and his intense agony, his friend, Swami Ramanapadananda, suggested that he should go and see Sri Ramana Maharshi who was then considered to be an enlightened soul, and an embodiment of the Hindu mystical tradition.

UG was not sure if it would be of any help to him. He thought he was finished with holy men; they only said, 'Do more and more and you will get it.' He believed he had performed the required sadhana; whatever he had done was enough. In fact there was nothing to these sadhanas, for they left you only in greater conflict and confusion. He was finished. For he had realized that the solutions offered were no solutions, and that the solutions themselves were the problem. Still, on Ramanapadananda's suggestion, he read Paul Brunton's *Search in Secret India*, particularly the chapters related to Sri Ramana Maharshi. He was not convinced, yet, 'reluctantly, hesitatingly, unwillingly', he agreed to go and meet the great sage.

Devotees and truth-seekers believed that it was enough to sit there bathed in the enveloping silence, and feel the presence of the sage in one's heart. And now, UG sat there on the tiled floor and wondered: 'How can he help me?' Ramanapadananda had assured him that like hundreds of truth-seekers before, he too would experience a penetrating silence and all his questions would drop away, and a mere look from the Master would change him completely.

At last the sage looked up and their eyes met briefly. But nothing happened. The clock on the wall registered the passage of time. An hour had passed. The questions had remained and there was no sign of UG's distress coming to an end. Two hours passed, and then UG thought: 'All right, let me ask him some questions.' He wanted nothing less than the ultimate freedom, nothing less than moksha. But he asked, 'Is there anything like moksha?'

The sage answered in the affirmative.

'Can one be free sometimes and not free sometimes?'

'Either you are free, or you are not free at all.'

'Are there any levels to it?'

'No, no levels are possible, it is all one thing. Either you are there or not there at all.'

And then UG shot his final question. 'This thing called moksha, can you give it to me?'

Ramana answered with a counter-question: 'I can give it, but can you take it?'

No guru before had given such an answer. They had only advised him to do more of sadhana, more of what he had already done and finished with. But here was a guru, who was supposed to be an enlightened man, asking, 'Can you take it?'

The counter-question struck UG like a thunderbolt. It also seemed an extremely arrogant question. But UG's own arrogance was of Himalayan proportions: 'If there is any individual in this world who can take it, it is me.... If I can't take it, who else can take it?' Such was his frame of mind. However, the absolute conviction with which Ramana had fired the question at UG had its effect. He had asked more or less similar questions of many gurus during his seven years of sadhana, and he knew all the traditional answers. He had even stumbled upon certain mystical states, yet the questions had remained unanswered. What was that state that all those people—Buddha, Jesus and the whole gang— were in? Ramana was supposed to be in that state! But then Ramana was like any other man, born of woman, he couldn't be very different, could he? But people said that something had happened to him. What was that? What was there? He had to find out. And he knew in the very marrow of his bones, as it were, that nobody could give that state to him. 'I am on my own,' he told himself. 'I have to go on this uncharted sea without a compass, without a boat, with not even a raft to take me. I am going to find out for myself what that state is...'

★

The war years (1940s) were an extremely restless period for UG Krishnamurti. After quitting his BA Honours course at the Madras University, he was without a sense of direction. The meeting with Ramana had only deepened his anguish. The search, of course, did not end there, but he was going nowhere. The Theosophical Society seemed to be the way out, if only for want of a better option.

Even after leaving the university, UG continued to live in Adyar at the headquarters of the Theosophical Society. But now he worked as the press secretary to the president, Dr Arundale. He would read newspapers, magazines and journals that came to the library from all over the world and choose reports and articles of interest and importance to be read by Arundale later.

He was nearing twenty-five years of age. Sex had remained a nagging problem, yet he had not rushed into marriage. It was a natural biological urge, but most religious traditions taught one either to deny it or suppress it. Sex was seen as spiritually debilitating, and ultimately an obstacle on the path to moksha. UG, of course, did not believe in the denial of sex, although he had practised abstinence. He wanted to see what happened to the urge if he did not do anything about it. All this only made his situation more difficult, and he was troubled by guilt. He never consciously entertained any thoughts about girls, yet sexual images persisted. Meditation on gods and goddesses only gave him wet dreams. Study of holy books and avoidance of aphrodisiacs were of absolutely no help. The so-called mystical experiences he had had in the caves of Rishikesh had failed to dissolve the sexual urge in him.

It was time to stop fooling himself and reckon with the fact of sex, to come to terms with the body's urge which can never be false. And so, in 1943, he married a beautiful Brahmin girl chosen for him by his grandmother. The very next day after the wedding, however, he realized that he had blundered. In his words: 'I awoke the morning after my wedding night and knew without doubt that I had made the biggest mistake of my life.' But there was no way he could undo the mistake now. He remained married for seventeen years, and fathered four children.

After his marriage, UG moved out of the Theosophical Society headquarters and took a house on a street close to the Theosophical Society and Elliott Beach at Adyar. And he continued to work for the Theosophical Society. In 1946, Jinarajadasa was elected the president of the Theosophical Society, and for three years, UG worked under him as the joint secretary of the Indian section. Later, in recognition of his oratorical gift, he was made a national lecturer. For nearly seven years, he travelled extensively in India and Europe on lecture tours. He spoke on theosophy at practically every college and university in India. Then he went on a long tour to Europe and North America. Going through the lectures he gave in Europe and India, one is surprised to see how a man who was so thoroughly frustrated with his own religious search and experiences, who had grown cynical of all religious endeavours and goals, adapted himself to the philosophy and activities of the Theosophical Society. Did he really take up this work for want of a 'better occupation', as he had said once? Was it like his marriage, with no heart in what he was doing? Was it all inevitable that he had to go through the whole process, that there was very little to choose from, or that it really did not matter one way or another?

However, at the end of the seventh year as a lecturer of theosophy, he grew frustrated with the work. It seemed to him that what he had been doling out in his lecture was just 'second-hand information'. Anybody with some brains could do this work. It was not something true to his experience, true to his real self. And he quit the Theosophical Society.

UG's leaving coincided with J. Krishnamurti's visit to India to give his first talk after the war years, at Adyar. By his own admission, UG listened to JK's talks between 1947 and 1953. And from 1953, UG interacted with JK at a personal level, holding long conversations with him on several occasions. During that time, JK also met UG's wife and their children, and took a particular interest in the health of UG's eldest son, Vasant, who had been struck with polio.

JK was fifty-eight years old then, and UG running thirty-five. The relationship between UG and Krishnaji cannot exactly be categorized as one between a guru and a disciple, nor as one between two antagonists or rival gurus. But what comes through is that right from the beginning UG seemed to have had problems with JK's image as the World Teacher and his teachings. Often UG would react critically, harshly and scathingly against Krishnaji, exploding with fury like the mythical Shiva in a state of wrath, while Krishnaji would always behave like an English gentleman. But there is no denying the fact that Krishnaji and his teaching had had a great impact on UG, even if, gradually and progressively, he was to reject it all at the end.

Yet, every year for seven years, UG listened to Krishnaji, despite his doubts and troubles with Krishnaji's ideas and 'insights'. There really was something to JK's teachings, yet he felt that they were somehow not true to his own experience, that they were falsifying him. But he was not sure of himself; he was not certain yet if what he had come upon by and for himself was true either. He lacked clarity and conviction; also, there were too many doubts and questions, all of which were to dissolve and disappear in the heat of the explosive experience, or what UG would call the 'calamity', in 1967.

In 1953, UG planned to go to the USA to get medical treatment for his son, Vasant. On hearing about it, JK offered to try his hand at curing Vasant. On a few occasions, JK had had used his healing hands and is believed to have cured people of what were then considered to be almost incurable ailments. UG was sceptical, and he warned, 'I did hear a lot about your healing work. It doesn't work in this case. The cells in the boy's legs are dead.' Yet, in deference to his wife's wishes, he relented. But JK's healing technique of massaging the boy's legs did not improve the boy's condition. After the experiment failed, UG left for America with his wife and son in 1955, leaving behind their two daughters in the care of Kusuma Kumari's elder sister.

It was indeed, both politically and culturally, an interesting period to be in America. But to UG, America was like a transit camp, a sort of preparatory ground before stripping himself of everything and going adrift in Europe. Meanwhile he tried to be a good father and make himself useful.

The money he had taken with him to the USA was just enough to meet the expenses of his son's medical treatment. But it was worth it, thought UG, for his son couldn't have received better treatment anywhere else. The doctors assured him that Vasant would be able to walk in a year's time. It meant they had to stay in the USA for another year, perhaps longer; so, with his resources diminishing fast, UG had to do something to earn some money. He took up what he was best at— lecturing. Unlike in India where his lectures had been for free, here he was paid one hundred dollars per lecture. He now even had a manager to arrange his lectures.

Vasant's condition did improve considerably with the medical treatment, and he was able to walk, dragging his diseased foot, without using crutches. UG continued to lecture in different parts of America, including four notable lectures on the major religions of the world, at the University of St Louis in Washington state.

On UG's home front at that time, however, there was no major change. His relationship with his wife was as good as it could be between the likes of him and Kusuma Kumari. With all his eccentricities and his spiritual quest, UG was not a bad husband and father. Kusuma Kumari, of course, always remained a devoted wife and mother. The only major problem that erupted now and then in the family was regarding money. UG was never good at managing his financial affairs or in handling money.

He gave around sixty lectures a year and at the end of the second year, he not only felt exhausted but also quite depressed with the whole lecturing business. Two incidents stand out during this period. A couple of days after his lecture on 'The Meaning and Mystery of Pain', he was laid up with mumps. The discomfort was quite unbearable and the pain almost too excruciating, yet he refused to see a doctor. As always he was overcome by a terrific curiosity to see into the structure of pain, as it were; after all, just a couple of days ago, he had given a lecture on the meaning and mystery of pain. This sort of curiosity would again and again drive him to probe and experiment with himself to find things out for himself, the same curiosity that had years ago made him eat grass during his tapas in the caves of Rishikesh, if only to find out whether he could survive on it. The pain, however, became unbearable and he lost consciousness. The story goes that he was rushed to a nearby hospital, but the doctors were not too sure as to the type of treatment he required. He lay there on the hospital bed, his body turning cold, and it seemed he was on the verge of death. Half an hour passed, and then suddenly he regained consciousness. He felt no pain or discomfort now; the body had cured itself of the illness!

A year after this, he began to lose interest in lecturing and began to wonder if there could be some other way of earning his livelihood. His manager, Erma, was shocked. He had become a celebrity of sorts and was in demand everywhere, and there was of course good money to take home after every lecture. But UG refused; suddenly, he no longer had the will to work.

Now the onus of earning money for the family fell on Kusuma Kumari. Since she had degrees both in English and Sanskrit, she found a job as a research assistant with the *World Book Encyclopaedia*. At the time Kusuma Kumari was pregnant with their fourth child, and she was not exactly happy about going out to work for a living. But there was no choice. Her initial fascination with the American lifestyle was gone. In fact, coming from a traditional Indian background, despite her degree in English, she found it difficult to relate to Americans, who to her seemed distant, queer and somewhat intimidating. Now, working with them only added to her misery. Yet, she carried on stoically, and sometimes she would bring her work home. She was required to make notes and answer queries on several aspects of Indian cultural and religious practices. UG, although not a 'good husband' in a traditional way, did help her out in her research work, reading the necessary books and answering these queries for her.

UG now stayed home, attending to the household chores and the needs of their handicapped son, Vasant. Friends would drop in at UG's place and hold discussions with him for hours on theosophy and Indian philosophy. After the birth of their fourth child, Kumar (1958), when Kusuma Kumari resumed work, UG did the babysitting.

After working for about two years, Kusuma Kumari quit her job in frustration and decided to leave America. The thought of her two daughters, who had been left in the care of her elder sister in India, troubled her all the time. And now, with her fourth child growing up in an 'alien country', without the benefit of the love and care of the elders and family members, and with no big change in the condition of Vasant, she worried about the future of her two sons. And to make matters worse, her husband was no longer the man she was married to seventeen years ago. He had changed and changed drastically and now he lived like a stranger at home.

The inevitable happened at the end of the year 1959. Kusuma Kumari decided to leave America with her two sons, even if it meant leaving without her husband. Her imploring that he too must return with them to India had no impact on UG. He bought her the tickets and handed over all of the money that was left with him. Kusuma Kumari and her two sons flew to Madras, and then, somewhere on the way to Pulla, in the train, she lost the box that contained UG's books, documents and almost all the letters he had received from important people. It was as if all of UG's past was being systematically erased, and his return made impossible.

Now, with his wife gone back to India, if UG wanted to stay on in the country, he needed sponsorship. The problem was solved when the World University offered him a job. He had been recognized not only as a brilliant speaker, but also as one with a brilliant and well-informed mind. His talents were found to be useful by the university which had planned to open hostels for its students in several parts of the world. UG had no choice; he accepted the offer and made his first trip to India.

When UG first came to Madras to 'wind up' his 'show' at Adyar, Kusuma Kumari met him and tried to persuade him to join the family. It was to be UG's last meeting with his wife. She had brought all her children with the hope that UG would, at least for the sake of his children, change his mind. But he was hard as stone; there was no going back. He was finished with his past.

A month later, UG went to Russia, and from there flew to some of the Central European countries he had not visited before. It seems he was getting fed up with his work, and visited various cities in Central Europe, not to do 'business', but as a tourist, as one eager to touch and know every important place on the world map. Actually, he had begun to drift. And when finally he landed in London, he was almost finished!

In London, UG began to aimlessly wander about like one who had lost his head. Some describe UG's phase in London as 'the dark night of the soul'. UG disagrees, and most vehemently says that there was 'no heroic struggle with temptation and worldliness, no soul-wrestling with urges, no poetic climaxes, but just a simple withering away of the will'.

His 'will' beginning to crack, when UG arrived in England, the winter had set in. With whatever money he had been left with he managed to find a place in Kedagin Square Apartments on Knight Bridge Road. During the day, to escape from the shivering cold and the boredom of staring at the four walls of his room, he would slip into the British Museum and spend the whole day sitting at the table next to the one where Marx had done his research for *Das Kapital*. UG was, of course, not interested in doing any research or reading books. He had in fact stopped reading books on philosophy and religion some years ago. Yet, to pretend that he was there to read something, he would pick up a thesaurus of 'Underground Slang' and immerse himself in it for several hours. In the evenings, he would aimlessly wander the streets of London, reading signboards and the names and telephone numbers of the London call girls written or pasted on the walls, on telephone booths and even on trees.

Winter receded; the air grew warm and the day bright. The summer began and suddenly London had come alive. But nothing helped UG. Nothing changed. To make things worse he was running out of money. Still, if only to somehow keep himself going, he had to do something. So, whenever an opportunity came his way, he started doing palm-reading for the immigrants (mostly from India and Pakistan), and at times, even giving cooking lessons for a fee. He could have, of course, managed to live on 'the unemployment dole', but he didn't. It was a desperate situation. And he couldn't help asking himself why he had become 'a bum living on the charity of people'. It was quite insane! But he seemed to lack the will even to think of an alternative. He just let himself be blown like a leaf 'here, there and everywhere'.

It was around this time that his wife died in India, the news of which reached UG almost six months late. There was nothing he could do except write to his children expressing his sympathy over the irreparable loss of their mother.

And he drifted along, seeing and not seeing, hearing and not hearing, almost like one who had lost his head. At times, he felt tired, but no hunger. And one day, he realized he had only five pence left in his pocket. He was finished. There was no place to go and there seemed nothing he could do. But, as his luck would have it, help came to him in the form of Swami Ghanananda, the head of the Ramakrishna Mission in London. It was during this time certain changes began to appear in UG's body. In 1953, he had brushed aside the mystical experiences he had undergone in the caves of Rishikesh and his 'near-death experience' at Adyar as of no great consequence. But now, it seems that all these experiences were to converge and build up as it were, and steadily begin to alter his being. From the traditional Hindu perspective it may be interpreted as the awakening of Kundalini energy, the 'serpent power'. One day, while sitting in the meditation room of the Ramakrishna mission, he came upon the following experience. It was only the beginning. In his own words:

I was sitting doing nothing, looking at all those people, pitying them. These people are meditating. Why do they want to go in for *samadhi*? They are not going to get anything—have been through all that—they are kidding themselves. What can I do to save them from wasting all their lives, doing all that kind of thing? It is not going to lead them anywhere. I was sitting there and in my mind there was nothing—there was only blankness—when I felt something very strange: there was some kind of movement inside of my body. Some energy was coming up from the penis and out through the head, as if there was a hole. It was moving in circles in a clockwise direction and then in a counter clockwise direction. It was like the Wills cigarette advertisement at the airport. It was such a funny thing for me. But I didn't relate it to anything at all. I was a finished man. Somebody was feeding me, somebody was taking care of me, there was no thought of the morrow. Yet inside of me something was happening....

Indeed, the 'new man' was in the making, it was as if he was programmed for it from birth, or some mysterious force was slowly but surely leading him to it. But it was not going to be what he had imagined or thought it would be like. And that is the most mind-boggling, most enigmatic, part of his story.

In any case, his stay in London was over. He quit Ramakrishna Mission, moved on and landed up in Paris. He turned in his airline ticket to India and made a handy 350 dollars. For another three months he let his hair down and stayed at a hotel in Paris. And as he had done before in London, he wandered the streets of Paris and lived on varieties of French cheese, a habit that continued throughout his life, though in very small quantities in later years.

And again, as it happened in London, at the end of three months he ran out of money. There were no immigrants from India here for him to give cooking lessons to and make some money on the side, and no friends to approach for help either. However, with whatever little money he could scrape up, UG took a chance and reached Geneva. Again, like an amnesaic, he took a room in a hotel, and started wandering about.

Two weeks passed and yet again he found himself without money even to buy his meals, let alone pay the hotel bills. He had reached the end of his tether and there seemed no way out except going to the Indian consulate and requesting the authorities there to send him back to India.

Fortunately, he still had his scrapbook with him which saved him from being thrown out of the consulate. Reading through the praises heaped on UG by the American press, which included the high opinions of the notable Norman Cousins, and Dr S. Radhakrishnan, who was at the time the Indian ambassador to Russia, the vice-consul was quite impressed. But he was helpless, since UG could not be flown back to India at the expense of the government. The only alternative was for UG to write to his people in India and get some money. At that time, the head of Sri Ramakrishna Mission in Geneva, Swami Nityabodhananda, happened to be there in the vice-consul's chamber. The swamiji straightaway offered UG 400 francs to clear all his bills, and then turning to the vice-consul, he advised him not to treat UG as an ordinary person and to see what best he could do to help him. It seems the 'inscrutable power of Sri Ramakrishna' had yet again come to the rescue of UG.

Among the staff of the consulate was a rather unusual woman, Valentine de Kerven. She was sixty-three years old then and UG was seventeen years younger than she. Something about UG touched a deep chord in her. Talking to him a little later, her impulse or sudden resolve to help this strange man from India only grew stronger; she told UG that she could arrange for his stay in Switzerland, and if he really didn't want to go back to India, he shouldn't. For UG it was like a new lease of life and he accepted the offer without a second thought. In point of fact, there was no choice and UG let himself flow with the tide.

A few months later, Valentine gave up her job and the two lived like friends who had been separated for ages but were now reunited on the cusp of a new age. The pension Valentine received was not large but was sufficient to take care of their household expenses and travel. Upon UG's suggestion, she sold almost all her jewellery and antique art pieces she had collected over the years and put the money in the bank. Later, Valentine also set up a separate fund for UG's travels.

Valentine took care of UG, but had no idea of what was to come. The next four years were relatively calm. With all the time in the world and no pressing tasks to attend to, UG and Valentine went travelling outside Geneva. For UG, the search had nearly come to an end. He ate, slept, read *Time* magazine, occasionally travelled, and went for long walks either alone or with Valentine. It was what may be called the period of 'incubation'. The body was preparing itself for the 'metamorphosis' that would challenge the very foundation of human thought built over centuries.

Though all his search for truth, for moksha, was at an end and he was not seeking anything spiritual or mystical, strange, 'funny' things had started happening to him. If he rubbed his palms or any part of his body, there was a sparkle, like a phosphorous glow. And when he rolled on his bed with unbearable pain in his head, again there would be sparks. It was electricity. The body had become an electromagnetic field. And he started suffering from constant headaches or from what he calls 'terrible pain in the brain'. But UG did not discuss what was happening to him with Valentine. However, with all these physical changes and bouts of severe headaches that went on for over three years, UG began to appear much younger than his age. In photographs of him taken at that time, he truly looks like a young man of eighteen or twenty. But this was to change and he would start ageing after the completion of his forty-ninth birthday.

Every summer JK came to Saanen to hold his talks and discussions. With the exception of a few occasions when UG was dragged to these talks by his friends, UG kept a respectful distance from JK and his admirers. But then it so happened that almost every evening, inquisitive seekers would drop in at the chalet (where UG was living) to chat with UG. The chat would invariably turn into a fierce conversation on spiritual matters and UG would debunk the many spiritual concepts thrown at him and generally tear apart JK's teachings. And then gradually even Krishnamurtiites started to drop in on UG; if some came out of sheer curiosity to see who the 'other Krishnamurti' was, the others came either to clarify their doubts or challenge UG with ideas gleaned from JK's talks. This was to become a pattern every summer. Even JK's close associates would sometimes amble into the chalet, if only to quench their curiosity, among them Madame Scaravelli and David Bohm. Some, after extended conversations with UG, were to turn their backs on JK and become UG's close friends.

With all this, ironic and even mysterious as it may seem, on 13 August 1967, UG was dragged to listen to JK's last talk of the summer. UG sat there, under the huge tent, listening and not listening. At some point JK started saying: '... in that silence there is no mind; there is action...'

Stunned, UG listened, and suddenly it all seemed funny. JK was actually describing *his* state of being! How could that be? But it was true. So, 'I am in that state!' UG thought to himself. If that was so, then what the hell had he been doing all these thirty-odd years, listening to all these people, struggling, wanting to attain the state of Jesus, of Buddha, when in fact he had already been there! 'So I am in that state'; the self-assertion, along with a sense of huge wonder, continued for a while. And then it suddenly seemed ridiculous to sit there listening to JK's description of *his* state of being. He got up and walked out of the tent. But he was not finished. He was in that state, certainly—state of the Buddha and all the enlightened masters. But what exactly was that state? The next moment the question transformed itself into yet another question: 'How do I know that I am in that state?' The question burned through him like a maddening fury. 'How do I know I am in that state of the Buddha, the state I very much wanted and demanded from everybody? How do I know?'

The next day, still consumed by the question burning through his whole body as it were, he sat on a little wooden bench under a wild chestnut tree overlooking Saanenland with its seven hills and seven valleys bathed in blue light. The question persisted; the whole of his being was possessed by that single question: 'How do I know?' In other words, he had become the question. And it went on thus: 'How do I know that I am in that state? There is some kind of peculiar division inside of me: there is somebody who knows that he is in that state. The knowledge of that state—what I have read, what I have experienced, what they have talked about—it is this knowledge that is looking at that state, so it is only this knowledge that has projected that state. I said to myself: "Look here, old chap, after forty years you have not moved one step; you are there in square number one. It is the same knowledge that projected that state there when you asked this question. You are in the same situation asking the same question, *how do I know*? Because it is this knowledge, the description of the state by those people, that has created this state for you. You are kidding yourself. You are a damned fool." But still there was some kind of a peculiar feeling that this was the state. And yet again the question "How do I know that this is the state?"—I didn't have any answer for that question—it was like a question in a whirlpool—it went on and on and on...'

Then suddenly the question disappeared. He was finished truly and wholly. It was not emptiness, it was not blankness, it was not the void of Buddhism, and it was not the state that all the enlightened persons were supposed to be in. The question just disappeared.

The disappearance of the question marked the extinction of thought—thought crystallized and strengthened over centuries by cultures and religions. The 'I' linking up the thoughts, 'the psychic coordinator collating, comparing and matching all the sensory input so that it could use the body and its relation for its own separative continuity' was suddenly gone. Now, the link broken, the continuity of thought snapped, exploded, releasing tremendous energy: repairing, cleansing, invigorating, cathartic...

UG deliberately calls it a *Calamity* for he doesn't want people, particularly the religious kind, to interpret it as something blissful, full of beatitude, love, ecstasy, or even as 'Enlightenment'. No. It is physical, physiological; a torture. It is a calamity from that point of view.

For the next seven days, seven bewildering changes took place and catapulted him into what he calls the 'Natural State'. It took another six months for the whole painful process to disappear altogether.

It was a cellular revolution, a full-scale biological mutation. It was the birth of the 'individual' in the natural state.

★

Towards the end of 1967, UG visited Sringeri in Karnataka and happened to meet the Sankaracharya of Sringeri. Upon hearing of the bewildering physical changes come upon UG, the Sankaracharya, Sri Abhinava Vidya Tirtha Swami, had no doubt that UG was a *jivanmukta* and he is believed to have said, 'I don't know of these things in my own personal experience.... It is very rare that the body survives the shock of such a thoughtless state. According to the scriptures, within three days or seventy-two hours after such an event the body dies. If the body could sustain its vital force and not die off, it must surely be for the sake of saving humanity.'

UG did not think he was a saviour. What had happened to him was not something he had sought, and it had happened despite all his search and sadhana. Now he just wished to stay put in some quiet place and let things be. The peaceful environs of Sringeri, on the banks of the Tunga River, seemed an appropriate place for him to retire. He listened silently to the swamiji for some time and then quietly broached the subject of his retirement. The Sankaracharya is reported to have said, 'I will be responsible for getting you any place around here, if you so wish. But your idea of living alone will never work. Whether you stay in a jungle or in a mountain cave, people won't stop coming to see you.'

It was truly said. One could not hide a sun, nor could the sun choose to go incognito. UG abandoned his resolve to stay away from people. But the question remained: 'What is there to say after a thing like this?' Days passed, and then suddenly it occurred to him:

'I will say it exactly the way it is.'

UG gave his first public talk at the Indian Institute of World Culture in Bangalore, in the month of May 1972. He never again gave any public talk, nor would he accept invitations to speak at universities or institutions. But he could not stop people from meeting and talking to him. He responded to their queries and answered their questions in the way only he could. During his lifetime, UG travelled to practically every country in the world. And this man with 'no message', 'no teaching' probably met and talked to more people than can be counted.

UG usually stayed with friends or in small rented apartments, but never in one place for more than six months. He gave no lectures or discourses. He had no organization, no office, no secretary, and no fixed address. Despite his endless repetition that he had 'no message for mankind', ironically, yet also naturally, thousands of people the world over felt otherwise and flocked to see and listen to his 'anti-teaching'. The 'shop' was kept open from early morning to late evening for people to feel free to come without any prior appointment, and feel free to go whenever they wanted. 'This is how it should be. There should be no special duration, prior appointment, and such,' UG said, and his hosts everywhere maintained the rule without fail.

Wherever he went and stayed, people met him in increasing numbers. There was absolutely no restriction. People could walk in and walk out as in a shopping mall. But there were no wares sold in this shop. People were of course welcome to ask him questions, even questions they dare not ask their parents, their spouses or their intimate friends, let alone their gurus and intellectuals. 'Why do you speak? Where do you get money to travel so much? What do you mean you are neither man nor woman? What is there in your pyjamas? What is love? Do you have sexual urges? Do you have dreams? Why do you criticize and condemn the spiritual gurus? What is moksha? Aren't you an enlightened man? What is your teaching? Do you have a message?' And so on and on. And he answered them all in the way only he could, and in his own inimitable style.

He didn't preach, for there was nothing to preach, nothing there to be changed. The questions thrown at him were often shot down. It was like skeet shooting. As Jeffrey Masson (the author of *Final Analysis: The Making and Unmaking of a Psychoanalyst* and several other popular works) rightly puts it, '...everything he says or does is the mirror-image of what a traditional guru does, in reverse.' He discouraged you from touching his feet, he questioned, subverted and laughed at your so-called spiritual sadhanas, your great ideals, if you had any, and used every trick possible to stop you speaking further and going back to him again. If you found him rude, insulting and blasphemous and felt hurt, then you were lost, you had entirely missed the 'point', and missed the man. You went to him not to 'receive' but to lose, to drop your heavy baggage of ideas, to free yourself from, if you could, non-existent gods and goals. He was a blaze that burned and exploded everything that falsified the unitary movement of life.

27

In the last few years UG had wanted to do something other than answer tiresome questions, for he found all questions (except in the technical area, which is something else) were variations of basically the same question revolving around the ideas of 'being' and 'becoming'. He would curtly yet simply say, 'Becoming something other than what you are is the cause of your misery.... You will remain a man of violence as long as you follow some idea of becoming.... You can't divide these things into two. The process you adopt to reach what you call being is also a becoming process. You are always in the becoming process, no matter what you call it. If you want to be yourself and not somebody else, that also is a becoming process. There is nothing to do about this. Anything you do to put yourself in that state of being is a becoming process. That is all that I am pointing out,' and that left people with nothing to say.

The conversation comes to an end. He has spoken enough! He has said what he wanted to say a million times. There is utter silence. It is embarrassing; it is also a tremendous relief from the burden of knowing. And UG would start playing his enigmatic little 'games', or invite friends (all are friends, no disciples, no followers) to sing, to dance, and to share jokes. Now, either one drops one's questions and abandons one's 'becoming', or one gets up and leaves. The room explodes with laughter: funny, silly, dark, and apocalyptic! We all mock and laugh at everything, mock heroes and lovers, thinkers and politicians, scientists and thieves, kings and sages, including ourselves, at our own silly yet agonizing struggle for non-existent things. We convulse with laughter. And suddenly, it seems, at last we are delivered from the tyranny of knowledge, beauty, goodness, truth, and God.

★

Truly, there was no teaching. A teaching implies a method or a system, a technique or a new way of thinking to be applied in order to bring about a transformation in our way of life. What UG was saying, he insisted, was outside the field of teachability. In point of fact, there was no teacher, no taught and thereby no teaching. There was no symbolism, no metaphysics, no mysticism involved in his words. He meant what he said, literally. There was nothing new in the language of UG. He did not coin any new words like philosophers and scientists do; he used simple, commonplace words, free of metaphysical overtones and spiritual content, to describe life in pure and simple physical and physiological terms so that it was de-psychologized and demystified, and the implication of what came through is quite revolutionary, to say the least.

Generally, in his freewheeling chats he did two things:

First, in physical and physiological terms he described the way he, the body, was functioning. He called it the natural state. It is the state of 'primordial awareness without primitivism', or the 'undivided state of consciousness', where all desires and fear, and the search for happiness and pleasure, God and truth, have come to an end. He insisted that it is not the state of a God-realized man or 'enlightenment'. It is not a state of bliss or supreme happiness either. There is only the throb, the pulse, the beat of life. There thoughts emerge in response to stimuli or a question, and then burn themselves up, releasing energy. There is no soul, no atman, only the body, and the body is immortal. It is an acausal state of 'not-knowing', of wonder. And this is the way *you*, UG stated, stripped of the machinations of thought, are also functioning.

Second, he described the way we function, caught in a world of opposites, constantly struggling to become something other than what we are, and in search of non-existent gods and goals. How we all think and function in a 'thought sphere' just as we all share the same atmosphere for breathing. How and why we have no freedom of action, unless and until thought comes to an end—but then, it is not in the interest of thought to end itself. Thought is self-protective and fascist in nature, and it'll use every trick under the sun to give momentum to its own continuity. Thought controls, moulds, and shapes our ideas and actions. Idea and action—they are one and the same. All our actions are born out of ideas. Our ideas are thoughts passed on to us from generation to generation. And this thought is not the instrument to help us to live in harmony with the life around us. That is why we create all these ecological problems, problems of pollution, and the problem of possibly destroying ourselves with the most destructive weapons that we have invented. There is no way out. The planet is not in danger. We are in danger...

★

Who is this UG? What is he? Is it possible to say anything and describe him without making any comparisons, without locating him or his utterances, in the realm of the 'known'?

It is true that when UG rejects the notion of soul or atman and declares that our search for permanence is the cause of our suffering, he sounds like the Buddha; when he negates all concepts and knowledge systems including his own statements, we may recall the great Buddhist, Nagarjuna, who negated everything including his own act of negation; when he blasts all spiritual discourses as 'poppycock' and thrashes the spiritual masters as 'misguided fools', we may think of the fiery and abusive words of the great ninth-century mystic of China, Rinzai Gigen, who declared, 'I have no dharma to give…. There is no Buddha, no dharma, no training and no realization…. If you meet the Buddha on the road, kill him!' When he speaks of 'affection' as 'thuds' felt in the spot where the thymus gland is located, we may relate it to Sri Ramana's declaration that the 'true heart' is located on the right side of the chest; and when he speaks of 'wonder' and the state of 'not knowing' we may wonder if this is what the Mother (of Pondicherry) tried to describe in her report of the bodily changes she had experienced between 1962 and 1973. Likewise we may connect some of his radical statements to certain expressions or declarations in the *Avadhuta Gita*, *Ashtavakra Gita*, the Upanishads and Zen koans, or compare them with the teachings of J. Krishnamurti, Nisargadatta Maharaj and even the postmodern 'deconstructionists'. Or, persons grounded in nuclear physics may find similarities or parallels between UG's statements and the observations made in quantum physics. We could go on making such connections and comparisons but still it doesn't help us to get a handle on the mystery that is UG.

Of course, UG warns us against relating, for instance, his statements about time and space, order and chaos, birth and death to the observations made by scientists since, according to him, they are mere concepts to them and 'they are observing certain things only through the mirror of their own thinking. The scientist is influencing what he is looking at. Whatever theories he comes up with are only theories; they are not facts to him.' And as regards the past spiritual masters he said most emphatically, 'I don't give a hoot for a sixth-century-BC Buddha, let alone all the other claimants we have in our midst. Do not compare what I am saying with what he, or other religious authorities, has said. If you give what I am saying any spiritual overtones, any religious flavour at all, you are missing the point.'

Does it mean that UG is utterly unique, without a parallel in the history of humankind, or that we should just listen to the utterly new and cathartic voice of the 'natural state' and not put whatever he says in any particular frame whether traditional or modern? How then can one understand his admonitions, his mind-boggling statements? Indeed, *how* is the problem and the beginning of mischief, since it throws us back into the old 'frames' of traditional discourses. Yet, we cannot help but ask questions. We cannot but respond to the challenge, albeit cautiously and without putting this 'wild bird in constant flight' into a cage, or on a pedestal.

Now, what does it mean to have a body that is in tune with the cosmos and be affected by whatever is happening in nature? What does it mean to be in a 'declutched state' or 'state of not knowing', or to feel all sounds emerging from within and have no sense of division at all? Was UG in the state of 'primordial awareness'; was he the end result of the evolutionary process? Is this what the spiritual masters of the past hinted at but could not clearly articulate in the limited vocabulary of their times? Is this what the mystics and the religious gurus speculated about, but erred in institutionalizing the 'teachings', in building knowledge systems and inventing methods to reach it? Is then 'liberation' all about reactivation of the thymus, pituitary and pineal glands? Is it a biological mutation? In short, is 'enlightenment' physical after all?

Truly, UG brought something utterly new and revolutionary into the world, into our consciousness, the implication and impact of which cannot be known today. His is the voice that is at once explosive, subversive and cathartic. In 'bits and pieces' we may yet find echoes of his voice in the teachings of the past masters. Perhaps we can say there was a need for the masters and they came in answer to the anguish and cries of their times, and marked a leap in human consciousness and the emergence of new ways of being and doing things. They have served their purpose and are gone. Period. Newton has to give way to Einstein and of course Einstein is not the last word in physics. That is not to say we must forget Newton or the past masters. Our learning can never stop. But there's no need to continue to build temples and set up organizations for them, and look upon them as perfect models. As UG would say, 'There is no point in reviving all those things and starting revivalistic movements. That is dead, finished.... All of them have totally failed. Otherwise we wouldn't be where we are today. If there is anything to their claims, we would have created a better and happier world.... We are partly responsible for this situation because we want to be victimized by them. What is the point in blaming those people? There is no point in blaming ourselves either because it is a two-way game: we play the game and they play the game. But... you can't come into your own being until you are free from the whole thing surrounding the concept of self. To be really on your own, the whole basis of spiritual life, which is erroneous, has to be destroyed. It does not mean that you become fanatical or violent, burning down temples, tearing down the idols, destroying the holy books like a bunch of drunks. It is not that at all...'

Of course that is not the way. We cannot destroy the past, for, we are the past. But we can refuse to be victims and stop playing games with ourselves. Religions have failed to solve our problems, and politics, that 'warty outgrowth of religious thinking', hasn't done better. Our problem lies in our solutions. No wonder UG challenged the very foundation of our cultures, and in particular, our so-called spiritual practices of 'awakening'. Now, in the light of what UG says, can we really critically re-examine our past, de-psychologize and demystify our religious discourses and political culture, and possibly put ourselves on a different track wherein the search and struggle for non-existent gods and goals have come to an end?

Read on. UG mirrors reality as it is. It'll be extremely difficult to agree with all that he said, but then it'll be even more difficult to disagree with him.

THROWING AWAY THE CRUTCHES

The Biological Mutation and Thereafter:
The Way UG (The Body) Functions or the Natural State, in UG's Own Voice*

--⇒ ⇐--

The following excerpt is from the discussion UG had with the doctors and psychologists from NIMHANS (*National Institute of Mental Health and Neuroscience, Bangalore*) *and intellectuals who met him in Bangalore in the year 1976. Here, in this report, he is referring to his experiences in Gstaad (1967–1970), while he was staying with Valentine.*

There was no search in me, no seeking after something, but something funny was going on...

During that time (I call it the 'incubation') all kinds of things were happening to me inside—headaches, constant headaches, terrible pains here in the brain. I swallowed I don't know how many tens of thousands of aspirins. Nothing gave me relief. It was not migraine or any of those known headaches, but tremendous headaches. Those aspirin pills and fifteen to twenty cups of coffee every day to free myself! One day Valentine said, 'What! You are taking fifteen cups of coffee every day. Do you know what it means in terms of money? It is three or four hundred francs per month. What is this?' Anyway, it was such a terrible thing for me.

All kinds of funny things happened to me. I remember when I rubbed my body like this, there was a sparkle, like a phosphorous glow, on the body. She used to run out of her bedroom to see—she thought there were cars going that way in the middle of the night. Every time

---

*   From *The Mystique of Enlightenment*

I rolled in my bed there was a sparkling of light, [*laughs*] and it was so funny for me—'What is this?' It was electricity—that is why I say it is an electromagnetic field. At first I thought it was because of my nylon clothes and static electricity; but then I stopped using nylon. I was a very sceptical heretic, to the tips of my toes; I never believed in anything; even if I saw some miracle happen before me, I didn't accept that at all—such was the make-up of this man. It never occurred to me that anything of that sort was in the making for me.

Very strange things happened to me, but I *never* related those things to liberation or freedom or moksha, because by that time the whole thing had gone out of my system. I had arrived at a point where I said to myself, 'Buddha deluded himself and deluded others. *All* those teachers and saviours of mankind were *damned* fools—they fooled themselves—so I'm not interested in this kind of thing anymore,' so it went out of my system *completely*. It went on and on in its own way—*peculiar* things—but never did I say to myself, 'Well, [*laughs*] I am getting there, I am *nearer* to that.' There is no nearness to that, there is no far-away-ness from that, there is no closeness to that. Nobody is nearer to that because he is different, he is prepared. There's no readiness for that; it just hits you like a ton of bricks.

Then [April 1967] I happened to be in Paris when J. Krishnamurti also happened to be there. Some of my friends suggested 'Why don't you go and listen to your old friend? He is here giving a talk.' All right, I said, I haven't heard him for so many years—almost twenty years—let me go and listen. When I got there they demanded two francs from me. I said, 'I am not ready to pay two francs to listen to J. Krishnamurti. No, come on, let us go and do something foolish. Let's go to a striptease joint, the "Folies Bergere" or the "Casino de Paris". Come on, let us go there for twenty francs.' So, there we were at the 'Casino de Paris' watching the show. I had a very strange experience at that time: I didn't know whether I was the dancer or whether there was some other dancer dancing on the stage. A very strange experience for me: a peculiar kind of movement, here, inside of me (this is now something natural for me). There was no division: there was nobody who was looking at the dancer. The question of whether I was the dancer, or whether there was a dancer out there on the stage, puzzled me. This kind of peculiar experience of the absence of division between me and the dancer, puzzled me and bothered me for some time—then we came out.

The question 'What is that state?' had a tremendous intensity for me—not an emotional intensity—the more I tried to find an answer, the more I failed to find an answer, the more intensity the question had. It's like (I always give this simile) rice chaff. If a heap of rice chaff is ignited, it continues burning inside; you don't see any fire outside, but when you touch it, it burns you of course. In exactly the same way the question was going on and on and on: 'What is that state? I want it. Finished. Krishnamurti said, "You have no way," but still I want to know what that state is, the state in which Buddha was, Sankara was, and all those teachers were.

Then [July 1967] there arrived another phase. Krishnamurti was again there in Saanen giving talks. My friends dragged me there and said, 'Now at least it is a free business. Why don't you come and listen?' I said, 'All right, I'll come and listen.' When I listened to him, something funny happened to me—a peculiar kind of feeling that he was describing my state and not his state. Why did I want to know his state? He was describing something, some movements, some awareness, some silence. 'In that silence there is no mind; there is action'—all kinds of things. So I told myself, 'I am in that state. What the hell have I been doing these thirty or forty years, listening to all these people and struggling, wanting to understand his state or the state of somebody else, Buddha or Jesus? I am in that state. Now I am in that state.' So, then I walked out of the tent and never looked back.

Then—very strange—that question 'What is that state?' transformed itself into another question: 'How do I know that I am in that state, the state of Buddha, the state I very much wanted and demanded from everybody? I am in that state, but how do I know?' The next day [UG's forty-ninth birthday] I was sitting on a bench under a tree overlooking one of the most beautiful spots in the whole world, the seven hills and seven valleys [of Saanenland]. I was sitting there. Not that the question was there; the whole of my being was that question: 'How do I know that I am in that state?' There is some kind of peculiar division inside of me: there is somebody who knows that he is in that state. The knowledge of that state—what I have read, what I have experienced, what they have talked about—it is this knowledge that is looking at that state, so it is only this knowledge that has projected that state. I said to myself: Look here, old chap, after forty years you have not moved one step; you are there in square number one. It is the same knowledge that projected your mind there when you asked this question. You are in the same situation asking the same question, "How do I know?" because it is this knowledge, the description of the state by those people, that has created this state for you. You are kidding yourself. You are a damned fool.' So, nothing. But still there was some kind of a peculiar feeling that this was the state.

The second question 'How do I know that this is the state?'—I didn't have any answer for that question—it was like a question in a whirlpool—it went on and on and on. Then *suddenly* the question disappeared. Nothing happened; the question just disappeared. I didn't say to myself, 'Oh, my God! Now I have found the answer.' Even that state disappeared—the state I thought I was in, the state of Buddha, Jesus—even that has disappeared. The question has disappeared. The whole thing is finished for me, and that's all, you see. From then on, never did I say to myself, 'Now I have the answer to all those questions.' That state of which I had said 'This is the state'—that state disappeared. The question disappeared. Finished, you see. It is not emptiness, it is not blankness, it is not the void, it is not any of those things; the question disappeared suddenly, and that is all.

*

(The disappearance of his fundamental question, on discovering that it had no answer, was a physiological phenomenon, UG says, 'a sudden "explosion" inside, blasting, as it were, every cell, every nerve and every gland in my body.' And with that 'explosion', the illusion that there is continuity of thought, that there is a centre, an 'I' linking up the thoughts, was not there any more.)

Then thought cannot link up. The linking gets broken, and once it is broken it is finished. Then it is not once that thought explodes; every time a thought arises, it explodes. So, this continuity comes to an end, and thought falls into its natural rhythm.

Since then I have no questions of any kind, because the questions cannot stay there any more. The only questions I have are very simple questions ('How do I go to Hyderabad?' for example) to function in this world—and people *have* answers for these questions. For those questions, nobody has any answers—so there are no questions any more.

Everything in the head has tightened—there was no room for anything there inside of my brain. For the first time I became conscious of my head with everything 'tight' inside of it. So, these *vasanas* [past desires] or whatever you call them—they do try to show their heads sometimes, but then the brain cells are so 'tight' that it has no opportunity to fool around there any more. The division cannot stay there—it's a physical impossibility; you don't have to do a thing about it, you see. That is why I say that when this 'explosion' takes place (I use the word 'explosion' because it's like a nuclear explosion) it leaves behind chain reactions. Every cell in your body, the cells in the very marrow of your bones, have to undergo this 'change'—I don't want to use that word— it's an *irreversible* change. There's no question of your going back. There's no question of a 'fall' for this man at all. *Irreversible*: an alchemy of some sort.

It is like a nuclear explosion, you see—it shatters the whole body. It is not an easy thing; it is the end of the man—such a shattering thing that it blasts every cell, every nerve in your body. I went through terrible physical torture at that moment. Not that you experience the 'explosion'; you can't experience the 'explosion'—but it's after-effects, the 'fallout', is the thing that changes the whole chemistry of your body.

★

Q: Sir, you must have experienced, if I may use the words, higher planes....

UG: You are talking of planes? There are no planes—no planes, no levels. You see, there is one very strange thing that happens as a result of this 'explosion' or whatever you want to call it: at no time does the thought that I am different from you come into this consciousness. Never. Never does that thought come into my consciousness and tell me that you are different from me or I am different from you, because there is no point here, there is no centre here. Only with reference to this centre do you create all the other points.

Q: In some way, you must certainly be different from other people.

UG: Physiologically, probably.

Q: You said that tremendous chemical changes have taken place in you. How do you know this? Were you ever examined, or is this an inference?

UG: The after-effects of that ['explosion'], the way the senses are operating now without any coordinator or centre—that's all I can say. Another thing: the chemistry has changed—I can say that because unless that alchemy or change in the whole chemistry takes place, there is no way of freeing this organism from thought, from the continuity of thought. So, since there is no continuity of thought, you can very easily say that something has happened, but what actually has happened? I have no way of experiencing this at all.

Q: It may be that the mind is playing games and that I may merely think I am an 'exploded man'.

UG: I am not trying to sell anything here. It is impossible for you to simulate this. This is a thing that has happened outside the field, the area, in which I expected, dreamed and wanted change, so I don't call this a 'change'. I really don't know what has happened to me. What I am telling you is the way I am functioning. There seems to be some difference between the way you are functioning and the way I am functioning, but basically there can't be any difference. How can there be any difference between you and me? There can't be; but from the way we are trying to express ourselves, there seems to be. I have the feeling that there is some difference, and what that difference is is all that I am trying to understand. So, this is the way I am functioning.

★

(UG noticed, during the week following the 'explosion', fundamental changes in the functioning of his senses. On the last day his body went through 'a process of physical death', and eventually these changes became permanent features.)

Then began the changes—from the next day onwards, for seven days— every day one change. First I discovered the softness of the skin, the blinking of the eyes stopped, and then changes in taste, smell and hearing—these five changes I noticed. Maybe they were there even before, and I only noticed them for the first time.

[*On the first day*] I noticed that my skin was soft like silk and had a peculiar kind of glow, a golden colour. I was shaving, and each time I tried to shave, the razor slipped. I changed blades, but it was no use. I touched my face. My sense of touch was different, you see, also the way I held the razor. Especially my skin—my skin was soft as silk and had this golden glow. I didn't relate this to anything at all; I just observed it.

[*On the second day*] I became aware for the first time that my mind was in what I call a 'declutched state'. I was upstairs in the kitchen and Valentine had prepared tomato soup. I looked at it, and I didn't know what it was. She told me it was tomato soup, and I tasted it, and I recognized 'This is how tomato soup tastes.' Then I swallowed the soup, and then I returned to this odd frame of mind—though 'frame of mind' is not the word for it; it was a frame of 'not mind'—in which I forgot again. I asked again 'What is that?' Again she said it was tomato soup. Again I tasted it. Again I swallowed and forgot. I played with this for some time. It was such a funny business for me then, this 'declutched state'; now it has become normal. I no longer spend time in reverie, worry, conceptualization and the other kinds of thinking that most people do when they're alone. My mind is only engaged when it's needed, for instance when you ask questions, or when I have to fix the tape recorder or something like that. The rest of the time my mind is in the 'declutched state'. Of course now I have my memory back—I lost it at first, but now I have it back—but my memory is in the background and only comes into play when it's needed, automatically. When it's not needed, there is no mind here, there is no thought, there is only life.

[*On the third day*] some friends invited themselves over for dinner, and I said 'All right, I'll prepare something.' But somehow I couldn't smell or taste properly. I became gradually aware that these two senses had been transformed. Every time some odour entered my nostrils it irritated my olfactory centre in just about the same way—whether it came from the most expensive scent or from cow dung, it was the same irritation. And then, every time I tasted something, I tasted the dominant ingredient only—the taste of the other ingredients came slowly after. From that moment perfume made no sense to me, and spicy food had no appeal for me. I could taste only the dominant spice, the chili or whatever it was.

[*On the fourth day*] something happened to the eyes. We were sitting in the 'Rialto' restaurant, and I became aware of a tremendous sort of 'vistavision', like a concave mirror. Things coming towards me, moved into me, as it were; and things going away from me, seemed to move from inside me. It was such a puzzle to me—it was as if my eyes were a gigantic camera, changing focus without my doing anything. Now I am used to the puzzle. Nowadays that is how I see. When you drive me around in your Mini, I am like a cameraman dallying along, and the cars in the other direction go into me, and the cars that pass us come out of me, and when my eyes fix on something they fix on it with total attention, like a camera. Another thing about my eyes: when we came back from the restaurant I came home and looked in the mirror to see what was odd about my eyes, to see how they were 'fixed'. I looked in the mirror for a long time, and then I observed that my eyelids were not blinking. For half an hour or forty-five minutes I looked into the mirror—still no blinking of the eyes. Instinctive blinking was over for me, and it still is.

[*On the fifth day*] I noticed a change in hearing. When I heard the barking of a dog, the barking originated inside me. And the same with the mooing of the cow, the whistle of the train—suddenly all sounds originated inside me, as it were—coming from within, and not from outside—they still do.

Five senses changed in five days, and *on the sixth day* I was lying down on a sofa—Valentine was there in the kitchen—and suddenly my body disappeared. There was no body there. I looked at my hand. (Crazy thing—you would certainly put me in the mental hospital.) I looked at it—'Is this my hand?'

There was no questioning here, but the whole situation was like that—that is all I am describing. So I touched this body—*nothing*—I didn't feel there was anything there except the touch, you see, the point of contact. Then I called Valentine: 'Do you see my body on this sofa? Nothing inside of me says that this is my body.' She touched it—'This is your body.' And yet that assurance didn't give me any comfort or satisfaction—'What is this funny business? My body is missing.' My body had gone away, and it has never come back. The points of contact are all that is there for the body—nothing else is there for me—because the seeing is altogether independent of the sense of touch here. So it is *not* possible for me to create a complete image of my body even, because where there's no sense of touch there are *missing* points here in the consciousness.

[*On the seventh day*] I was again lying on the same sofa, relaxing, enjoying the 'declutched state'. Valentine would come in, I would recognize her as Valentine; she would go out of the room—finish, blank, no Valentine—'What is this? I can't even imagine what Valentine looks like.' I would listen to the sounds coming from inside me, I could not relate. I had discovered that all my senses were without any coordinating thing inside: the coordinator was missing.

I felt something happening inside of me: the life energy drawing to a focal point from different parts of my body. I said to myself, 'Now you have come to the end of your life. You are going to die.' Then I called Valentine and said, 'I am going to die, Valentine, and you will have to do something with this body. Hand it over to the doctors— maybe they will use it. I don't believe in burning or burial or any of

those things. In your own interest you have to dispose of this body—
one day it will stink—so, why not give it away?' She said 'You are a
foreigner. The Swiss government won't take your body. Forget about
it.' Then she went away. And then this whole business of the frightening
movement of the life force coming to a point, as it were. I was lying
down on the sofa. Her bed was empty, so I moved over to that bed and
stretched myself, getting ready. She ignored me and went away. She
said, 'One day you say this thing has changed, another day this thing
has changed, a third day this thing has changed. What is this whole
business?' She was not interested in any of those things—never was she
interested in any of these religious matters—never heard of those things.
'You say you are going to die. You are not going to die. You are all
right, hale and healthy.'

She went away. Then I stretched myself, and this was going on and
on and on. The whole life energy was moving to some focal point—
where it was, I don't know. Then a point arrived where the whole
thing looked as if the aperture of a camera was trying to close itself. (It
is the only simile that I can think of. The way I am describing this is
quite different from the way things happened at that time, because
there was nobody there thinking in such terms. All this was part of my
experience, otherwise I wouldn't be able to talk about it.) So, the aperture
was trying to close itself, and something was there trying to keep it
open. Then after a while there was no will to do anything, not even to
prevent the aperture closing itself. Suddenly, as it were, it closed. I don't
know what happened after that.

This process lasted for forty-nine minutes—this process of dying. It
was like a physical death, you see. Even now it happens to me: the
hands and feet become so cold, the body becomes stiff, the heartbeat
slows down, the breathing slows down, and then there is a gasping for
breath. Up to a point you are there, you breathe your last breath, as it
were, and then you are finished. What happens after that, nobody knows.

When I came out of that, somebody said there was a telephone call
for me. I came out and went downstairs to answer it. I was in a daze. I
didn't know what had happened. It was a physical death. What brought
me back to life, I don't know. How long it lasted, I don't know. I can't

say anything about that, because the experiencer was finished: there was nobody to experience that death at all.... So, that was the end of it. I got up.

★

I didn't feel that I was a newborn baby—no question of enlightenment at all—but the things that had astonished me that week, the changes in taste, seeing and so on, had become permanent fixtures. I call all these events the 'calamity'. I call it the 'calamity' because from the point of view of one who thinks this is something fantastic, blissful, full of beatitude, love, ecstasy and all that kind of a thing, this is physical torture—this is a calamity from that point of view. Not a calamity to me, but a calamity to those who have an image that something marvellous is going to happen. It's something like: you imagine New York, you dream about it, you want to be there. When you are actually there, nothing of it is there; it is a godforsaken place, and even the devils have probably forsaken that place. It's not the thing that you had sought and wanted so much, but totally different. What is there, you really don't know—you have no way of knowing anything about that—there is no image here. In that sense I can never tell myself or anybody, 'I'm an enlightened man, a liberated man, a free man; I'm going to liberate mankind.' Free from what? How can I liberate somebody else. There's no question of liberating anybody. For that, I must have an image that I am a free man, you understand?

★

Then, on the eighth day, I was sitting on the sofa and suddenly there was an outburst of tremendous energy—tremendous energy shaking the whole body, and along with the body, the sofa, the chalet and the whole universe, as it were—shaking, vibrating. You can't create that movement at all. It was sudden.

Whether it was coming from outside or inside, from below or above, I don't know—I couldn't locate the spot; it was all over. It lasted for hours and hours. I couldn't bear it but there was nothing I could do to stop it; there was a total helplessness. This went on and on, day after day, day after day. Whenever I sat it started—this vibration like an epileptic fit or something. Not even an epileptic fit; it went on for days and days.

(For three days UG lay on his bed, his body contorted with pain—it was, he says, as if he felt pain in every cell of his body, one after the other. Similar outbursts of energy occurred intermittently throughout the next six months, whenever he lay down or relaxed.)

The body was not able to.... The body feels the pain. That's a very painful process. Very painful. It is a physical pain because the body has limitations—it has a form, a shape of its own, so when there is an outburst of energy, which is not your energy or my energy or God's (or call it by any name you like), it is like a river in spate. The energy that is operating there does not feel the limitations of the body; it is not interested; it has its own momentum. It is a very painful thing. It is not that ecstatic, blissful beatitude and all that rubbish—stuff and nonsense!—it is really a painful thing. Oh, I suffered for months and months after that; before that too. Everybody has. Even Ramana Maharshi suffered after that.

A great cascade—not one, but thousands of cascades—it went on and on and on for months and months. It's a very painful experience—painful in the sense that the energy has a peculiar operation of its own. H'm, you know, you have at the airport a Wills cigarette advertisement. There is an atom: lines going like that. [*UG demonstrates.*] It is clockwise, anticlockwise, and then it is this way and then this way and then this way. Like an atom it moves inside—not in one part of your body; the *whole* body. It is as if a wet towel were being wrung to get rid of the water—it is like that, the whole of your body—it's such a painful thing.

It goes on even now. You can't invite it; you can't ask it to come; you can't do anything. It gives you the feeling that it is enveloping you, that it is descending on you. Descending from where? Where is it coming from? How is it coming? Every time it is new—very strange—every time it comes in a different way, so you don't know what is happening.

You lie down on your bed, and suddenly it begins—it begins to move slowly like ants. I'd think there were bugs in my bed, jump out, look— [*laughs*] no bugs—then I'd go back—then again.... The hairs are electrified, so it slowly moves.

There were pains all over the body. Thought has controlled this body to such an extent that when that loosens, the whole metabolism is agog. The whole thing was changing in its own way without my doing anything. And then the movement of the hands changed. Usually your hands turn this way. [*UG demonstrates.*] Here, this wrist joint had terrible pains for six months until it turned itself, and all the movements are now like this. That is why they say my movements are mudras [mystical gestures]. The movements of the hands are quite different now than before. Then there were pains in the marrow of the bones. Every cell started changing, and it went on and on for six months.

And then the sex hormones started changing. I didn't know whether I was a man or a woman—'What is this business?' I asked myself— suddenly there was a breast on the left-hand side. All kinds of things— I don't want to go into details—there is a complete record of all these things. It went on and on and on. It took three years for this body to fall into a new rhythm of its own.

★

(Up and down his torso, neck and head, at those points which Indian holy men call chakras, UG's friends observed swellings of various shapes and colours, which came and went at intervals. On his lower abdomen the swellings were horizontal, cigar-shaped bands. Above the navel was a hard, almond-shaped swelling. A hard, blue swelling, like a large medallion in the middle of his chest was surmounted by another smaller, brownish-red, medallion-shaped swelling at the base of his throat. These two 'medallions' were as though suspended from a varicoloured, swollen ring—blue, brownish and light yellow—around his neck, as in pictures of the Hindu gods. There were also other similarities between the swellings and the depictions of Indian religious art: his throat was swollen to a shape that made his chin seem to rest on the head of a cobra, as in the

*traditional images of Siva; just above the bridge of the nose was a white
lotus-shaped swelling; all over the head the small blood vessels expanded,
forming patterns like the stylized lumps on the heads of Buddha statues.
Like the horns of Moses and the Taoist mystics, two large, hard swellings
periodically came and went. The arteries in his neck expanded and rose,
blue and snake-like, into his head.)*

I do not want to be an exhibitionist, but many of you are doctors.
There is something to the symbolism they have in India—the cobra.
Do you see the swellings here? …they take the shape of a cobra. Yesterday
was the new moon. The body is affected by everything that is happening
around you; it is not separate from what is happening around you.
Whatever is happening there is also happening here—there is only the
physical response. Your body is affected by everything that is happening
around you; and you can't prevent this, for the simple reason that the
armour that you have built around yourself is destroyed, so it is very
vulnerable to everything that is happening there. With the phases of the
moon—full moon, half moon, quarter moon—these swellings here take
the shape of a cobra. Maybe that is the reason why some people have
created all these images—Siva and all those kinds of things. But why
should it take the shape of a cobra? I have asked many doctors why this
swelling is here, but nobody could give me a satisfactory answer. I don't
know if there are any glands or anything here.

★

There are certain glands … I have discussed this so many times with
doctors who are doing research into the ductless glands. Those glands
are what the Hindus call chakras. These ductless glands are located in
exactly the same spots where the Hindus speculated the chakras are.
There is one gland here which is called the 'thymus gland'. That is very
active when you are a child—very active—it has feelings, extraordinary
feelings. When you reach the age of puberty it becomes dormant—
that's what they say. When again this kind of a thing happens, when
you are reborn, that gland is automatically activated, so all the feelings

are there. Feelings are not thoughts, not emotions; you feel for somebody. If somebody hurts himself there, that hurt is felt here—not as a pain, but there is a feeling, you see—you automatically say 'Ah!' This actually happened to me when I was staying in a coffee plantation: a mother started beating a child, a little child, you know. She was mad, hopping mad, and she hit the child so hard, the child almost turned blue. And somebody asked me, 'Why did you not interfere and stop her?' I was standing there—I was so puzzled, you see. 'Who should I take pity on, the mother or the child?'—that was my answer—'Who is responsible?' Both were in a ridiculous situation: the mother could not control her anger, and the child was so helpless and innocent. This went on—it was moving from one to the other—and then I found all those things [marks] on my back. So I was also part of that. (I am not saying this just to claim something.)

That is possible because consciousness cannot be divided. Anything that is happening there is affecting you—this is affection, you understand? There is no question of your sitting in judgement on anybody; the situation happens to be that, so you are affected by that. You are affected by everything that is happening there.

Q: In the entire universe?

UG: That is too big, you see. Anything that is happening within your field of consciousness. Consciousness is, of course, not limited. If he is hurt there, you also are hurt here. If you are hurt, there is an immediate response there. I can't say about the universe, the whole universe, but in your field of consciousness, in the limited field in which you are operating at that particular moment, you are responding ...

And all the other glands also here.... there are so many glands here; for example, the pituitary—'third eye', '*ajña chakra*', they call it (the literal meaning of 'ajña' is 'command'). When once the interference of thought is finished, it is taken over by this gland: it is this gland that gives the instructions or orders to the body; not thought any more; thought cannot interfere. (That is why they call it that, probably. I'm not interpreting or any such thing; perhaps this gives you an idea.) But you have built an armour, created an armour with this thought, and you don't allow yourself to be affected by things.

★

Since there is nobody who uses this thought as a self-protective mechanism, it burns itself up. Thought undergoes combustion, ionization (if I may use your scientific term). Thought is, after all, vibration. So, when this kind of ionization of thought takes place, it throws out, sometimes it covers the whole body with, an ash-like substance. Your body is covered with that when there is no need for thought at all. When you don't use it, what happens to that thought? It burns itself out—that is the energy—it's combustion.

The body gets heated, you know. There is tremendous heat in the body as a result of this, and so the skin is covered—your face, your feet, everything—with this ash-like substance. That's one of the reasons why I express it in pure and simple physical and physiological terms. It has no psychological content at all, it has no mystical content, it has no religious overtones at all, as I see it. I am bound to say that, and I don't care whether you accept it or not, it is of no importance to me.

★

This kind of a thing must have happened to so many people. I say this happens to one in a billion, and you are that one in a billion. It is not something that one is specially prepared for. There are no purificatory methods necessary, there is no sadhana necessary for this kind of a thing to happen—no preparation of any kind. The consciousness is so pure that whatever you are doing in the direction of purifying that consciousness is adding impurity to it.

Consciousness has to flush itself out: it has to purge itself of *every* trace of holiness, *every* trace of unholiness, *everything*. Even what you consider 'sacred and holy' is a contamination in that consciousness. It is not through any volition of yours; when once the frontiers are broken— not through any effort of yours, not through any volition of yours—the floodgates are open and everything goes out. In that process of flushing out, you have all these visions. It's not a vision outside there or inside of you; suddenly you yourself, the whole consciousness, takes the shape of Buddha, Jesus, Mahavira, Mohammed, Socrates—only those people who have come into this state; not great men, not the leaders of mankind— it is very strange—but only those people to whom this kind of a thing happened.

One of them was a coloured man (not exactly a coloured man), and during that time I could tell people how he looked. Then some woman with breasts, flowing hair—naked. I was told that there were two saints here in India—Akkamahadevi and Lalleswari—they were women, naked women. Suddenly you have these two breasts, the flowing hair— even the organs change into female organs.

But still there is a division there—you, and the form the consciousness has assumed, the form of Buddha, say, or Jesus Christ or God knows what—the same situation: 'How do I know I am in that state?' But that division cannot stay long; it disappears and something else comes. Hundreds of people—probably something happened to so many hundreds of people. This is part of history—so many rishis, some Westerners, monks, so many women, and sometimes very strange things. You see, all that people have experienced before you is part of your consciousness. I use the expression 'the saints go marching out'; in Christianity they have a hymn 'When the Saints Go Marching In'. They run out of your consciousness because they cannot stay there any more, because all that is impurity, a contamination there.

You can say (I can't make any definite statement) probably it is because of the impact on the human consciousness of the 'explosions' of all those saints, sages and saviours of mankind that there is this dissatisfaction in you, that whatever is there is all the time trying to burst out, as it were. Maybe that is so—I can't say anything about it. You can say that they are there because they are pushing you to this point, and once the purpose is achieved they have finished their job and they go away—that is only speculation on my part. But this flushing out of everything good and bad, holy and unholy, sacred and profane has got to happen, otherwise your consciousness is *still* contaminated, *still* impure. During that time it goes on and on and on—there are hundreds and thousands of them—then, you see, you are put back into that primeval, primordial state of consciousness. Once it has become pure, *of and by itself,* nothing can touch it, *nothing* can contaminate that any more. All the past up to that point is there, but it cannot influence your actions any more.

All these visions and everything were happening for three years after the 'calamity'. Now the whole thing is finished. The divided state of consciousness cannot function at all any more; it is always in the undivided state of consciousness—nothing can touch that. Anything can happen—the thought can be a good thought, a bad thought, the telephone number of a London prostitute.... During my wanderings in London, I used to look at those telephone numbers fixed to the trees. I was not interested in going to the prostitute, but those things, the numbers, interested me. I had nothing else to do, no books to read, nothing to do but look at those numbers. One number gets fixed in there, it comes there, it repeats itself. It doesn't matter what comes there—good, bad, holy, unholy. Who is there to say 'This is good; that is bad?'—the whole thing is finished. That is why I have to use the phrase 'religious experience' (not in the sense in which you use the word 'religion'): it puts you back to the source. You are back in that primeval, primordial, pure state of consciousness—call it 'awareness' or whatever you like. In that state things are happening, and there is nobody who is interested, nobody who is looking at them. They come and go in their own way, like the Ganges water flowing: the sewerage water comes in, half-burnt corpses, both good things and bad things—everything—but that water is always pure.

★

The most puzzling and bewildering part of the whole thing was when the sensory activities began their independent careers. There was no coordinator linking the senses, so we had terrible problems—Valentine had to go through the whole business. We'd go for a walk, and I'd look at a flower and ask, 'What is that?' She'd say, 'That is a flower.' I'd take a few more steps, look at a cow and ask, 'What is that?' Like a baby, I had to relearn everything all over (not actually relearn, but all the knowledge was in the background and never came to the forefront, you see). It started—the whole business—'What is this crazy business? I have to put it in words'; not that I felt I was in a crazy state. I was a very sane man, acting sanely, everything going on, and yet this ridiculous business of asking about everything, 'What is this? What is that?' That's all; no other questions. Valentine also didn't know what to make of the whole business. She even went to a leading psychiatrist in Geneva. She rushed to him—she wanted to understand, but at the same time she felt that there was nothing crazy about me. If I'd done one crazy thing she would have left me. Never; only strange things, you see. 'What is that?' 'That is a cow.' 'What is that?' 'That is that.' It went on and on and on, and it was too much for her and too much for me. When she met the psychiatrist, he said, 'Unless we see the person, we can't tell anything. Bring him.' But I knew that something really fantastic had happened inside—what it was, I didn't know, but that didn't bother me. 'Why ask if that's a cow? What's the difference whether it is a cow, a donkey or a horse?'—that bewildering situation continued for a long time—all the knowledge was in the background. It's the same situation even now, but I don't ask those questions any more. When I am looking at something, I really don't know what I'm looking at—that is why I say it is a state of not knowing. I really don't know. That is why I say that once you are there, through some luck, some strange chance, from then on everything happens in its own way. You are always in a state of samadhi; there is no question of going in and out of it; you are always there. I don't want to use that word, so I say it is a state of not knowing. You really don't know what you are looking at.

★

I can't do anything about it—there is no question of my going back or anything; it is all finished—it is operating and functioning in a different way. (I have to use the words 'different way' to give you a feel of it.)

There *seems* to be some difference. You see, my difficulty with the people who come to see me is this: they don't seem to be able to understand the way I am functioning, and I don't seem to be able to understand the way they are functioning. How can we carry on a dialogue? Both of us have to stop. How can there be a dialogue between us both? I am talking like a raving maniac. All my talking totally unrelated, just like a maniac's—the difference is only a hair's breadth—that is why I say you either flip or fly at that moment.

There is *no* difference, absolutely no difference. Somehow, you see, by some luck, by some strange chance, this kind of thing happens (I have to use the word 'happens' to give you a feel about that) and the whole thing is finished for you.

Q: Are even those who have 'realized' different from one another?

UG: Yes, because the background is different. The background is the only thing that can express itself. What else is there? My expression of it is the background: how I struggled, my path, the path I followed, how I rejected the paths of others—up to that point I can say what I did or what I did not do—so, that did not help me in any way.

Q: But one like you is different from us?

UG: He's different, not only from you but from all the others who are supposed to be in this state, because of his background.

Q: Although everyone who is supposed to have undergone this 'explosion' is unique, in the sense that each one is expressing his own background, there do seem to be some common characteristics.

UG: That is not my concern; it seems to be yours. I never compare myself to somebody else.

★

And that is all there to it. My biography is over. There is nothing more to write about, and never will be. If people come and ask me questions, I answer; if they don't, it makes no difference to me. I have not set myself up in the 'holy business' of liberating people. I have no particular message for mankind, except to say that all holy systems for obtaining enlightenment are bunk, and that all talk of arriving at a psychological mutation through awareness is poppycock. Psychological mutation is impossible. The natural state can happen only through biological mutation.

--->===>   <====<---

The Natural State

This state is a physical condition of your being. It is not some kind of psychological mutation. It is not a state of mind into which you can fall one day, and out of it the next day. You can't imagine the extent to which, as you are now, thought pervades and interferes with the functioning of every cell in your body. Coming into your natural state will blast every cell, every gland, every nerve. It is a chemical change. An alchemy of some sort takes place. But this state has nothing to do with the experiences of chemical drugs such as LSD. Those are experiences; this is not.

★

This state is a state of not knowing; you really don't know what you are looking at. I may look at the clock on the wall for half an hour—still I do not read the time. I don't know it is a clock. All there is inside is wonderment: 'What is this that I am looking at?' Not that the question actually phrases itself like that in words: the whole of my being is like a single, big question mark. It is a state of wonder, of wondering, because I just do not know what I am looking at. The knowledge about it—all that I have learned—is held in the background unless there is a demand. It is in the 'declutched state'. If you ask the time, I will say 'It's a quarter past three' or whatever—it comes quickly like an arrow—then I am back in the state of not knowing, of wonder.

★

You can never understand the tremendous peace that is always there within you, that is your natural state. Your trying to create a peaceful state of mind is in fact creating disturbance within you. You can only talk of peace, create a state of mind and say to yourself that you are very peaceful—but that is not peace; that is violence. So there is no use in practising peace, there is no reason to practise silence. Real silence is explosive; it is not the dead state of mind that spiritual seekers think. 'Oh, I am at peace with myself! There is silence, a tremendous silence! I experience silence!'—that doesn't mean anything at all. This is volcanic in its nature: it's bubbling all the time—the energy, the life—that is its quality. You may ask how I know. I don't know. Life is aware of itself, if we can put it that way—it is conscious of itself.

★

When I talk of 'feeling', I do not mean the same thing that you do. Actually, feeling is a physical response, a thud in the thymus. The thymus, one of the endocrine glands, is located under the breastbone. The doctors tell us that it is active through childhood until puberty and then becomes dormant. When you come into your natural state, this gland is reactivated. Sensations are felt there; you don't translate them as 'good' or 'bad'; they are just a thud. If there is a movement outside of you—a clock pendulum swinging, or a bird flying across your field of vision— that movement is also felt in the thymus. The whole of your being is that movement or vibrates with that sound; there is no separation. This does not mean that you identify yourself with that bird or whatever— 'I am that flying bird.' There is no 'you' there, nor is there any object. What causes that sensation, you don't know. You do not even know that it is a sensation.

'Affection' means that you are affected by everything, not that some emotion flows from you towards something. The natural state is a state of great sensitivity—but this is a physical sensitivity of the senses, not some kind of emotional compassion or tenderness for others. There is compassion only in the sense that there are no 'others' for me, and so there is no separation.

★

Is there in you an entity which you call the 'I' or the 'mind' or the 'self'? Is there a coordinator who is coordinating what you are looking at with what you are listening to, what you are smelling with what you are tasting, and so on? Or is there anything which links together the various sensations originating from a single sense—the flow of impulses from the eyes, for example? Actually, there is always a gap between any two sensations. The coordinator bridges that gap: he establishes himself as an illusion of continuity.

In the natural state there is no entity who is coordinating the messages from the different senses. Each sense is functioning independently in its own way. When there is a demand from outside which makes it necessary to coordinate one or two or all of the senses and come up with a response, still there is no coordinator, but there is a temporary state of coordination. There is no continuity; when the demand has been met, again there is only the uncoordinated, disconnected, disjointed functioning of the senses. This is always the case. Once the continuity is blown apart—not that it was ever there; but the illusory continuity— it's finished once and for all.

Can this make any sense to you? It cannot. All that you know lies within the framework of your experience, which is of thought. This state is not an experience. I am only trying to give you a 'feel' of it, which is, unfortunately, misleading.

When there is no coordinator, there is no linking of sensations, there is no translating of sensations; they stay pure and simple sensations. I do not even know that they are sensations. I may look at you as you are talking. The eyes will focus on your mouth because that is what is moving, and the ears will receive the sound vibrations. There is nothing inside which links up the two and says that it is you talking. I may be looking at a spring bubbling out of the earth and hear the water, but there is nothing to say that the noise being heard is the sound of water, or that that sound is in any way connected with what I am seeing. I may be looking at my foot, but nothing says that this is my foot. When I am walking, I see my feet moving—it is such a funny thing: 'What is that which is moving?'

What functions is a primordial consciousness, untouched by thought.

★

The eyes are like a very sensitive camera. The physiologists say that light reflected off objects strikes the retina of the eye and the sensation goes through the optic nerve to the brain. The faculty of sight, of seeing, is simply a physical phenomenon. It makes no difference to the eyes whether they are focused on a snow-capped mountain or on a garbage can: they produce sensations in exactly the same way. The eyes look on everyone and everything without discrimination.

You have a feeling that there is a 'cameraman' who is directing the eyes. But left to themselves—when there is no 'cameraman'—the eyes do not linger, but are moving all the time. They are drawn by the things outside. Movement attracts them, or brightness or a colour which stands out from whatever is around it. There is no 'I' looking; mountains, flowers, trees, cows, all look at me. The consciousness is like a mirror, reflecting whatever is there outside. The depth, the distance, the colour, everything is there, but there is nobody who is translating these things. Unless there is a demand for knowledge about what I am looking at, there is no separation, no distance from what is there. It may not actually be possible to count the hairs on the head of someone sitting across the room, but there is a kind of clarity which seems as if I could.

The eyes do not blink, except when there is sudden danger—this is something very natural because the things outside are demanding attention all the time. Then, when the eyes are tired, a built-in mechanism in the body cuts them out—they may be open, but they are blurred. But if the eyes stay open all the time, if the reflex action of blinking is not operating, they become dry and you will go blind; so there are some glands beyond the outer corners of the eyes, which are not activated in your case, which act as a watering mechanism. Tears flow all the time from the outer corners. Ignorant people have described them as 'tears of joy' or 'tears of bliss'. There is nothing divine about them. By practising not blinking, one will not arrive in this state; one will only strain the eyes. And there are neurotics in mental hospitals whose eyes do not blink for one reason or another—for them it is a pathological condition. But once you are in your natural state, by some luck or some strange chance, all this happens in its own way.

★

The personality does not change when you come into this state. You are, after all, a computer machine, which reacts as it has been programmed. It is in fact your present effort to change yourself that is taking you away from yourself and keeping you from functioning in the natural way. The personality will remain the same. Don't expect such a man to become free from anger or idiosyncrasies. Don't expect some kind of spiritual humility. Such a man may be the most arrogant person you have ever met, because he is touching life at a unique place where no man has touched before.

It is for this reason that each person who comes into this state expresses it in a unique way, in terms relevant to his time. It is also for this reason that if two or more people are living in this state at the same time, they will never get together. They won't dance in the streets hand in hand: 'We are all self-realized men! We belong!'

★

There must be a living contact. If you walk out of the room, you disappear from my consciousness. Where you are, or why you are not here—these questions do not arise. There are no images here—there is no room for them—the sensory apparatus is completely occupied with the things I am looking at now. There must be a living contact with

59

those things that are in the room, not thoughts about things that are not here. And so, if you are totally 'tuned in' to the sensory activity, there is no room for fears about who will feed you tomorrow, or for speculation about God, Truth and Reality.

This is not a state of omniscience, wherein all of man's eternal questions are answered; rather it is a state in which the questioning has stopped. It has stopped because those questions have no relation to the way the organism is functioning, and the way the organism is functioning leaves no room for those questions.

★

My body exists for other people; it does not exist for me; there are only isolated points of contact, impulses of touch which are not tied together by thought. So the body is not different from the objects around it; it is a set of sensations like any other. Your body does not belong to you.

Perhaps I can give you the 'feel' of this. I sleep four hours at night, no matter what time I go to bed. Then I lie in bed until morning fully awake. I don't know what is lying there in the bed; I don't know whether I'm lying on my left side or my right side—for hours and hours I lie like this. If there is any noise outside—a bird or something—it just echoes in me. I listen to the 'flub-dub-flub-dub' of my heart and don't know what it is. There is no body between the two sheets—the form of the body is not there. If the question is asked, 'What is in there?' there is only an awareness of the points of contact, where the body is in contact with the bed and the sheets, and where it is in contact with itself, at the crossing of the legs, for example. There are only the sensations of touch from these points of contact, and the rest of the body is not there. There is some kind of heaviness, probably the gravitational pull, something very vague. There is nothing inside which links up these things. Even if the eyes are open and looking at the whole body, there are still only the points of contact, and they have no connection with what I am looking at. If I want to try to link up these points of contact into the shape of my own body, probably I will succeed, but by the time it is completed the body is back in the same situation of different points of contact. The linkage cannot stay. It is the same sort of thing when I'm sitting or standing. There is no body.

★

The body has an extraordinary mechanism for renewing itself. This is necessary because the senses in the natural state are functioning at the peak of their sensitivity all the time. So, when the senses become tired, the body goes through death. This is real physical death, not some mental state. It can happen one or more times a day. You do not decide to go through this death; it descends upon you. It feels at first as if you have been given an anaesthetic: the senses become increasingly dull, the heartbeat slows, the feet and hands become ice-cold, and the whole body becomes stiff like a corpse. Energy flows from all over the body towards some point. It happens differently every time. The whole process takes forty-eight or forty-nine minutes. During this time the stream of thoughts continues, but there is no reading of the thoughts.

At the end of this period you 'conk out': the stream of thought is cut. There is no way of knowing how long that cut lasts—it is not an experience. There is nothing you can say about that time of being 'conked out'—that can never become part of your conscious existence or conscious thinking. You don't know what brings you back from death. If you had any will at that moment, you could decide not to come back. When the 'conking out' is over, the stream of thought picks up exactly where it left off. Dullness is over; clarity is back. The body feels very stiff—slowly it begins to move of its own accord, limbering itself up. The movements are more like the Chinese T'ai Chi than like Hatha Yoga. The disciples observed the things that were happening to the teachers, probably, and embodied them and taught hundreds of postures—but they are all worthless; it is an extraordinary movement. Those who have observed my body moving say it looks like the motions of a newly born baby. This 'conking out' gives a total renewal of the senses, glands and nervous system: after it they function at the peak of their sensitivity.

★

My talking comes out in response to the questions which are asked. I cannot sit and give a talk on the natural state—that is an artificial situation for me. There is nobody who is thinking thoughts and then coming out with answers. When you throw a ball at me, the ball bounces back, and that is what you call an 'answer'. But I don't give any answers; this state is expressing itself. I really don't know what I'm saying, and what I'm saying is of no importance. You may transcribe my own talking, but it will make no sense to me—it is a dead thing.

What is here, this natural state, is a living thing. It cannot be captured by me, let alone by you. It's like a flower. (This simile is all I can give.) It just blooms. It's there. As long as it is there, it has a fragrance which is different and distinct from that of every other flower. You may not recognize it. You may or may not write odes or sonnets about it. A wandering cow might eat it, or it may be chopped down by a hay cutter, or it fades and is finished—that's the end of it. It's of no importance. You can't preserve its perfume; whatever you preserve of this is only a synthetic, a chemical perfume, not the living thing. Preserving the expressions, teachings or words of such a man has no meaning. This state has only contemporary value, contemporary expression.

★

This state is not in your interest. You are only interested in continuity. You want to continue, probably on a different level, and to function in a different dimension, but you want to continue somehow. You wouldn't touch this with a barge pole. This is going to liquidate what you call 'you,' all of you—higher self, lower self, soul, Atman, conscious, subconscious—all of that. You come to a point, and then you say, 'I need time.' So sadhana (inquiry and religious endeavour) comes into the picture, and you say to yourself, 'Tomorrow I will understand.' This structure is born of time and functions in time, but does not come to an end through time. If you don't understand now, you are not going to understand tomorrow. What is there to understand? Why do you want to understand what I am saying? You can't understand what I am saying. It is an exercise in futility on your part to try to relate the description of how I am functioning to the way you are functioning. This is a thing which I cannot communicate. Nor is any communication necessary. No dialogue is possible. When the 'you' is not there, when the question is not there, what is is understanding. You are finished. You'll walk out. You will never listen to anybody describing his state or ask any questions about understanding at all.

What you are looking for does not exist. You would rather tread an enchanted ground with beatific visions of a radical transformation of that non-existent self of yours into a state of being which is conjured up by some bewitching phrases. That takes you away from your natural state—it is a movement away from yourself. To be yourself requires extraordinary intelligence. You are 'blessed' with that intelligence; nobody need give it to you, nobody can take it away from you. He who lets that express itself in its own way is a natural man.

◦━━● ●━━◦

The public talk given at the Indian Institute of World Culture in Bangalore, in the month of May 1972.

…I was trapped into this kind of a thing. I don't like to give talks at all. You all seem to be very fond of listening to speeches, talks, lectures, discussions, discourses, conversations, and so on. I do not know if at any time you realize for yourself and by yourself that you never listen to anybody or anything in this world. You always listen to yourself. I really don't know what to say. I don't know what you want to listen to and what I am expected to do. This is supposed to be a discourse and a dialogue. I very often point out to those who come to see me and talk things over that no dialogue is possible and no dialogue is necessary. It may sound very strange to you, but, nevertheless, the fact does remain that no dialogue is possible and yet no dialogue is necessary.

If you will permit me, I will say a few words, to set the ball rolling, as it were. I am going to say a few words about the state of not knowing. How can anybody say anything about the 'state of not knowing?' I have necessarily to use words. Can we use words without indulging in abstract concepts? I say we can. But I do not, at the same time, mean that it is a non-verbal conceptualization. That is a funny thing—there is no such thing as non-verbal conceptualization at all. But, perhaps, a few words like this will enable you to understand [that] the methods of thought prevent you from understanding the limitations of thought as a means to directly experience life and its movements.

This 'state of not knowing' is not [just] my particular state. This is as much your natural state as it is mine. It is not the state of a God-realized man; it is not the state of a Self-realized man. It is not the state of a holy man. It is the natural state of every one of you here. But since you are looking to somebody else and you are reaching out for some kind of a state of liberation, freedom, or moksha—I don't know what words you want to use—you are lost. But, how can one understand the limitations of thought? Naturally, the only instrument we have is the instrument of thought. But what is thought? I can give you a lot of definitions, and you know a lot of definitions about thought. I can say that thought is just matter; thought is vibration; and we are all functioning in this sphere of thought. And we pick up these thoughts because this human organism is an electro-magnetic field. And this electro-magnetic field is the product of culture. It may sound very inappropriate on this occasion to say that in order to be in your natural state, all that man has thought and felt before you must be swept aside and must be brushed aside. And that means the culture in which you are brought up must go down the drain or out of the window. Is it possible? It is possible. But, at the same time, it is so difficult, because you are the product of that culture and you are that. You are not different from that. You cannot separate yourself from that culture. And yet, this culture is the stumbling block for us to be in our natural state. Can this 'Natural State' be captured, contained and expressed through words? It cannot. It is not a conscious state of your existence. It can never become part of your conscious thinking. And then why do I talk of this state of not knowing? For all practical purposes it does not exist at all. It can never become part of your conscious thinking.

Here, I have to explain what I mean by the word 'consciousness'. I don't know. When do you become conscious of a thing? Only when the thought comes in between what is there in front of you and what is supposed to be there inside of you. That is consciousness. So, you have to necessarily use thought to become conscious of the things around you, or the persons around you. Otherwise, you are not conscious of the things at all. And, at the same time, you are not unconscious. But there is an area where you are neither conscious nor unconscious. But that 'consciousness'—if I may use that word—expresses itself in its own way; and what prevents that consciousness to express itself in its own way is the movement of thought. What can anyone do about this thought? It has a tremendous momentum of millions and millions of years. Can I do anything about that thought? Can I stop it? Can I mould it? Can I shape it? Can I do anything about it? But yet, our culture, our civilization, our education—all these have forced us to use that instrument to get something for us. So, can that instrument be used to understand its own nature? It is not possible. And yet, when you see the tremendous nature of this movement of thought, and that there isn't anything that you can do about it, it naturally slows down and falls in its natural pattern. When I say that, I do not, of course, mean what these people in India talk about—that thought must be used in order to get into a thoughtless state or into a meditative state. But there is no such thing as a thoughtless state at all. Thoughts are there; they will be there all the time. Thoughts will disappear only when you become a dead corpse—let me use these two words—'dead corpse'. Otherwise, thoughts are there and they are going to be there. If all the religious teachers tell us that you are going into a 'thoughtless state', they are taking us all for a ride. They can promise you that in that thoughtless state—in that state of silence, in that state of quietness, or in that state of a 'Quiet Mind', or whatever phrase you want to use—there will be this real 'bliss', 'beatitude', 'love', 'religious joy', and 'ecstatic state of being'. All that is balderdash. Because, that state—if there is any state like the state of bliss—it can never become part of your consciousness. It can never become part of your conscious existence. So, you might as well throw the whole thing—the whole crap of these ideas, concepts and abstractions about the blissful states—into a cocked hat.

So, what is one to do? Can anybody help you? No outside agency can help you. That means a complete and total rejection, as I said in the beginning, of all that man has thought and felt before you. As long as there is any trace of knowledge, in any shape, in any form, in your consciousness, you are living in a divided state of consciousness. He [Mr Kothari] referred to my coming into a state of 'not knowing' or 'the calamity', as I myself refer to it. What happened? I don't know. Suddenly thought has fallen into its natural state. The continuity has come to an end. So, what I am saying is not the product of thinking. It is not manufactured by my thought structure inside. Nor is it a logically ascertained premise. But what is happening here is only the expression of that state of being where you do not know what is happening. You do not know how this organism is functioning. This is a pure and simple physical and physiological state of being. It has no religious undertones or overtones. It has no mystical content whatsoever. And, at the same time, this extraordinary thing, the extraordinary intelligence that is there, which is a product of centuries of human evolution, is able to express itself and deal with any problem and any situation without creating problems for us.

Q: May I interrupt you? I was told by people who are around you that when this calamity befell you, you couldn't recognize even ordinary things. You were asking like a newborn child, 'What is this?' Even if there was a flower in front of you, you did not know if that was a flower. Then you would ask, 'What is this?' And the Swiss lady who was keeping house for you, who was looking after you, Valentine, (she is here with us), said, 'This is a flower.' Then you would ask again, 'What is this?' You mean to say that at the time when the calamity took place, all recognition was gone?

UG: Not only then, but even now, as I said, this is a state of 'not knowing'. Since the memory is there in the background, it begins to operate when there is a demand for it. That demand is created by an outside agency, because there is no entity here. There is no centre here.

There is no self here. There is no Atman here. There is no soul here at all. You may not agree. You may not accept it, but that unfortunately happens to be a fact. The totality of thoughts and feelings is not there. But [in you] there is an illusion that there is a totality of your feelings and thoughts. This human organism is responding to the challenges from outside. You are functioning in the sphere—so, thousands and thousands, perhaps millions and millions of sensations are bombarding this body. Since there is no centre here, since there is no mind here, since there is nothing here, what is it that is happening? What is happening here [is that] this human organism is responding to the challenges, or to the stimuli, if I may put it that way. So, there is nobody here who is translating these sensations in terms of past experiences. But there is a living contact with the things around. That is all that is there. One sensation after another is hitting this organism. And at the same time there is no coordinator here. This state of not knowing is not in relationship to your Brahman, or your Nirguna Brahman or Saguna Brahman or any such thing. This state of not knowing is in its relationship to the things that are there around you. You may be looking at a flower. You may think that it is a crazy state. Perhaps it is—I don't know. You do not know what you are looking at. But when there is a demand for that—and that demand always comes from outside, [asking] what is that, and then the knowledge, the information that is there, locked up in this organism comes and says that it is a rose, that this is a microphone, that's a man, that's a woman, and so on and so forth. This is not because there is a drive from inside, but the outside challenge brings out this answer. So, I say that this action is always taking place outside of this organism, not inside. How do I know that these sensations are bombarding or hitting this organism all the time? It is only because there is a consciousness which is conscious of itself and there is nobody who is conscious of the things that are happening. This is a living organism and that living state is functioning in its own natural way.

Mr Kothari: UG, it appears to me this Nirguna Brahman, Atman, whatever it is—when somebody uses the word *Bhuma*, another uses the word 'unknown', the third man says 'akal' [the timeless], the fourth one says something else—all of them say that this cannot be described, 'Neti, Neti.' Probably they meant the same thing; I don't know. I think they meant probably what you are saying as 'totality'. As I understand it, Brahman means 'totality'. If I would translate this state into terms of those times, probably it is the same thing as being in the state of Brahman and [it is] thought which is limiting the 'alpa', which is limiting the 'bhuma', which is limiting the limitless, since it does not function like that, creating an individuality within you. Maybe I am wrong, maybe I am translating, but I say that it is possible that the person who listens to you doesn't know the old terms. You are not going to use the old terms, because the new terms are your terms. And every teacher, every person who has come into some state like this has generally used a different term, a different word, according to his background. But personally I think you mean the same thing. This is a commentary on what you are saying.

UG: What do you want me to say? [*Laughter*] If they have understood what there is, they wouldn't be here. They wouldn't go to anybody. They wouldn't ask these questions at all. If they translate what I am saying, in terms of their particular fancy or their particular background, that's their tragedy; it would be their misery. It hasn't helped them. This is my question: Has it helped you? Why are you hung up on these phrases? They are after all phrases. When once you realize, when once this is understood—how this mechanism is operating, how automatic it is, how mechanical it is, you will realize that all these phrases have no meaning at all. You may very well ask me why I am using these phrases: [it is] because you and I have created this unfortunate situation where you have put me here on the dais and asked me to talk, and naturally, as I said in the beginning, I have to use words. So, the moment I stop talking, the whole thing has come to a stop inside. Is that so? It is so here (in my case), because there is no continuity of thought.

...There is nothing to achieve, there is nothing to accomplish, nothing to attain, and no destination to arrive at. And what prevents what is there, this living state, from expressing itself in its own way is the movement of thought which is there only for the purposes of

functioning in this world. When the movement of thought is not there—
I have to use the clauses in terms of time—but time is thought. When
thought is there, time is there. When thought is there, sex is there,
when thought is there, God is there. When thought is not there, there is
no God, there is no sex, nothing is there. But the drug of virtues you
practise, the practice of virtues is not a foundation for it at all. And the
practice of abstinence, continence, and celibacy is not the path to it.
But if you want to indulge in them and feel greatly superior, it's your
own business. I am not here to reform you. I am not here to lead you
anywhere. But this is a fact. You have to understand a fact as a fact. It is
not a logically ascertained thing, it is not a rational thing [so as] to
understand it rationally. A fact is a movement. Truth is movement.
Reality is movement. But I don't want to use these words, because they
are all loaded words. You know all about them. The unfortunate thing
about the whole business is that you know a lot about these things, and
that is the misery of you all. This is a thing which you do not know at
all. I am not claiming that I know it. I myself don't know. That is why
I say I don't know. It's a state of not knowing. Let alone God, let alone
reality, ultimate or otherwise, I don't know what I am looking at—the
very person who has been with me all the time, day and night. That is
my situation. If I tell this to a psychiatrist, he will probably put me on
a couch and say something is radically wrong with me. Probably I am
functioning like any other human being. He doesn't understand that.
That's his problem, it is not my problem any more. So, all your search—
for truth, God, reality—you use any phrase you like, is a false thing.
You are all on a merry-go-round, and you want to go round and
round and round.

…You want to imitate the life of Jesus, you want to imitate the life
of Buddha, you want to imitate the life of Sankara. You can't do it,
because you don't know what is there behind. You will end up changing
your robes, from rose to saffron, saffron to yellow, or from yellow to
rose, depending upon your particular fancy. How can you ask for a
thing which you do not know? How can you search for a thing which
you do not know? That is my question. So, search has no meaning at all.
Only when the search comes to an end, what there is will express itself,

in its own way. You cannot tamper with that. You cannot manipulate that. You cannot manipulate the action of the thing which is there, which has an extraordinary intelligence.

...I am making assertions, statements and conclusions—you will object to them. Take it or leave it. I don't expect you to accept anything that I am saying. You are not in a position to accept or reject it. You can reject it because it does not fit into the particular framework of your philosophy—Sankara, Gaudapada, Ramanuja, Madhavacharya, God knows what—we have too many of them here. So how can you understand this? The only thing to do is to throw in the towel. Turn your back on the whole business. That is why, it takes extraordinary courage, not the courage or the bravado of these people who climb Mount Everest or try to swim across the English Channel, or cross the Pacific or Atlantic—whatever their fancy—on a raft. That is not what I mean. What I mean is the courage. You quote your Bhagavad Gita, or your Brahma Sutras, '*kaschid dhirah*'. All these phrases. What do they mean? '*Abhayam Brahma.*' [Fearless is Brahman.] Why do you all repeat these phrases? It has no meaning. It's a mechanical thing. 'How are you?' 'I am all right, I am fine. Just fine. I couldn't be better.' In America, you know, [they say] 'How are you this morning?' 'I am just fine. I couldn't be better.' In exactly the same way, you throw these phrases at everybody. If you understand the way this mechanical structure is functioning inside of you, you see the absurdity of the whole business of discussing these matters everlastingly. Can you throw the whole business out of the window and walk out?

Mr Kothari: Not now...

UG: Yes, throw stones at me and walk out.

Mr Kothari: They don't have any.

UG: My interest is to send you packing, as the expression has it. If you can do that, you will never go to listen to anybody.

That's enough, I suppose. I haven't said anything. What all you think

I have said is a 'bag'. You think it makes sense. How can it make sense? If you think that it makes sense, you haven't understood a thing. If you think that it doesn't make any sense, you haven't understood it either. It's just words, words, words.... I am not trying to be clever with all these phrases. I don't know a thing about it. Am I talking, am I saying anything? This is like the howling of a jackal, barking of a dog or the braying of an ass. If you can put this on that level and just listen to this vibration, you are out, you will walk out, and you will never listen to anybody in your lifetime. Finish. It doesn't have to be the talk of a self-realized man. You will realize that there is no self to realize. That's all.

⋯⊨◉ ◉⊨⋯

Why Do I Speak?

Why do I speak? Am I speaking? You know, it may sound very funny to you. I have nothing to say and what I am saying is not born out of my thinking. You may not accept this. But it is not a logically ascertained premise that I am putting across. It may sound very funny to you and you have put me in a very precarious position by asking me why I am talking. Am I talking? Really I am not, you see. There is nobody who is talking here. I use this simile of a ventriloquist. He is actually carrying on both sides of the dialogue but we attribute one side of it to the dummy in front of him. In exactly the same way, all your questions are born out of the answers you already have. Any answer anybody gives should put an end to your questions. But it does not. And we are not ready to accept the fact that all the questions are born out of the answers. If the questions go, the answers we take for granted also go with them. But we are not ready to throw the answers away because sentiment comes into the picture. The tremendous investment we have made and the faith we have in the teachers, are also at stake. Therefore, we are not ready to brush aside the answers.

Actually we do not want answers for our questions. The assumption that the questions are different from the questioner is also false. If the answer goes, the questioner also goes. The questioner is nothing but the answers. That is really the problem. We are not ready to accept this answer because it will put an end to the answers which we have accepted for ages as the real answers.

I am just singing my song; then I go. Whether someone listens to me or not it is not my concern. If nobody comes and talks it is alright with me. Believe me, my talking is only incidental. It is not aimed at liberating anyone. If you are not here it's all the same for me. I am not selling anything.

You may infer a rational meaning in what I say or do but it is your doing not mine. I am not interested in anyone's search for happiness, romance or escape. There is no experience here. So how can there be these dramatic, crazy experiences? I have no way of separating myself from events. The event and I are one and the same. I have no teaching. There is nothing to preserve. Teaching implies something that can be used to bring about change. Sorry, there is no teaching here, just disjointed, disconnected sentences. What is there is only your interpretation, nothing else. For this reason there is not now nor will there ever be any kind of copyright for whatever I am saying. I have no claims.

You may very well ask why the hell I am still talking. I emphatically assure you that, in my case, it is not at all in the nature of self-fulfilment. My motive for talking is quite different from what you think it is. It is not that I am eager to help you understand or that I feel that I must help you, not at all. My motive is direct and temporary. You arrive seeking understanding, while I am only interested in making it crystal clear that there is nothing to understand. As long as you want to understand, so long there will be this awkward relationship between two individuals. I am always emphasizing that somehow the truth has to dawn upon you that there is nothing to understand. As long as you think, accept and believe that there is something to understand, and make that understanding a goal to be placed before you, demanding search and struggle, you are lost and will live in misery. The search is invalid because it is based upon questions which in turn are based upon false knowledge. Your knowledge has not freed you from your problems.

★

I don't want many people. I am trying to avoid all the seekers and if there are any finders they don't need my help. By allowing myself to be surrounded by those people I am inadvertently participating in the illusion that by carrying on a dialogue or a conversation with me they are getting something. So I discourage people. Even if they just come and sit around me I try to point out the ridiculous nature of this get-together. I try to finish it by saying, 'Nice meeting you all,' but still they don't go. They would sit with me for hours and hours. Even if I get up and go away they would be still there sitting and talking. They would be talking about what I did or did not say or what they thought I had said.

Still they keep coming back. Most of those who come to see me are religious buffs of all shapes, sizes and colours. Unless they have some sort of background in all this they can't be interested in this kind of thing. They only come to receive some confirmation from me about what they are interested in but they find that they are not getting anything from me. Still they continue to come. You have no idea of how many thousands of people have passed through the precincts of my homes.

Some of them are intelligent enough to realize that they are not going to get anything from me and that there is no point in hanging around. Others are not ready to accept what I emphasize, overemphasize and assert all the time, that whatever has happened to me has happened despite everything I did. Some friends who have been with me for years say that they still have the hope that they are going to get something from me. This, in short, is the story of my life. If you destroy the authority of others, you in your own way become an authority.

My first sentence is negated by the second sentence, and the next sentence negates the second. If you want to understand what I am saying you must listen to me in disconnected frames, the same way that I talk. That's the way I am listening to you. Each is a separate, independent frame. Then you don't see any contradictions.

My interest is not to knock off what others have said (that is too easy) but to knock off what I am saying. More precisely, I am trying to stop what you are making out of what I am saying. This is why my talking sounds contradictory to others. I am forced by the nature of your listening to always negate the first statement with another statement. Then the second statement is negated by a third and so on. My aim is not some comfy dialectical thesis but the total negation of everything that can be expressed.

Anything you try to make out of my statements is not it. You sense a freshness, a living quality, to what is being said here. That is so, but this cannot be used for anything. It is worthless. All you can do with it is to try to organize it, create organizations, open schools, publish holy books, celebrate birthdays, sanctify holy temples and the like, thus destroying any life it may have had in it. No individual can be helped by such things. They only help those who would live by the gullibility of others.

In other words, I am trying to free you not from the past, the conditioning, but rather from what I am saying. I am not suggesting any way out because there is no way. I have stumbled into this and freed myself from the paths of others. I can't make the same mistake they did. I will never suggest that anyone use me as a model or follow in my footsteps.

My path can never be your path. If you attempt to make this your path you will get caught in a rut. No matter how refreshing, revolutionary or fantastic, it is still a rut, a copy, a second-hand thing. I myself do not know how I stumbled into this, so how do you expect me to give it to another? My mission, if there is any, is to debunk every statement I have ever made. If you take seriously and try to use or apply what I have said you will be in danger.

Is There a Teaching/Message?

There is no teaching of mine, and never shall be one. 'Teaching' is not the word for it. A teaching implies a method or a system, a technique or a new way of thinking to be applied in order to bring about a transformation in your way of life. What I am saying is outside the field of teachability; it is simply a description of the way I am functioning. It is just a description of the natural state of man—this is the way you, stripped of the machinations of thought, are also functioning.

The natural state is not the state of a self-realized, God-realized man, it is not a thing to be achieved or attained, it is not a thing to be willed into existence; it is *there*—it is the living state. This state is just the functional activity of life. By 'life' I do not mean something abstract; it is the life of the senses, functioning naturally without the interference of thought. Thought is an interloper, which thrusts itself into the affairs of the senses. It has a profit motive: thought directs the activity of the senses to get something out of them, and uses them to give continuity to itself.

Your natural state has no relationship whatsoever with the religious states of bliss, beatitude and ecstasy; they lie within the field of experience. Those who have led man on his search for religiousness throughout the centuries have perhaps experienced those religious states. So can you. They are thought-induced states of being, and as they come, so do they go. Krishna Consciousness, Buddha Consciousness, Christ Consciousness, or what have you, are all trips in the wrong direction: they are all within the field of time. The timeless can never be experienced, can never be grasped, contained, much less given expression to, by any man. That beaten track will lead you nowhere. There is no oasis situated yonder; you are stuck with the mirage.

I've no message to give to the world. Whatever happens to me is such that you can't share it with the world. That's the reason why I don't get up on a platform or give any lectures—it's not that I can't give lectures; I've lectured everywhere in the world—I've nothing to say. And I don't like to sit in one place, surrounded by people asking set questions. I never initiate any discussions; people come and sit round me—they can do what they like. If somebody asks me a question suddenly, I try to answer, emphasizing and pointing out that there is no answer to that question. So, I merely rephrase, restructure and throw the same question back at you. It's not game playing, because I'm not interested in winning you over to my point of view. It's not a question of offering opinions—of course I do have my opinions on everything from disease to divinity, but they're as worthless as anybody else's.

What I say you must not take literally. So much trouble has been created by people taking it all literally. You must test every word, every phrase, and see if it bears any relation to the way you are functioning. You must test it, but you are not in a position to accept it—unfortunately this is a fact, take it or leave it. By writing it down, you will do more harm than good. You see, I am in a very difficult position: I cannot help you, whatever I say is misleading.

What I am saying has no logic. If it has a logic, it has a logic of its own—I don't know anything about it. But you have necessarily to fit me into the logical structure of your thought; otherwise the logical structure there, the rational thing, comes to an end. You see, you have to rationalize—that is what you are. But this has nothing to do with rationality, it has nothing to do with your logic—that doesn't mean that it is illogical or irrational.

I have not set myself up in the holy business of liberating people. I have no particular message for mankind except to say that all holy systems for obtaining enlightenment are bunk and that all talk of arriving at a psychological mutation through awareness is poppycock. Psychological mutation is impossible. The natural state can happen only through biological mutation.

I have no teaching. There is nothing to preserve. Teaching implies something that can be used to bring about change. Sorry, there is no teaching here, just disjointed, disconnected sentences. What is there is only your interpretation, nothing else. For this reason there is not now nor will there ever be any kind of copyright for whatever I am saying. I have no claims.

My teaching, if that is the word you want to use, has no copyright. You are free to reproduce, distribute, interpret, misinterpret, distort, garble, do what you like, even claim authorship, without my consent or the permission of anybody.

You come here and throw all these things at me. I am not actually giving you any answers. I am only trying to focus or spotlight the whole thing and say, 'This is the way you look at these things; but look at them this (other) way. Then you will be able to find out the solutions for yourself without anyone's help.' That is all. My interest is to point out to you that you can walk, and please throw away all those crutches. If you are really handicapped, I wouldn't advise you to do any such thing. But you are made to feel by other people that you are handicapped so that they could sell you those crutches. Throw them away and you can walk. That's all that I can say. 'If I fall...'—that is your fear. Put the crutches away, and you are not going to fall.

Your very listening has destroyed the revolutionary nature of this [his] breakthrough and has made this a part of knowledge, tradition, because you are the tradition. The listening mechanism that is operating there in you is the tradition. ...By the time this has been accepted, the need has been created for somebody else to come and blast it. That is why I am talking. The very expression of this has created the need for something new to happen. That is its nature. That is the purpose, if there is any purpose, not to create a following but to create something new there. Something new is saving you from the burden of the past. The moment it is given expression to, it is old. Why be like those handing over the torch from one person to another and maintaining the hierarchical structure.

⤙⥤　⥢⤚

Is There Such a Thing as Enlightenment?

There is no such thing as enlightenment. You may say that every teacher and all the saints and saviours of mankind have been asserting for centuries upon centuries that there is enlightenment and that they are enlightened. Throw them all in one bunch into the river! I don't care. To realize that there is no enlightenment at all is enlightenment.

But actually an enlightened man or a free man, if there is one, is not interested in freeing or enlightening anybody. This is because he has no way of knowing that he is a free man, that he is an enlightened man. It is not something that can be shared with somebody, because it is not in the area of experience at all.

Does such a thing as enlightenment exist? To me what does exist is a purely physical process. There is nothing mystical or spiritual about it. If I close the eyes some light penetrates through the eyelids. If I cover the eyelids there is still light inside. There seems to be some kind of a hole in the forehead which doesn't show but through which something penetrates. In India that light is golden, in Europe it is blue. There is also some kind of light penetration through the back of the head. It's as if there is a hole running through between those spots in front and back of the skull. There is nothing inside but this light. If you cover those points there is complete, total darkness. This light doesn't do anything or help the body to function in any way, it's just there.

This state is a state of not knowing. You really don't know what you are looking at. All there is inside is wonderment. It is a state of wonder because I just do not know what I am looking at. The knowledge about it, all that I have learned, is held in the background unless there is a demand. When required it comes quickly like an arrow, then I am back in the state of not knowing, of wonder.

I don't know if I have made myself clear. The reason why I am emphasizing the physical aspect is not with the idea of selling something but to emphasize and express what you call enlightenment, liberation, transformation, in pure and simple physical and physiological terms. There is absolutely no religious content to it, and no mystical overtones or undertones to the functioning of the body. Unfortunately, for centuries the whole thing has been interpreted in religious terms and that has caused misery for us all.

I am not interested in propagating this. This is not something which you can make happen, nor is it possible for me to create that hunger which is essential to understand anything. I am repeating this over and over again but repetition has its own charm. You are assuming that you are hungering for spiritual attainments and you are reaching out for your goals. Naturally, there are so many people in the marketplace, all these saints, selling all kinds of shoddy goods. They say it is for the welfare of mankind and that they do it out of compassion and all that kind of thing. What I am trying to say is that you are satisfied with the crumbs they throw at you. They promise that one day they are going to deliver to you a full loaf of bread. That is just a promise. They cannot deliver the goods at all. There is no use waiting for something to happen to satisfy your hunger. The hunger has to burn itself up. Literally, it has to burn itself out.

★

The whole mystique of enlightenment is based upon the idea of transforming yourself. I cannot convey or transmit my certainty that you, and all the authorities down through the centuries, are false. They, and the spiritual goods they peddle, are utterly false.

Just let me warn you that if what you are aiming at, enlightenment, really happens you will die. There will be a physical death because there has to be a physical death to be in that state. It happens when you touch life at a point where nobody has touched it before. Nobody can teach you that.

When enlightenment comes it wipes out everything. That is something which cannot be made to happen through your effort or through the grace of anybody, through the help of even a god walking on the face of this earth claiming that he has specially descended from wherever for your sake and for the sake of mankind. That is just absolute gibberish.

★

People call me an 'enlightened man'—I detest that term—they can't find any other word to describe the way I am functioning. At the same time, I point out that there is no such thing as enlightenment at all. I say that because all my life I've searched and wanted to be an enlightened man, and I discovered that there is no such thing as enlightenment at all, and so the question whether a particular person is enlightened or not doesn't arise. I don't give a hoot for a sixth-century-BC Buddha, let alone all the other claimants we have in our midst. They are a bunch of exploiters, thriving on the gullibility of the people. There is no power outside of man. Man has created God out of fear. So the problem is fear and not God.

◆━◉ ◉━◆

Is There a Beyond or Timelessness?

Is there a beyond? Because you are not interested in the everyday things and the happenings around you, you have invented a thing called the 'beyond', or 'timelessness', or 'God', 'Truth', 'Reality', 'Brahman', 'enlightenment', or whatever, and you search for that. There may not be any beyond. You don't know a thing about that beyond; whatever you know is what you have been told, the knowledge you have about that. So you are projecting that knowledge. What you call 'beyond' is created by the knowledge you have about that beyond; and whatever knowledge you have about a beyond is exactly what you will experience. The knowledge creates the experience, and the experience then strengthens the knowledge. What you know can never be the beyond. Whatever you experience is not the beyond. If there is any beyond, this movement of 'you' is absent. The absence of this movement probably is the beyond, but the beyond can never be experienced by you; it is when the 'you' is not there. Why are you trying to experience a thing that cannot be experienced?

The fictitious beyond, created by thought out of fear, is really the demand for more of the same in modified form. This demand for repetition of the same thing over and over again is the demand for permanence.

> There is nothing there inside you but the totality of this knowledge you have accumulated. That is what you are. You cannot even directly experience the reality of the world in which you are functioning, much less some world beyond. There is no world beyond space and time. It is your invention based upon the vague promises of the holy men.

In the natural state the movement of self is absent. The absence of this movement probably is the beyond but that can never be experienced by you. It is when the you is not there. The moment you translate, the you is there. You look at something and recognize it. Thought interferes with the sensation by translating. You are either thinking about something which is totally unrelated to the way the senses are functioning at the moment or else labelling. That is all that is there. The word separates you from what you are looking at, thereby creating the you. Otherwise, there is no space between the two.

⋅→▭ ▭←⋅

The Search for God Is the Search for Permanent Happiness.

Man has to be saved from God—that is very essential because ... I don't mean God in the sense in which you use the word 'God'; I mean all that 'God' stands for, not only God, but all that is associated with that concept of God—even karma, reincarnation, rebirth, life after death, the whole thing, the whole business of what you call the 'great heritage of India'—all that, you see. Man has to be saved from the heritage of India. Not only the people; the country has to be saved from that heritage. (Not by revolution, not the way they have done it in the communist countries—that's not the way. I don't know why; you see, this is a very tricky subject.) Otherwise there is no hope for the individual and no hope for the country.

★

That messy thing called the mind has created many destructive things, and by far the most destructive of them all is God. To me the question of God is irrelevant and immaterial. We have no use for God. More people have been killed in the name of God than in the two world wars put together. In Japan, millions of people died in the name of the sacred Buddha. Christians and Muslims have done the same. Even in India, five thousand Jains were massacred in a single day. Yours is not a peaceful nation. Read your own history—it's full of violence from the beginning to the end. Man is merely a biological being. There is no spiritual side to his nature. There is no such thing.... All the virtues, principles, beliefs, ideas and spiritual values are mere affectations. They haven't succeeded in changing anything in you. You're still the brute that you have always been. When will you begin to see the truth that the philosophy of 'Love thy neighbour as thyself' is not what stops you from killing indiscriminately but it's the terror of the fact that if you kill your neighbour you too will also be destroyed along with him that stops you from killing.

★

God is the ultimate pleasure, uninterrupted happiness. No such thing exists. Your wanting something that does not exist is the root of your problem. Transformation, moksha, liberation, and all that stuff are just variations on the same theme: permanent happiness.

★

We have used God to justify the killing of millions and millions of people. We exploit God. You don't want to read your own history. It's full of violence from the beginning to the end.

> God is irrelevant... there's no power outside of man. It is the same power, the same life, that is functioning there in you. Something is trying to express itself and the culture is pushing it down. When once it throws the culture out it expresses itself in its own way.

⊶⊷

Religion Is a Neurological Problem

Religion is not a contractual arrangement, either public or private. It has nothing to do with the social structure or its management. Religious authority wants to continue its hold on the people, but religion is entirely an individual affair. The saints and saviours have only succeeded in setting you adrift in life with pain and misery and the restless feeling that there must be something more meaningful or interesting to do with one's life.

★

'Religion', 'God', 'Soul', 'Beatitudes', 'moksha', are all just words, ideas used to keep your psychological continuity intact. When these thoughts are not there, what is left is the simple, harmonious physical functioning of the organism.

Love, compassion, ahimsa, understanding, bliss, all these things which religion and psychology have placed before man, are only adding to the strain of the body. *All* cultures, whether of the Orient or of the Occident, have created this lopsided situation for mankind and turned man into a neurotic individual.

★

Man has already messed up his life, and religion has made it worse. It is religion that really made a mess of man's life.

> You cannot exonerate the founders and leaders of religions. The teachings of all those teachers and saviours of mankind have resulted in only violence. Everybody talked of peace and love, while their followers practised violence.

Religion is not going to save man; neither atheism nor communism nor any of those systems. Not only the teachings but the teachers themselves have sown the seeds of this violence that we have in this world. You can't put them on a pedestal and say that they should be exonerated. The man who talked of love is responsible because love and hate go together. So how can you exonerate them? Why do you want to revive religion? What for? I am not condemning any particular thing. All are responsible for that. Talk of love is one of the most absurd things. There must be two. Wherever there is a division there is this destruction. Kindness needs two. You are kind to somebody or you are kind to yourself. There is a division there in your consciousness. Anything that is born out of that division is a protective mechanism and in the long run it is destructive.

*

Man has created religion because it gives him a cover. You see, good and bad, right and wrong are like the two ends of the spectrum, one cannot exist independent of the other. When once you are finished with this duality (I am using the word with much caution although I don't like to use it), when you are no longer caught up in the dichotomy of right and wrong or good and bad, you can never do anything wrong. As long as you are caught up in it the danger is that you will always do wrong and if you don't do wrong it is because you are a frightened chicken. It is out of this cowardice that the whole religious thinking is born.

*

The whole structure of religious thought is built on the foundation of discipline. Discipline to me means a sort of masochism. We are all masochists. We torture ourselves because we think that suffering is a means to achieve our spiritual goals. That's unfortunate. Life is difficult so discipline sounds very attractive to people. We admire those who have suffered a lot to achieve their goals. As a matter of fact, the whole religious thinking is built on the foundation of suffering. Those who impose that kind of discipline on us are sadists and we are all being masochists in accepting that. We torture ourselves in the hope of achieving something.

*

Whatever man experiences—self-awareness, self-consciousness—he has sown the seeds of his total destruction. All those religions have come out of that divisive consciousness in man. All the teachings of those teachers will inevitably destroy mankind. There is no point in reviving all those things and starting revivalistic movements. That is dead, finished. Anything that is born out of this division in your consciousness is destructive, is violence. It is so because it is trying to protect not this living organism, not life, but the continuity of thought. And through that it can maintain the status quo of your culture or whatever you want to call it, the society. The problems are neurological.

*

Your highly praised inventiveness springs from your thinking, which is essentially a protective mechanism. The mind has invented both religion and dynamite to protect what it regards as its best interests. There is no good or bad in this sense. Don't you see? All these bad, brutal, terrible people who should have been eliminated long ago are thriving and successful. Don't think that you can get off this merry-go-round or that by pretending to be spiritually superior you are avoiding any complicity. You are that.

⇥⇒ ⇐⇤

Why Is There Fundamentalism?

The self-consciousness that occurred in the human species may be a necessary thing, I don't know. I am not claiming that I have a special insight into the workings of nature. You see for yourself. That's why I say that the very foundation of the human culture is to kill and to be killed. It has happened so. If one is interested in looking at history right from the beginning, the whole foundation of humanity is built on the idea that those who are not with us are against us. That's what is operating in human thinking. So to kill and to be killed in the name of God, represented by the church in the West and all the other religious thinking here in the East, was the order of the day. That's why there is fundamentalism.

★

We are slaves to our ideas and beliefs. We are not ready to throw them out. If we succeed in throwing them out we replace them with another set of beliefs, another body of discipline. Those who are marching into the battlefield and are ready to be killed today—in the name of democracy, in the name of freedom, in the name of communism—are no different from those who threw themselves to the lions in the arenas. The Romans watched that fun with great joy. How are we different from them? Not a bit. We love it. To kill and to be killed is the foundation of our culture.... The Chinese—what horrors they have committed, you will be surprised. They killed scholars and religious people. They burned and buried the books of Confucius and other teachers.

The whole culture of our civilization is built on external violence, killing, and getting killed, first in the name of God as symbolized by the church, then by religious institutions, and finally, in the name of political ideologies as symbolized by the state. Killing is basic to our culture. Our culture is not based on harmony with nature.

We have used God to justify the killing of millions and millions of people. We exploit God. That's the positive aspect of it, not the negative. In the name of God we have killed more people than in the two world wars put together. In Japan, millions of people died in the name of the sacred Buddha. Here in India, five thousand Jains were massacred in a single day. This is not a peaceful nation! You don't want to read your own history—it's full of violence from the beginning to the end.

⊶⚌◉　◉⚌⊷

Holy Men and Holy Business

We have been brainwashed for centuries by holy men that we must control our thoughts. Without thinking you would become a corpse. Without thinking the holy men wouldn't have any means of telling us to control our thoughts. They would go broke. They have become rich telling others to control their thoughts.

The whole religious business is nothing but moral codes of conduct: you must be generous, compassionate, loving, while all the time you remain greedy and callous. Codes of conduct are set by society in its own interests, sacred or profane. There is nothing religious about it. The religious man puts the priest, the censor, inside you. Now the policeman has been institutionalized and placed outside you. Religious codes and strictures are no longer necessary; it is all in the civil and criminal codes. You needn't bother with these religious people anymore;

they are obsolete. But they don't want to lose their hold over people. It is their business; their livelihood is at stake. There is no difference between the policeman and the religious man. It is a little more difficult with the policeman, for, unlike the inner authority sponsored by the holy men, he lies outside you and must be bribed. The secular leaders tell you one way, the holy men another way. It makes no difference: as long as you are searching for peace of mind, you will have a tormented mind. If you try not to search, or if you continue to search, you will remain the same. You have to stop.

★

It is not only your past. It's the entire past, entire existence of every human being and every form of life. It is not such an easy thing. It is like trying to stop this flow of the river through all those artificial means. It will inundate the whole thing.

★

Understanding yourself is one of the greatest jokes, perpetrated on the gullible and credulous people everywhere, not only by the purveyors of ancient wisdom— the holy men— but also by the modern scientists. The psychologists love to talk about self-knowledge, self-actualization, living from moment to moment, and such rot. These absurd ideas are thrown at us as if they are something new.

You have been brainwashed by all those holy men, gurus, teachers and the so-called enlightened people that the past should die, should come to an end. 'If you attain this, life would be hunky-dory—full of sweetness.' You have fallen for all that romantic stuff. If you try to suppress the past and try to be in the present, it will drive you crazy. You are trying to control something which is beyond your control.

★

The holy men talk very lightly of money as if it has no importance for them, when in fact it is one of the most important things in their lives. These holy men are greedy, jealous, and vindictive bastards, just like everybody else. You want to live through your work, and through your children. These people want to live through their religious institutions.

What these gurus in the marketplace do is to sell you some ice packs and provide you with some comforters.

★

I was telling my friends yesterday about the simile we had in one of our books. Those who go to listen to spiritual discourses, those who read books of a religious nature, and those who are looking beyond for something are like the monkeys who sit around the red ochre trying to warm themselves. You know what red ochre is. It is red in colour, just like flame, but there is no warmth.

There isn't anything that you can get from any religious or spiritual discourses. What I have been trying to point out to those that come to listen to me and care to listen to me is that there is nothing to achieve, nothing to accomplish, and nothing to attain. What is it that you want? And what is it that you are searching for? That is my question. If you are searching for anything, if you want anything, the first thing you must do is to throw away lock, stock and barrel and book, bell and the candle, the stuff you are hanging on to. You have to throw the whole lot into the cocked hat. Otherwise, there isn't any chance for you to be yourself. If you follow any path—it doesn't matter what that path is— it is leading you astray. It is putting you on the wrong path. If you make anything out of what I have been saying, you are lost, body and soul. And, if there is a God, out of sheer mercy He should save you all and save you from me and persons like me. One thing I make very clear: I am not here to liberate you at all. What is it that you want to liberate yourself from? You are trying to ask for a thing which you have.

★

You are not interested in solving the problem because that will put an end to you. You want the problems to remain. You want the hunger to remain because if you are not hungry you will not seek this food from all these holy men. What they are giving you are some scraps, bits of food, and you are satisfied.

⋆⫘ ⫘⋆

Meditation Is Warfare

Meditation is a self-centred activity. It is strengthening the very self you want to be free from. What are you meditating for? You want to be free from something. What are you to meditate on? All right, thought is a noise, sound. What is sound? You look at this and you say, 'This is a tape recorder,' so thought is sound. There is a continuous flow of thoughts, and you are linking up all these thoughts all the time, and this is the noise you can't stand. Why can't you stand that noise? So, by repeating mantras, you create a louder noise, and you submerge the noise of thought, and then you are at peace with yourself. You think that something marvellous is happening to you.

You have also been told that through meditation you can bring selfishness to an end. Actually, you are not meditating at all, just thinking about selflessness, and doing nothing to be selfless. I have taken that as an example, but all other examples are variations of the same thing. All activity along these lines is exactly the same. You must accept the simple fact that you do not want to be free from selfishness.

★

Meditation is warfare. You sit for meditation while there is a battle raging within you. The result is violent, evil thoughts welling up inside you. Next, you try to control or direct these brutal thoughts, making more effort and violence for yourself in the process.

Expansion of consciousness is nothing, but you give so much importance to that. Drugs will make it a lot easier than all these meditations and yogas. I am not recommending drugs but they are the same. Doctors say that drugs will damage the brain but meditation will also damage the brain if it is done very seriously. They have gone crazy, jumped into rivers and killed themselves. They did all kinds of things, locked themselves up in caves because they couldn't face it.

★

You see, it is not possible for you to watch your thoughts. It is not possible for you to watch every step you take, it will drive you crazy.

> All your experiences, all your meditations, all your prayer, all that you do, is self-centred. It is strengthening the self, adding momentum, gathering momentum, so it is taking you in the opposite direction. Whatever you do to be free from the self also is a self-centred activity.

⊷⧲ ⧳⊶

You Cannot Find the Seat of Human Consciousness

Krishna Consciousness, Buddha Consciousness, Christ Consciousness, or what have you, are all trips in the wrong direction: they are all within the field of time. The timeless can never be experienced, can never be grasped, contained, much less given expression to, by any man.

★

This consciousness which is functioning in me, in you, in the garden slug and earthworm outside, is the same. In me it has no frontiers; in you there are frontiers—you are enclosed in that. Where is the seat of human consciousness?

You have no way at all of finding out for yourself the seat of human consciousness, because it is all over, and you are not separate from that consciousness. Even with all the experiments that the brain physiologists and psychologists are doing, wasting millions and millions of dollars just to find out the seat of human consciousness, they will never be able to find it out at all. Nor will it be possible for anybody to find out the content of the whole thing—it is too vast. The genetic is only part of it. It is much more than the genetic.

Culture is part of this human consciousness, so everything that man has experienced and felt before you is part of that consciousness. It is really a mystery. All the experiences—not necessarily just your experiences during your span of thirty, forty or fifty years, but the animal consciousness, the plant consciousness, the bird consciousness—all that is part of this consciousness.

Whatever you experience, however profound that experience may be, is the result of the knowledge that is part of your consciousness. Somebody must have, somewhere along the line, experienced the bliss, beatitude—call it 'ecstasy', call it by whatever name you like, but somebody somewhere along the line—not necessarily you—must have experienced that, and that experience is part of your consciousness. You have to come to a point where there is no such thing as a new experience at all: somebody has experienced it before, so it is not yours.

The consciousness of the body does not exist. There is no such thing as consciousness at all. The one thing that helps us to become conscious of the non-existing body, for all practical purposes, is the knowledge that is given to us. Without that knowledge you have no way of creating your own body and experiencing it. I am questioning the very idea of consciousness, let alone the subconscious, the unconscious, the different levels of consciousness, and higher states of consciousness. I don't see that there is any such thing as consciousness. I become conscious of this [touching the arm of the chair] only through the knowledge that I have of it. The touch does not tell me anything except when I translate it within the framework of knowledge. Otherwise I have no way of experiencing that touch at all. The way these senses are operating here is quite different from the way we are made to believe. The eye is looking at the movement of your hand, and is not saying anything about that activity, except observing what is going on there.

⊷⇒ ⇐⊶

What Is Awareness?

I am not particularly fond of the word 'awareness'. It is misused. It is a rubbed coin, and everybody uses it to justify some of his actions, instead of admitting that he did something wrong. Sometimes you say, 'I was not aware of what was going on there.' But awareness is an integral part of the activity of this human organism. This activity is not only specifically in the human organism but in all forms of life—the pig and the dog. The cat just looks at you, and is in a state of choiceless awareness. To turn that awareness into an instrument which you can use to bring about a change is to falsify that. Awareness is an integral part of the activity of the living organism.

★

Awareness is not a divided state. There are not two states, awareness and something else. There are not two things. It is not that you are aware of something. Awareness is simply the action of the brain. The idea that you can use awareness to bring about some happier state of affairs, some sort of transformation or God-knows-what, is absurd. Awareness cannot be used to bring about a change in yourself or the world around you.

All this rubbish about the conscious and the unconscious, awareness and the self, is all a product of modern psychology. The idea that you can use awareness to get somewhere psychologically is very damaging. After more than a hundred years we seem unable to free ourselves from the psychological rubbish, Freud and the whole gang. Just what exactly do you mean by consciousness? You are conscious, aware, only through thought. The other animals use thought. The dog, for example, can recognize its owner in a simple manner. They recognize without using language. Humans have added to the structure of thought, making it much more complex.

If you could be in a state of awareness for a single moment once in your life the continuity would be snapped, the illusion of the experiencing structure, the you, would collapse and everything would fall into the natural rhythm. In this state you do not know what you are looking at. That is awareness.

※

There Is No Self, No Soul

The belief that there is a centre here, that there is a spirit here, that there is a soul here, is what is responsible for that belief that there must be something beyond.

Is there any such thing as soul? Is there any such thing as the 'I'? Is there any such thing as the psyche? Whatever you see there, whatever you experience there, is created only by the knowledge you have of that self.

There is no self, there is no I, there is no spirit, there is no soul, and there is no mind. That knocks off the whole list, and you have no way of finding out what you are left with.

Ideas of soul and life after death are born out of the demand for permanence. That's the basis of man's religious thinking. All religious thinking is born out of the demand for permanence.

> Religion, God, soul, are all just words, ideas used to keep your psychological continuity intact. When these thoughts are not there, what is left is the simple, harmonious physical functioning of the organism.

★

When you actually do see and perceive for the first time that there is no self to realize, no psyche to purify, no soul to liberate, it will come as a tremendous shock to that instrument. You have invested everything in that—the soul, mind, psyche, whatever you wish to call it—and suddenly it is exploded as a myth. It is difficult for you to look at reality, at your actual situation. One look does the trick. You are finished.

★

I may say that there is nothing to be changed, but the revolutionary teachers come and tell us that there is something there, in which you have to bring about a radical revolution, then we assume there is such a thing as soul, spirit or the self. What I assert all the time is that I haven't found anything like the self or soul there. This question haunted me all my life and suddenly it hit me, 'There is no self to realize. What the hell have I been doing all this time?' You see, that hits you like lightning. Once that hits you, the whole mechanism of the body that is controlled by this thought is shattered. What is left is the tremendous living organism with an intelligence of its own. What you are left with is the pulse, the beat and the throb of life.

⊶⊜ ⊜⊷

Mind Is a Myth

There is no such thing as an unconditioned mind; the mind is conditioned. It is absurd, you see, to.... If there is a mind, it is bound to be conditioned. There is no such thing as an open mind.

To me there is no such thing as mind; mind is a myth. Since there is no such thing as mind, the 'mutation of mind' that J. Krishnamurti is talking about has no meaning. There is nothing there to be transformed, radically or otherwise. There is no self to be realized. The whole religious structure that has been built on this foundation collapses because there is nothing there to realize.

The whole Buddhist philosophy is built on the foundation of that 'no mind'. Yet they have created tremendous techniques of freeing themselves from the mind. All the Zen techniques of meditation try to free you from the mind. But the very instrument that we are using to free ourselves from, the thing called 'mind', *is* the mind. Mind is nothing other than what you are doing to free yourself from the mind. But when it once dawns on you, by some strange chance or miracle, that the instrument that you are using to understand everything is not the instrument, and that there is no other instrument, it hits you like a bolt of lightning.

★

The separation between mind and body must come to an end. Actually, there is no separation. I have no objection to the word mind but it is not in one particular location or area. Every cell in your system has a mind of its own and its functioning or working is quite different from that of the other cells.

> Mind or thought is not yours or mine. It is our common inheritance. There is no such thing as your mind and my mind (it is in that sense mind is a myth). There is only mind, the totality of all that has been known, felt and experienced by man, handed down from generation to generation. We are all thinking and functioning in that thought sphere just as we all share the same atmosphere for breathing.

⊷☰◉　◉☰⊶

Thought Is Bourgeois

Thought in its birth, in its origin, in its content, in its expression, and in its action is very fascist. When I use the word 'fascist' I use it not in the political sense but to mean that thought controls and shapes our thinking and our actions. So it is a very protective mechanism. It has no doubt helped us to be what we are today. It has helped us to create our high-tech and technology. It has made our life very comfortable. It has also made it possible for us to discover the laws of nature. But thought is a very protective mechanism and is interested in its own survival. At the same time, thought is opposed fundamentally to the functioning of this living organism.

It is thought that has invented the ideas of cause and effect. There may not be any such thing as a cause at all. Every event is an individual and independent event. We link up all these events and try to create a story of our lives. But actually every event is an independent event. If we accept the fact that every event is an independent event in our lives, it creates a tremendous problem of maintaining what we call identity. And identity is the most important factor in our lives. We are able to maintain this identity through the constant use of memory, which is also thought. This constant use of memory or identity, or whatever you call it, is consuming a tremendous amount of energy, and it leaves us with no energy to deal with the problems of our living. Is there any way that we can free ourselves from the identity? As I said, thought can only create problems; it cannot help us to solve them. Through dialectical thinking about thinking itself we are only sharpening that instrument. All philosophies help us only to sharpen this instrument.

Thought is very essential for us to survive in this world. But it cannot help us in achieving the goals that we have placed before ourselves. The goals are unachievable through the help of thought. The quest for happiness, as you mentioned, is impossible because there is no such thing as permanent happiness. There are moments of happiness, and there are moments of unhappiness. But the demand to be in a permanent state of happiness is the enemy of this body. This body is interested in maintaining its sensitivity of the sensory perceptions and also the sensitivity of the nervous system. That is very essential for the survival of this body. If we use that instrument of thought for trying to achieve the impossible goal of permanent happiness, the sensitivity of this body is destroyed. Therefore, the body is rejecting all that we are interested in—permanent happiness and permanent pleasure. So, we are not going to succeed in that attempt to be in a permanent state of happiness.

> You have, through ideation and mentation, created your own thoughts which you consider to be yours, just as when different colours are mixed into various hues, but all of them can be reduced to the seven basic colours found in nature. What you think are your thoughts are actually just combinations and permutations of the thoughts of others.

Thought to me is matter. Therefore, all our spiritual goals are materialistic in their value. And this is the conflict that is going on there. In this process, the totality of man's experiences created what we call a separate identity and a separate mind. But actually if you want to experience anything, be it your own body, or your own experiences, you have no way of experiencing them without the use of the knowledge that is passed on to us.

★

All the problems are artificially created by the various structures created by human thinking. There is some sort of (I can't make a definitive statement) neurological problem in the human body. Human thinking is born out of this neurological defect in the human species. Anything that is born out of human thinking is destructive. Thought is destructive. Thought is a protective mechanism. It draws frontiers around itself, and it wants to protect itself. It is for the same reason that we also draw lines on this planet and extend them as far as we can. Do you think these frontiers are going to disappear? They are not. Those who have entrenched themselves, those who have had the monopoly of all the world's resources so far and for so long, if they are threatened to be dislodged, what they would do is anybody's guess. All the destructive weapons that we have today are here only to protect that monopoly.

★

But actually the question 'Is there a thought?' is born out of the assumption that there is a thought there. But what you will find there is all about thought and not thought. All about thought is what is put in there by the culture. That is put in by the people who are telling us that it is very essential for you to free yourself from whatever you are trying to free yourself from through that instrument. My interest is to emphasize that that is not the instrument, and there is no other instrument. And when once this hits you, dawns upon you that thought is not the instrument, and that there is no other instrument, then there is no need for you to find out if any other instrument is necessary. No need for any other instrument. This very same structure that we are using, the instrument which we are using, has in a very ingenious way invented all kinds of things like intuition, right insight, right this, that, and the other. And to say that through this very insight we have come to understand something is the stumbling block. All insights, however extraordinary they may be, are worthless, because it is thought that has created what we call insight, and through that it is maintaining its continuity and status quo.

★

Where does thought come from? Is it from inside, or outside? Where is the seat of human consciousness? So, for purposes of communication, or just to give a feel about it, I say there is a 'thought sphere'. In that 'thought sphere' we are all functioning, and each of us probably has an 'antenna', or what you call an 'aerial' or something, which is the creation of the culture into which we are born. It is that that is picking up these particular thoughts. You have no way at all of finding out for yourself the seat of human consciousness, because it is all over, and you are not separate from that consciousness. Even with all the experiments that the brain physiologists and psychologists are doing, wasting millions and millions of dollars just to find out the seat of human consciousness, they will never be able to find it out at all. I am not making a dogmatic statement or any such thing.

★

Thought can never capture the movement of life, it is much too slow. It is like lightning and thunder. They occur simultaneously, but sound, travelling slower than light, reaches you later, creating the illusion of two separate events. It is only the natural physiological sensations and perceptions that can move with the flow of life.

★

There is no such thing as looking at something without the interference of knowledge. To look you need space, and thought creates that space. So space itself, as a dimension, exists only as a creation of thought. Thought has also tried to theorize about the space it has created, inventing the 'time–space continuum'. Time is an independent reference or frame. There is no necessary continuity between it and space. Thought has also invented the opposite of time, the 'now', the 'eternal now'. The present exists only as an idea. The moment you attempt to look at the present, it has already been brought into the framework of the past. Thought will use any trick under the sun to give momentum to its own continuity. Its essential technique is to repeat the same thing over and over again; this gives it an illusion of permanency. This permanency is shattered the moment the falseness of the past–present–future continuum is seen. The future can be nothing but the modified continuity of the past.

⊷⇒◎ ◎⇐⊷

Feeling Too Is Thought

Feeling is also thought. We want to feel that feelings are more important than thoughts, but there is no way you can experience a feeling without translating that within the framework of the knowledge that you have. Take for example that you tell yourself that you are happy. You don't even know that the sensation that is there is happiness. But you capture that sensation within the framework of the knowledge you have of what you call a state of happiness, and the other state, that of unhappiness. What I am trying to say is that it is the knowledge that you have about yourself which has created the self there and helps you to experience yourself as an entity there.

> You think the thoughts of your society, feel the feelings of your society and experience the experiences of your society. There is no new experience.

All your relationships, knowledge and experiences, all your emotions and feelings, all that romantic stuff, belongs entirely to society, not to you. You are not an individual at all. Only when you are free from what every man and woman has thought and felt before you will you become an individual. Such an individual will not burn books that men have made with great care. He would not be a rebel. All the accumulated knowledge, experience and suffering of mankind is inside of you. You must build a huge bonfire within you. Then you will become an individual. There is no other way.

⋆⟾ ⟾⋆

Knowledge and Experience

Whatever you experience—peace, bliss, silence, beatitude, ecstasy, joy, God knows what—will be old, second-hand. You already have knowledge about all of these things. The fact that you are in a blissful state or in a state of tremendous silence means that you know about it. You must know a thing in order to experience it. That knowledge is nothing marvellous or metaphysical; 'bench', 'bag', 'red bag', is the knowledge. Knowledge is something which is put into you by somebody else, and he got that from somebody else; it is not yours. Can you experience a simple thing like that bench that is sitting across from you? No, you only experience the knowledge you have about it. And the knowledge has come from some outside agency, always. You think the thoughts of your society, feel the feelings of your society and experience the experiences of your society; there is no new experience.

★

Knowledge is not something mysterious or mystical. You know that you are happy, and you have theories about the working of the fan, the light—this is the knowledge we are talking about. You introduce another knowledge, 'spiritual knowledge', but—spiritual knowledge, sensual knowledge—what is the difference? We give the names to them. Fantasies

101

about God are acceptable, but fantasies about sex are called 'sensual', 'physical'. There is no difference between the two; one is socially acceptable, the other is not. You are limiting knowledge to a particular area of experience, so then it becomes 'sensual', and the other becomes 'spiritual'? Everything is sensual.

★

You cannot communicate what you cannot experience. I don't want to use those words, because 'inexpressible' and 'incommunicable' imply that there is something which cannot be communicated, which cannot be expressed. I don't know. There is an assumption that there is something there which cannot be expressed, which cannot be communicated. There is nothing there. I don't want to say there is nothing there, because you will catch me—you will call it 'emptiness', 'void' and all that sort of thing.

> Whatever is experienced is thought-induced. Without knowledge you can't experience. And experience strengthens the knowledge. It is a vicious circle: the dog chasing its own tail.

Where, you ask, is this knowledge, the past? Is it in your brain? Where is it? It is all over your body. It is in every cell of your body.

⊷⊜ ⊜⊶

Is There Any Meaning and Purpose to Life?

'What is the meaning of life?' It is not life that we are really interested in but living. The problem of living has become a very tiring business— to live with somebody else, to live with our feelings, to live with our ideas. In other words, it is the value system that we have been thrown into. You see, the value system is false.

The heart does not for a moment know that it is pumping blood. It is not asking the question, 'Am I doing it right?' It is just functioning.

It does not ask the question, 'Is there any purpose?' To me, that question has no meaning. The questions, 'Is there any meaning?' 'Is there any purpose?' take away the living quality of life. You are living in a world of ideas.

Suppose I say that this meaninglessness is all there is for you, all there can ever be for you. What will you do? The false and absurd goal you have before you is responsible for that dissatisfaction and meaninglessness in you. Do you think life has any meaning? Obviously you don't. You have been told that there *is* meaning, that there *must* be a meaning to life. Your notion of the 'meaningful' keeps you from facing this issue, and makes you feel that life has no meaning. If the idea of the meaningful is dropped, you will see meaning in whatever you are doing in daily life.

★

Why should life have any meaning? Why should there be any purpose to living? Living itself is all that is there. Your search for spiritual meaning has made a problem out of living. You have been fed all this rubbish about the ideal, perfect, peaceful, purposeful way of life, and you devote your energies to thinking about that rather than living fully. In any case you are living, no matter what you are thinking about. Life has to go on.

Once a very old gentleman, ninety-five years old, who was considered to be a great spiritual man and who taught the great scriptures all the time to his followers, came to see me. He heard that I was there in that town. He came to me and asked me two questions. He asked me, 'What is the meaning of life? I have written hundreds of books telling people all about the meaning and purpose of life, quoting all the scriptures and interpreting them. I haven't understood the meaning of life. You are the one who can give an answer to me.' I told him, 'Look, you are ninety-five years old and you haven't understood the meaning of life. When are you going to understand the meaning of life? There may not be any meaning to life at all.' The next question he asked me was, 'I have lived ninety-five years and I am going to die one of these days. I want to know what will happen after my death.' I said, 'You may not live long to know anything about death. You have to die now. Are you ready to die?' As long as you are asking the question, 'What is death?' or 'What is there after death?' you are already dead. These are all dead questions. A living man would never ask those questions.

⊷⟾　⟾⊶

Creation and Destruction: The Reshuffling of Atoms

Why does nature deliberately want to first create and then destroy? Because nothing is ever born and nothing ever dies. What has created the space between creation and destruction or the time between the two, is thought. In nature there is no death or destruction at all. What occurs is the reshuffling of atoms. If there is a need or necessity to maintain the balance of energy in this universe, death occurs. You may not like it. Earthquakes may be condemned by us. Surely they cause misery to so many thousands and thousands of people. And all this humanitarian activity around the world—sending planeloads of supplies is really a commendable act. It helps those who are suffering there and those who have lost their property. But it is the same kind of activity that is responsible for killing millions and millions of people. What I am saying is that the destructive, war-making movement and the humanitarian movement on the other hand—are both born from the same source.

★

In the long run, earthquakes and the eruption of volcanoes are part of nature's way of creating something new. ...Of course, I am not saying that you should not do anything to help those people [affected by earthquakes].

In nature the positive and the negative don't exist at all. They don't exist at all. If they do, they exist in the same frame. That is what these scientists are all talking about. If you observe the universe, there is chaos in it. The moment you say there is chaos, in the same frame, there is also order. So, you cannot, for sure, say that there is order or chaos in the universe.

Both of them are occurring simultaneously. That is the way the living organism also operates. The moment thought is born, it cannot stay there. Thought is matter. When once the matter that is necessary for the survival of the living organism is created, that matter becomes part of energy. Similarly life and death are simultaneous processes. It is thought that has separated and created the two points of birth and death. Thought has created this space and this time. But actually, birth and death are simultaneous processes.

★

The military wars out there are the extension of what is going on all the time inside you. Why is there a war waging inside you? Because you search for peace. The instrument you are using in your attempt to be at peace with yourself is war. There is already peace in man. You need not search. The living organism is functioning in an extraordinarily peaceful way.

Man's search for truth is born out of this same search for peace. It only ends up disturbing and violating the peace that is already there in the body. So what we are left with is the war within and the war without. It's an extension of the same thing. Our search in this world for peace, being based upon warfare, will lead only to war, towards damnation. Humanity has polluted, destroyed and killed off everything, all on account of his wanting to be at the centre of the universe, of all creation.

Is There Such A Thing As Truth?

Truth is a movement. You can't capture it, contain it, give expression to it, or use it to advance your interests. The moment you capture it, it ceases to be the truth. What is the truth for me is something that cannot, under any circumstances, be communicated to you. The certainty here cannot be transmitted to another. For this reason the whole guru business is absolute nonsense. This has always been the case, not just now. Your self-denial is to enrich the priests. You deny yourself your basic needs while that man travels in a Rolls Royce car, eating like a king, and being treated like a potentate. He, and the others in the holy business, thrive on the stupidity and credulity of others. The politicians, similarly, thrive on the gullibility of man. It is the same everywhere.

★

Whatever you do in the pursuit of truth or reality takes you away from your own very natural state in which you always are. It's not something you can acquire, attain or accomplish as a result of your effort. All that you do makes it impossible for what already is there to express itself. That is why I call this your natural state. You're always in that state. What prevents what is there from expressing itself in its own way is the search. The search is always in the wrong direction.

★

Because you are not interested in the everyday things and happenings around you, you have invented the beyond, timelessness, God, truth, reality, enlightenment or whatever, and search for it.

★

There may not be any ultimate truth. You don't know a thing about it. Whatever you know is what you have been told, what you have heard, and you are projecting that information. What you call something is determined by the learning you have about it, and whatever knowledge you have about it is exactly what you will experience. The knowledge creates the experience and the experience then strengthens the knowledge. What you know can never be the ultimate reality.

> There is nothing there, only your relative, experiential data, your truth. There is no such thing as objective truth at all. There is nothing which exists outside or independent of our minds.

⋙   ⋘

There Is No Freedom of Action

I maintain that man has no freedom of action. I don't mean the fatalism that Indians have practised and are still practising: When I say that man has no freedom of action it is in relation to changing himself, to freeing himself from the burden of the past. It means that you have no way of acting except through the help of the knowledge that is passed on to you. It is in that sense, I said, no action is possible without thought.

So what is necessary is that the individual should free himself from the burden of the past, the great heritage you are talking about. Unless the individual frees himself from the burden of the past, he cannot come up with new solutions for the problems; he repeats the same old…. So it is up to the individual. He has to free himself from the *entire* past, the heritage which you are talking about—that is to say he has to break away from the cumulative wisdom of the ages—only then is it possible for him to come out with the solutions for the problems with which man is confronted today.

But that is not in his hands; there is nothing that he can do to free himself from the burden of the past. It is in that sense that I say he has no freedom of action. You have freedom to come here or not to come here, to study or teach economics or philosophy or something else—*there* you have a limited freedom. But you have no freedom to control the events of the world or shape the events of the world—*nobody* has that power, no nation has that power.

⋙   ⋘

Man Is Memory

The mind is (not that I am giving a new definition) the totality of man's experiences, thoughts, and feelings. There is no such thing as your mind or my mind. I have no objection if you want to call that totality of man's thoughts, feelings, and experiences by the name 'mind'. But how they are transmitted to us from generation to generation is the question. Is it through the medium of knowledge or is there any other way by which they are transmitted from generation to generation, say for example, through the genes? We don't have the answers yet. Then we come to the idea of memory. What is man? Man is memory. What is that memory? Is it something more than just to remember, to recall a specific thing at a specific time? To all this we have to have some more answers. How do the neurons operate in the brain? Is it all in one area? The other day I was talking to a neurosurgeon, a very young and bright fellow. He said that memory, or rather the neurons containing memory, are not in one area. The eye, the ear, the nose, all the five sensory organs in your body have a different sort of memory. But they don't yet know for sure. So we have to get more answers.

★

There is always a space between perception and memory. Memory is like sound. Sound is very slow, whereas light travels faster. All these sensory activities or perceptions are like light. They are very fast. But for some reason we have lost the capacity to kick that [memory] into the background and allow these things to move as fast as they occur in nature. Thought comes, captures it (the sensory perception), and says that it is this or that. That is what you call recognition, or naming, or whatever you want to call it. The moment you recognize this as the tape recorder, the name 'tape recorder' also is there. So recognition and naming are not two different things.

★

We maintain the separation and keep up a non-existing identity. That is the reason why you have to constantly use your memory, which is nothing but the neurons, to maintain your identity.

'Who am I?' 'What is the meaning of life?' 'Does God exist?' or 'Is there an afterlife?'—all these questions spring only from memory. That is why I ask whether you have a question of your own.

★

Can you become conscious of anything except through the medium of memory and thought? Memory is knowledge. Even your feelings are memory.

To attempt to be free from memory is withdrawal, and withdrawal is death.

⟶⟶ ⟵⟵

Do You Exist?

You don't exist. There is no individual there at all. Culture, society, or whatever you want to call it, has created 'you' and 'me' for the sole purpose of maintaining its own continuity. But, at the same time, we are made to believe that you have to become an individual. These two things have created this neurotic situation for us. There is no such thing as an individual, and there is no such thing as freedom of action. I am not talking of a fatalistic philosophy or any such thing. It is this fact that is frustrating us. The demand to fit ourselves into that value system is using a tremendous amount of energy, and there is nothing we can do to deal with the living problems here. All the energy is being consumed by the demands of the culture or society, or whatever you want to call it, to fit you into the framework of that value system. In the process, we are left with no energy to deal with the other problems. But these problems, that is, the living problems, are very simple.

After all, you don't exist, and I don't exist. You and I have been created by the totality of those experiences, and we have to use them in order to function sanely and intelligently in this world.

One thing that I always emphasize is that it is culture that has created us all for the sole purpose of maintaining its status quo and its continuity. So, in that sense, I do not see that there are any individuals at all. At the same time, the same culture has given us the hope that there is something that you can do to become an individual and that there is such a thing as free will. Actually, there is no free will at all.

→⇒○ ○⇐←

Do You Listen to Anybody?

You do not; you listen only to yourself. When you leave the sense of hearing alone, all that is there is the vibration of the sound—the words repeat themselves inside of you, as in an echo chamber. This sense is functioning in just the same way with you, except that you think the words you are hearing come from outside of you. Get this straight: You can never hear one word from anyone else, no matter how intimate you think your relationship with that person; you hear only your own translations, always. They are all your words you are hearing. All that the other person's words can possibly be to you is a noise, a vibration picked up by the ear-drum and transferred to the nerves which run to the brain. You are translating those vibrations all the time, trying to understand, because you want to get something out of what you are hearing. That is all right for a relationship with someone on the level of 'Here is some money; give me a half-kilo of carrots'—but that is the limit of your relationship, of your communication, with anybody. When there is no translation, all languages sound the same whether or not your particular knowledge structure 'speaks' a particular language. The only differences are in the spacing of the syllables and in the tune. Languages are melodic in different ways.

→⇒○ ○⇐←

Relationship Is Division

The problem is a problem of relationship. It is just not possible to establish any relationship with anything around you, including your near and dear ones, except on the level of what you can get out of the relationship. You see, the whole thing springs from this separation or isolation that human beings live in today. We are isolated from the rest of creation, the rest of life around us. We all live in individual frames. We try to establish a relationship at the level of 'What do I get out of that relationship?' We use others to try and fill this void that is created as a result of our isolation.

> We always want to fill this emptiness, this void, with all kinds of relationships with people around us. That is really the problem. We have to use everything—an idea, a person, anything we can get hold of, to establish relationships with others. Without relationships we are lost, and we don't see any meaning; we don't see any purpose.

We are not honest, decorous and decent enough to admit that all relationships are built on the foundation of, 'What do I get out of this relationship?' It is nothing but mutual gratification. If that is absent no relationship is possible. You keep the relationship going for social reasons or for reasons of children, property and security. All this is part and parcel of the relationship business but when it fails and does not give us what we really want we superimpose on it what we call love. So it is just not possible to have any relationship on any basis except on the level of mutual gratification.

The whole of culture has created this situation for us through its value system. The value system demands that relationships be based on love, but the most important elements are security and possessiveness. When your hold on the other weakens, the relationship wears out. You cannot maintain this lovey-dovey relationship all the time.

The relationship between a man and a woman is based on the images that the two create for themselves of each other. So the actual relationship between the two individuals is a relationship between the two images. But your image keeps changing and so does the other person's. To keep the image constant is just not possible. So when everything else fails we use this final, last card in the pack, love, with all the marvelous and romantic ideations around it.

⊷⇒ ⇐⊷

Marriage Is Possessiveness

The institution of marriage is not going to disappear. As long as we demand relationships, it will continue in some form or other. Basically, it is a question of possessiveness.

The marriage institution will somehow continue because it is not just the relationship between the two, but children and property are involved. And we use property and children as a pretext to give continuity to the institution of marriage. The problem is so complex and so complicated. It is not so easy for anybody to come up with answers to the age-old institution of marriage.

⊷⇒ ⇐⊷

Love Is Fascist

When everything fails, you use the last card, the trump in the pack of cards, and call it love. But it is not going to help us, and it has not helped us at all. Even religion has failed to free man from violence and from ten other different things that it is trying to free us from. You see, it is not a question of trying to find new concepts, new ideas, new thoughts, and new beliefs. But I am sure that the day has come for people to realize that all the weapons that we have built so far are redundant and that they cannot be used anymore. We have arrived at a point where you cannot destroy your adversary without destroying yourself. So it is that kind of terror, and not the love and brotherhood that have been preached for centuries, that will help us to live together.

What an amount of energy we are putting into making our relationship into a loving thing! It is a battle, it is a war. It is like preparing yourself all the time for war hoping that there will be peace, eternal peace, or this or that. You are tired of this battle, and you even settle for that horrible, non-loving relationship. And you hope and dream one day it will be nothing but love. 'Love thy neighbour as thyself ...' in the name of that how many millions of people have been killed? More than all the recent wars put together. How can you love thy neighbour as thyself? It is just not possible.

Love implies division, separation. As long as there is division, as long as there is a separation within you, you maintain that separation around you. When everything fails, you use the last card, the trump in the pack of cards, and call it love... We say: I love my country, I love my dog, I love my wife. What happens? You love your country, I love my country, and there is war.

It is not going to help us, and it has not helped us at all. Even religion has failed to free man from violence and from ten other different things that it is trying to free us from. You see, it is not a question of trying to find new concepts, new ideas, new thoughts, and new beliefs.

★

What, after all, is the world? The world is the relationship between two individuals. But that relationship is based on the foundation of 'What do I get out of a relationship?' Mutual gratification is the basis of all relationships. If you don't get what you want out of a relationship, it goes sour. What there is in the place of what you call a 'loving relationship' is hate.

★

The whole music of our age is all around that song, 'Love, Love, Love…'. But love is fascist in its nature, in its birth, in its expression and in its action. It cannot do us any good. We may talk of love but it doesn't mean anything.

⇥ ⇤

Isn't the Heart Different from the Mind?

You want to know? You are making this assumption that to have a 'heart' is better than to use your head. The whole religious thinking is built on the foundation of having a good heart and giving supremacy and importance to it, and not to what your 'head' is doing. But what I want to say is that the heart is there only to pump blood. It is not interested in your kindly deeds. If you indulge in kindly deeds, doing good unto others, having a good 'heart', you will only create problems for the heart. It is the beginning of your cardiac problems! That's going to be a real problem. It is your kindly deeds that are responsible for the cardiac arrests and heart failures, and not any [mal]functioning of the heart. The tremendous importance that we have given to the 'heart' is totally irrelevant. To make a distinction between the 'head' and the 'heart' is interesting, but in the long run it is not going to help us.

⇥ ⇤

Sex Is Thought

It is a very simple functioning of the living organism. The religious man has turned that into something big, and concentrated on the control of sex. After that the psychologists have turned that into something extraordinary.

You may ask: Is not sex a basic human requirement? Sex is dependent upon thought; the body itself has no sex. Only the genitals and perhaps the hormone balances differ between male and female. It is thought that says, 'I am a man, and that is a woman, an attractive woman.' It is thought that translates sex feelings in the body and says, 'These are sexual feelings.' And it is thought that provides the build-up without which no sex is possible: 'It would be more pleasurable to hold that woman's hand than just to look at her. It would be more pleasurable to kiss her than just to embrace her,' and so on. In the natural state there is no build-up of thought. Without that build-up, sex is impossible. And sex is tremendously violent to the body. The body normally is a very peaceful organism, and then you subject it to this tremendous tension and release, which feels pleasurable to you. Actually it is painful to the body.

But through suppression or attempts at sublimation of sex you will never come into this state. As long as you think of God, you will have thoughts of sex. Ask any religious seeker you may know who practises celibacy, whether he doesn't dream of women at night.

The peak of the sex experience is the one thing in life you have that comes close to being a first-hand experience; all of the rest of your experiences are second-hand, somebody else's. Why do you weave so many taboos and ideas around this? Why do you destroy the joy of sex? Not that I am advocating indulgence or promiscuity; but through abstinence and continence you will never achieve a thing.

⊷⇒◉ ◉⇐⊶

Sex Has to Be Put in Its Proper Place

Sexuality, if it is left to itself as it is in the case of other species, other forms of life, is merely a biological need because the living organism has this object to survive and produce one like itself. Anything you superimpose on that is totally unrelated to the living organism. But we have turned that, what you call sexual activity, which is biological in its nature, into a pleasure movement. I am not saying anything against the pleasure movement. I am not interested in saying that you should condemn that or become promiscuous or use sex as a means of spiritual attainment; no. It is a very simple functioning of the living organism. The religious man has turned that into something big and concentrated on the control of sex. After that the psychologists have turned that into something extraordinary. All commercialism is related to sex. How do you think it will fall into its proper place?

I am just pointing out the use to which we are putting that simple biological function. I am not condemning it. It is there, you see. Your talk of that as an expression of love has no meaning to me. We would love to put it that way because it is very comforting. If sex is used only for the biological purpose it is not really a devastating situation. If you leave it as it is it wouldn't be so horrible, the way you would like to put it, it would fall into its proper place. That is why we have invented all these other things—God, truth, and reality—which are nothing but ultimate pleasures.

Sex has to be put in its proper place as one of the natural functionings of the body. It is solely, mainly and wholly for the purpose of reproducing or procreating something like this. It has no other place in the functioning of the body. Thought always interferes with sex. It has become a pleasure movement. I am not saying anything against it. After that it goes. Thereafter, what you are left with is the natural functioning of the glands. So we have to revise all our ideas about this whole business of sex. We give a tremendous importance to sex and so the denial of it becomes such an obsession with people. In India, they even moved away from that denial and created what is called tantric sex. It was the highest pleasure that human beings could have, sex through tantra was considered the highest.

The fact is that the person is very much there even at the moment when there is peak sex experience. The experience has already been captured by your memory. Otherwise, you have no way of experiencing that as a peak moment. If that peak moment remained as a peak moment that would be just the end of sex. That would be the end of everything. The fact that you remember it as a peak moment and want to repeat it over and over again implies that it has already become part of your experiencing structure. You want it always and then want to extend it for longer and longer periods of time.

⊷⟹ ⟸⊶

Desire and Selfishness

Man is always selfish, and he will remain selfish as long as he practises selflessness as a virtue. I have nothing against selfish people. I don't want to talk about selflessness—it has no basis at all. You say, 'I will be a selfless man tomorrow. Tomorrow I will be a marvellous man'—but until tomorrow arrives (or the day after tomorrow, or the next life) you will remain selfish. What do you mean by 'selflessness'? You tell everybody to be selfless. What is the point? I have never said to anybody, 'Don't be selfish.' Be selfish, stay selfish!—that is my message. Wanting enlightenment is selfishness. The rich man's charity is also selfishness: he will be remembered as a generous man; you will put up a statue of him there.

> You have been told that you should practise desirelessness. You have practised desirelessness for thirty or forty years, but still desires are there. So something must be wrong somewhere. Nothing can be wrong with desire; something must be wrong with the one who has told you to practise desirelessness. This (desire) is a reality; that (desirelessness) is false—it is falsifying you. Desire is there. Desire as such can't be wrong, can't be false, because it is there.

You hope that you will be able to resolve the problem of desire through thinking, because of that model of a saint who you think has controlled or eliminated desire. If that man has no desire as you imagine, he is a corpse. Don't believe that man at all! Such a man builds some organization, and lives in luxury, which you pay for. You are maintaining him. He is doing it for his livelihood. There is always a fool in the world who falls for him. Once in a while he allows you to prostrate before him. You will be surprised if you live with him. You will get the shock of your life if you see him there. That is why they are all aloof—because they are afraid you will catch them some time or the other. The rich man is always afraid that you will touch him for money. So too the religious man—he never, never comes in contact with you. Seeing him is far more difficult than seeing the president of your country—that is a lot easier than seeing a holy man. He is not what he says he is, not what he claims he is.

As long as there is a living body, there will be desire. It is natural. Thought has interfered and tried to suppress, control, and moralize about desire, to the detriment of mankind. We are trying to solve the 'problem' of desire through thought. It is thinking that has created the problem. You somehow continue to hope and believe that the same instrument can solve your other problems as well. You hope against hope that thought will pull you through, but you will die in hope just as you have lived in hope. That is the refrain of my doom song.

⊷⊜ ⊜⊷

Politics Has Its Root in Religious Thinking

All the political ideologies, even your legal structures, are the warty outgrowth of the religious thinking of man. It is not so easy to flush out the whole series of experiences which have been accumulated through centuries, and which are based upon the religious thinking of man. There is a tendency to replace one belief with another belief, one illusion with another illusion. That is all we can do.

★

It is the constant demand for permanence which cripples society. Because we all seek permanence inwardly, we demand that those things which we perceive to lie outside ourselves—society, humanity, the nation and the world—also be permanent. We seek our permanence through them. All forms of permanence, whether personal or collective, are your own creation. They are all an extension of the very same demand for permanence. But nothing is permanent. Our efforts to make things permanent go entirely against the way of nature. Somehow you know that you will not succeed in your demand for permanence. Yet you persist.

★

Human nature being what it is, what can you expect? Falseness of human values has ended up in the church, the monarchy, and politics. We have elected and placed men in power, and with the very same power they will destroy everything. It is nothing but the power game. All heritage is born of a diseased mind. Man is corrupt and lays the blame at the feet of the coined word 'heritage'. The unwillingness to change with the changing times you call tradition.

> If religion doesn't hold the key, if political ideologies have failed, there must be some other solution, some other answer. These are extremely important questions to ask and find answers for, on which depends the fate of the whole world.

Traditional values and the military might of America cannot save anyone. You have grown up with the sense that America is the centre of the world. You were better at everything. Today the glory is gone; you are an also-ran. You are another England! This is a blot to your national image. You are being overtaken by others. I am as terrified if the US gets dumped from its throne as you will be; what you would do is anybody's guess.... The Russian revolution is a total failure. That revolution is only a revaluation of a value system. They replaced one system with another system of values. Which system will blow up the world? It matters not who is going to blow up the world. The solutions to the world's problems do not rest with your bureaucrats or the big boys. They are muddle-headed and low-grade morons; so are the other leaders of mankind. You can't get rid of them. You have delegated your power to them, placed them in the seats of power, and handed over the most destructive weapons to them. They are the defence that turned against you.

⊶⊜ ⊜⊶

Death of Ideologies

I have more faith in the scientific community than in all these jokers that are going around 'saving' mankind. We need to be saved from the self-appointed saviours of mankind. No, they are the ones who are responsible for the terrible situation we find ourselves in today. We don't realize that it is they who have created this mess for us. They had their day, and have utterly, totally failed. Still they refuse to take a back seat. That's it. We are stuck. You study the history of mankind: monarchies, revolutions, democracies, and more revolutions. Everything has failed us; everything is over. Not one ideology will survive. What's left for us? Democracy, the 'noble experiment', is over. Everything is over. We find ourselves in a situation where these issues will be decided by your boss.

Take the problem of starvation. One side says, 'My political system will solve the problem of starvation in this world,' and the other side says, 'No, mine will'; and both of them end up on the battlefield brandishing their atomic weapons. That is the reality of the situation. Everywhere, on every continent, there is confrontation.

The basic issue in the world is, of course, economic: Who will control the resources of this world? The nine rich nations of the world have been so used to controlling the resources of the world. They sit in Basel, Switzerland, and say, 'Here is the price you must take for your products. Take it or leave it.' A country like the United States may talk of freedom, democracy, and justice, but they would like to have military governments in countries like those of South America. They prefer to do business with militarized, authoritarian states. A military general is very useful to run those countries. That is a fact.

> The only answer to this human problem, if there is any answer, is not to be found through new ideas, new concepts or new ideologies but through bringing about a change in the chemistry of the human body.

⤙═➤ ⊙═⤙

Revolution Is Only Revaluation of the Old

What kind of a human being do you want on this globe? The human being modelled after the perfect being has totally failed. The model has not touched anything there. Your value system is the one that is responsible for the human malady, the human tragedy, forcing everybody to fit into that model. So, what do we do? You cannot do anything by destroying the value system, because you replace one value system with another. Even those who rebelled against religion, like those in the communist countries, have themselves created another kind of value system. So, revolution does not mean the end of anything. It is only a revaluation of our value system. So, that needs another revolution, and so on and on. There is no way.

★

Every human being is different. That is all I am saying. There is nobody like you anywhere in this world—I tell you, nobody! I am talking physiologically, you know. But we ignore that, and try to put everybody in a common mould and create what we call the greatest common factor. All the time you are trying to educate them and fit them into the value system. If that value system does not work, naturally revolutions take place. The whole idea of restructuring is nothing but a revaluation of the old value system. Revolution only means revaluation of our value system. It is the same thing. After a while things settle down, and then they go at it again. There is no improvement again. Or there is a slight improvement. But it is basically a modified continuity of the same. In that process what horrors we have committed, you know! Is it really worth all that? But you seem to think that it is. After killing so many people you go back to the same system, the same technique. What is the point?

★

The society in which we are living today considers certain actions as

121

socially acceptable and certain other actions antisocial. You may call yourself a rebel, a revolutionary and break away but you will certainly create another form no different and distinct from the structure in which you are caught up. There is no such thing as a revolution at all. What you call revolution is only a revaluation of your value system. The basic problem is the impossibility of fitting yourself into the framework, so you want to create another kind of a framework, a new way of thinking but basically and actually and fundamentally there is no difference between the two.

⋆⇒◉ ◉⇐⋆

Is Terror the Only Way?

I still maintain that it is not love, compassion, humanism, or brotherly sentiments that will save mankind. No, not at all. It is the sheer terror of extinction that can save us, if anything can. Each cell of a living organism cooperates with the cell next to it. It does not need any sentiment or declarations of undying love to do so. Each cell is wise enough to know that if its neighbour goes, it also goes. The cells stick together not out of brotherhood, love, and that kind of thing, but out of the urgent drive to survive. It is the same with us, but only on a larger scale. Soon we will all come to know one simple thing: If I try to destroy you, I will also be destroyed.

We have arrived at a point where you cannot destroy your adversary without destroying yourself. So it is that kind of terror, and not the love and brotherhood that have been preached for centuries, that will help us to live together. But this has to percolate to the level of human consciousness. (I don't want to use the words 'consciousness', or 'human consciousness', because there is no such thing as consciousness at all. I use that word only for purposes of communication.) Until this percolates to the level of human consciousness, in the sense that man sees that he cannot destroy his neighbour without destroying himself, I don't think it will help. I am sure that we have come to that point. Whenever and wherever you have an edge over your adversary or your neighbour, you will still continue to exercise what you have been holding on to for centuries. So how are you going to solve the problem? All utopias have failed.

Human nature is basically violent. Because thought is violent. Anything that is born out of thought is destructive. You may cover it up with all wonderful and romantic phrases: 'Love thy neighbour as thyself.' Don't forget that in the name of 'Love thy neighbour as thyself' millions and millions of people have died, more than in all the recent wars put together. But we now have come to a point where we can realize that violence is not the answer, that it is not the way to solve human problems. So, terror seems to be the only way. I am not talking of terrorists blowing up churches, temples, and all that kind of thing, but the terror that if you try to destroy your neighbour you will possibly destroy yourself. That realization has to come down to the level of the common man.

⊶⊜ ⊜⊰

What About the Sciences?

Science is as much a menace to mankind as any other system of thought. We have no doubt reaped immense benefit from the discoveries of science which has resulted in hi-tech and technology. But can you get away from this fact that its benefits have not percolated down to the common man? Science is as much an aberrant as religion is. Unfortunately it has become a handmaiden of the state and tool in the hands of the leaders of mankind.

*

Genetic engineering that the scientists are indulging in is not for the benefit of mankind. If they succeed, it will be handed over to the state. The state will use it to control everything and everyone. Brainwashing, which takes centuries, would be obsolete. Through a simple injection of genetically engineered substances into the body, the state can turn its citizens into bloodthirsty soldiers, mindless bureaucrats, or whatever type it wants.

★

Pure science is nothing but speculation. The scientists discuss formulas endlessly and provide us with some equations. But I am not at all taken in by the 'march of progress' and all that rot. The first trip I made to the US in the 1930s took more than a full day, and we had to stop everywhere. Later, the same trip took eighteen hours, then twelve hours, and even more recently six hours and three, and so on. And if the supersonic jets are put to commercial use we may be able to make the trip in one-and-a-half hours. All right, that's progress. But the same technology that makes fast international travel possible is making ever more deadly military fighter planes. How many of these planes are we using for faster and more comfortable travel from one point to another? And how many more hundreds of planes are we using to destroy life and property? You call this progress? I don't know. As the comforts increase, we come to depend upon them, and are loath to give up anything we have.

★

Gimmicks like yoga and meditation will only help you to escape into that feeling of wellness. It is one of those hypes you fall for, more so if they are sold in the name of science. How much of science is there in their claims is anybody's guess. Everything that has the stamp of science turns you into a fanatic and a health food junkie. It used to be three out of four. Now it is, 'Nine out of ten doctors recommend....' You can be sure that whatever they recommend are the very things that will destroy your health. Doctors need to be educated, and you will be better off listening to 'the tenth' one. When you have lost faith in everything, health becomes an obsession. Nutritional wisdom cannot stop the ageing process. One day through genetic engineering the process of ageing can be delayed; but it cannot be stopped. You may feel well and look more attractive. There is no such thing as the fountain of youth. War against ageing is a lost battle.

⊷⟾⊜　⊜⟾⊷

Anger Is Energy

You never look at the problem. What is the problem? Anger, for example. I don't want to discuss all those silly things which these people have been discussing for centuries. Anger. Where is that anger? Can you separate the anger from the functioning of this body? It's like a wave in the ocean. Can you separate the waves from the ocean? You can sit there and wait until the waves subside, so that you can have a swim in the ocean, like King Canute who sat there for years and years hoping that those waves in the ocean would disappear so that he could have a swim in a calm ocean. That will never happen.

You can sit there and learn all about how these waves, the high tide and the low tide (the scientists have given us all kinds of explanations), but the knowledge about that is not going to be of any help to you. You are not really dealing with anger at all.

Where do you feel the anger, first of all? Where do you feel all these so-called problems you want to be free from? ... the desires? The burning desires. The desire burns you. Hunger burns you. So, the solutions you have or the means of fulfilling them (desire and hunger) are very simple and makes it impossible for that to burn itself out in your system. Where do you feel the fear? You feel it here in the pit of your stomach. It is part of the body. The body cannot take those high and low tides of energy that is there in your body. So you are wanting to suppress it for some spiritual or social reasons. You are not going to succeed.

Anger is energy, a tremendous outburst of energy. And by destroying that energy through any means, you are destroying the very expression of life itself. It becomes a problem only when you try to do something with that energy. When it is absorbed by the system, you will not do the things that you think you will do if the anger is left alone. You are actually not dealing with the anger, but the frustration. Or to avoid such a situation which has resulted in clumsiness in your relationships or in your understanding of yourself. You want to be prepared to meet such situations as and when they arise in the future.

The instrument which you are using has been used by you every time there is an outburst of anger. Yet you have not succeeded in freeing yourself from the anger. You won't come into the position of anything extraordinary, other than this instrument which you have been using all these years, and at the same time you hope that somehow this very thing will help you to be free from the anger tomorrow. It is the same hope.

You are not dealing with anger. You will never deal with this anger at all as long as you are interested in finding out a way of not hitting the person who is coming with a knife. You have to protect yourself, that is essential. I am not saying for a moment that your anger makes it impossible for you to deal with that situation. Don't say that it's non-violence or you should not hurt somebody else. He is hurting you. Even in the Bible, it is an eye for an eye, a tooth for a tooth. You never practise that. Of course, they practise it on a larger scale, but in daily life they say it is something terrible to do. I don't see any problem with that at all. What is the problem?

★

There is no point in discussing those hypothetical situations for the simple reason that the person who is hopping mad with anger, burning with anger, will not seek and discuss the question of anger. That is amazing. That's the time to deal with those things, when you are really burning with anger, burning with desire, burning with all those things that you want to be free from. Otherwise, it becomes a classroom discussion. Somebody talking on the anatomy of anger, the anatomy of how the anger arises, or the anatomy of love. It's too ridiculous. Or, they offer solutions which don't work when there is a real situation. That's the reason why I don't discuss all these things. No problem.

There's no problem for the individual. When he's mad with anger—that's the time for him to deal with it. It stops the thinking.

★

There is no way of separating yourself from the problem. That's what you are trying to do. That is what I mean by saying that you are putting anger out there and trying to look and deal with it as if it is an object outside of you. When you separate yourself, the only result is that exactly what you fear would happen. That is inevitable. So you have no way of controlling that at all. Is there anything that you can do to prevent this separation from what you are? It is a horrible thing to realize that you are yourself anger and whatever you do to stop that, prevent it, or do something about it, is false. That (preventing, etc.) will be tomorrow or in your next life—not now. So that is what you are.

★

You are not a spiritual man or a religious man. You can imagine that you are a religious man, because you are trying to control your anger, or trying to be free from anger, or trying to be less and less angry as the years go by. All that makes you feel that you are not that vicious man whom you avoid. You are no different. You are not any more spiritual than the people whom you condemn. Tomorrow you are going to be a marvellous person, you will be free from anger. What do you want me to do in the meantime? Admire you? Because you have put on the label that you are a spiritual man or that you have put on fancy robes? What do you want me to do? For that you want me to admire you? There is nothing there to be admired because you are as vicious as anybody else in this world. If you condemn that...? Condemning that has no meaning. Adopting a posture which is totally unrelated to what is happening there has no meaning either.

So, how can you put on this posture or adopt some kind of an attitude and feel superior to the animals. The animals are better than the humans. If there is anger, it [the animal] acts and that [killing] is

127

only for the purpose of survival. If you kill your fellow man for feeding yourself that is a moral act—only for that purpose, because if you look around, one form of life lives on another form of life. And if you talk of vegetarianism and kill millions of people, that is the most immoral, unpardonable act that a civilized culture of human beings can ever do. Do you see the absurdity of the two? You condemn this [killing]. And you love the animals. What for?

⋅→▭ ▭←⋅

Suffering Is the Foundation of Religion

Suffering is the foundation on which the whole Christian religion is based…. Suffering as a means to reach your goal. What you are left with is only the suffering, and you make a great big thing out of suffering, and yet you are not anywhere near the goal, whatever is the nature of your goal … So you suffer in the hope of getting a permanent seat there in heaven—non-existent heaven. You are going through hell now in the hope of reaching heaven after your death. What for? So suffer. All religions emphasize that. Bear the pain, the endurance of pain is the means. You go through hell in the hope of having paradise at the end of your life, or the end of a series of lives if you want to believe that. I am just pointing out the absurdity of talking about these things. The religious [teaching] has no meaning when you are pushed into a corner. Then you will behave exactly like anybody else. So this culture, your values, religious or otherwise, haven't touched a bit there.

> The search for moksha (liberation) is the dukkha (suffering) of all dukkhas. There's no end to that—you will keep searching for this eternally—you are not going to get it. Even if you get what you want, and experience bliss, beatitude, God knows what, there is always more and more of it. Silence you experience, but you want permanent silence, you want always to be in silence. But in the very nature of things, there is no permanence at all.

The mind is a disease. Any medicine that you try is only going to prolong the suffering. Its only effect is to keep the disease going a little longer. The death of the mind will free you from suffering at once. But you do not want to die. Actually, you seem to enjoy the suffering, and that is why you continue looking for some medicines which will give you relief. Of course, the doctors and medicine makers have to make a living and will take full advantage of your hopeless situation.

★

It is not that I am indifferent to the suffering man. I suffer with the suffering man and am happy with the happy man. You seem to get pleasure out of the suffering of somebody. But why don't you get the same pleasure when you see a rich man throwing his weight around? They are the same. This you call pleasure and that you call jealousy or envy. But I don't see any difference between the two. I see suffering. Individually, there isn't anything that I can do. And at the same time I don't want to use this (suffering) for my self-aggrandizement, my self-fulfilment. The problem is there, and we are individually responsible for it. Yet we don't want to accept the responsibility for creating the problems. The problems are not created by nature. It is we who have created the problems. There is plenty, there is bounty, in nature; but we take away what rightfully belongs to everybody and then say that you should give charity. That's too absurd!

Why Are You So Afraid of Death?

What you call 'yourself' is fear. The 'you' is born out of fear; it lives in fear, functions in fear and dies in fear.... It is fear that makes you believe that you are living and that you will be dead. What we do not want is the fear to come to an end. That is why we have invented all these new minds, new sciences, new talks, therapies, choiceless awareness and various other gimmicks.

★

When there is an actual physical danger, the danger of the extinction of your physical body (which you think is yours), everything that it has as its resource gets thrown into that situation and the body tries to survive in that particular moment. Have you ever noticed that when there is a real physical danger your thinking mechanism is never there to help you? Never there. So you can plan ahead for every possible situation and be prepared to meet every kind of situation in your life, but actually when there is a physical danger, all your planning and all that you have thought about to be prepared to meet every kind of danger and every kind of situation is just not there. The body has to fall back on its own resources. If for some reason it cannot renew itself and survive in that particular situation, it goes merrily and gracefully. It knows that nothing is lost.

★

The balance of energy in nature has to be maintained for some reason. I don't know why. So death occurs only when there is a need for the atoms to maintain the balance of energy in the universe. It is nothing but a reshuffling of atoms. This organism has no way of finding out that it was born at a particular point of time and is going to die at another point of time, and also that it is living at this moment and not dead.

You shall not taste of death, for there is no death for you: You cannot experience your own death. Are you born? Life and death cannot be separated; you have no chance whatever of knowing for yourself where one begins and the other ends. You can experience the death of another, but not your own. The only death is physical death; there is no psychological death.

Your experiencing structure cannot conceive of any event that it will not experience. It even expects to preside over its own dissolution, and so it wonders what death will feel like—it tries to project the feeling of what it will be like not to feel. But in order to anticipate a future experience, your structure needs knowledge, a similar past experience it can call upon for reference. You cannot remember what it felt like not to exist before you were born, and you cannot remember your own birth, so you have no basis for projecting your future non-existence. As long as you have known life, you have known yourself, you have been there, so, to you, you have a feeling of eternity. To justify this feeling of eternity, your structure begins to convince itself that there will be a life after death for you—heaven, reincarnation, transmigration of souls, or whatever. What is it that you think reincarnates? Where is that soul of yours? Can you taste it, touch it, show it to me? What is there inside of you that goes to heaven? What is there? There is nothing inside of you but fear.

★

Creation and destruction are going on simultaneously. The birth and death of thought happen simultaneously. That is why I insist that there is no such thing as death at all. Even the body does not die. It can change form but does not cease altogether. Because death really does not exist it is impossible for you to experience it. What you do experience is the void or emptiness you feel upon the disappearance of someone's body. Death can never be experienced and neither can birth for that matter. In your natural state, where the body is allowed to function without the interference of thought, birth and death are going on all the time. There is no person and no space within to create a self. What is left, after the continuity of thought is blown away, is a disjointed and independent series of interactions. What happens in the environment around me happens in here. There is no division. When the armour you are wearing around you is stripped away, you find an extraordinary sensitivity of the senses that responds to the phases of the moon, the passage of the seasons and the movements of the other planets. There is simply no isolated, separate existence of its own here, only the throb of life.

★

The body knows that it is immortal. I very deliberately use the word immortal because nothing there comes to an end. When what you call clinical death takes place, the body breaks itself into its constituent elements. That's all that happens. It may not reconstitute again and create the same body, which you think is yours, but when it breaks itself into its constituent elements, it provides the basis for the continuity of life. It may not be of any consolation to the individual who is dying, but this body becomes food for the millions and millions of bacteria. So, even assuming for a moment that you resort to cremation, as they do in some countries, wherever you dump the ashes, the carbon which is the end result of the burned body, provides the basis for some tiny little flower coming out of the earth. So, nothing here is lost.

⊷⊜ ⊜⊶

Is There Anything to Vegetarianism?

If you talk of vegetarianism and kill millions of people, that is the most immoral, unpardonable act that a civilized culture of human beings can ever do. Do you see the absurdity of the two?

Vegetarianism for what? For some spiritual goals? One form of life lives off another. That's a fact, whether you like it or not. He [the questioner] says his cat is a vegetarian cat, it doesn't kill a fly. Because of its association with vegetarians it has become vegetarian. For health reasons maybe one should. I don't know, I don't see any adequate reason why one should be a vegetarian. Your body is not going to be any more pure than the meat-eating body. You go to India, those that have been vegetarians, they are not kind, they are not peaceful. You will be surprised. Vegetarians can be more aggressive than the meat eaters. Read the history of India—it is full of bloodshed, massacres, and assassinations—all in the name of religion. So it has nothing to do with spirituality—what you put in there (stomach) is not really the problem.

You feel good because you have given up meat-eating. But what's the difference? Why do you have to feel so good because you have given up meat-eating? That may be psychological, if I could use that word. If you want to go back to eating meat, it is a different story. If there is a craving, it creates a problem. If there is no craving, what's the difference whether you eat meat or vegetables? One form of life lives on another form of life. How many millions of bacteria are crawling all over your body—the flora and the fauna? You will be surprised, if they are magnified. They are as big as cockroaches. They live on you. When it becomes a corpse, they will have a field day on this body.

You want to eat macrobiotic food, and someone else wants to eat something else. These commercials sell you all kind of things. Why should we feed the body? The body needs some energy, and that energy you can have from anything you eat. Sawdust is enough for it, without the health food and vitamin C, or your brown rice and seaweed.

You can believe whatever you want to believe. Someone else believes something else. It is the belief that matters to people. You replace one belief with another. You eat ideas. You put ideas in your stomach. You can eat good ideas. Good luck to you.

The moment you ask, 'How to live' and 'What to eat?' you have created a problem.... Everything is cultural. All your tastes are cultivated tastes. The body does not know what you are eating. The problem is you eat more than what the body needs. It's the overeating that is the problem. You eat for pleasure. Eating has become a pleasure-seeking movement for us.

★

As far as I am concerned there is no difference between looking for varieties of food or looking for varieties of girls (or men, as the case may be).

--=● ●=--

What Are Psychic Powers?

Whatever is there is trying to express itself and blossom into a human being. The human being has lost all of the animal instincts, and he has

133

not developed the human instincts. What these people talk of—psychic powers, clairvoyance, clairaudience—they are all human instincts. And they are necessary because there are two things that the human organism is interested in. One: its survival at any cost. Why should it survive? I don't know; it is a foolish question to ask. That is one of the most important things: It has a survival mechanism of its own, which is quite different from the survival mechanism of the movement of thought. The second thing is to reproduce itself. It has to reproduce. These are the two fundamental characteristics of the human organism, the living organism.

—⇒○ ○⇐—

What Is Life?

You will never know what life is. Nobody can say anything about life. You can give definitions, but those definitions have no meaning. You can theorize about life, but that is a thing which is not of any value to you—it cannot help you to understand anything. So you don't ask questions like 'What is life?' you know. 'What is life?'—there is no answer to that question, so the question cannot stay there any longer. You really don't know, so the question disappears. You don't let that happen there, because you think there must be an answer. If you don't know the answer, you think there may be somebody in this world who can give an answer to that question. 'What is life?'—nobody can give an answer to that question—we really don't know. So the question cannot stay there; the question burns itself out, you see. The question is born out of thought, so when it burns itself out, what is there is energy. There's a combustion: thought burns itself out and gives physical energy. In the same way, when the question is burnt, along with it goes the questioner also. The question and the questioner are not two different things. When the question burns itself out, what is there is energy. You can't say anything about that energy—it is already manifesting itself, expressing itself in a boundless way; it has no limitations, no boundaries. It is not yours, not mine; it belongs to everybody. You are part of that. You are an expression of that. Just as the flower is an expression of life, you are another expression of life.

★

Life is one unitary movement, not two different movements. It's moving, it's a continuous flux, but you cannot look at that flux and say 'That is a flux.' ... This is just a pure and simple physiological functioning of the organism. Because there is life, there is a response. The response and the stimulus are not two different movements: you cannot separate the response from the stimulus. (The moment you separate the response from the stimulus, there is a division, it is a divisive consciousness that is in operation.) So, it is one movement.

→══ ══←

Life Is Like a Great Big Dream

In a way the whole of life is like a great big dream. I am looking at you but I really don't know anything about you. This is a dream, a dream world. There is no reality to it at all. When the experiencing structure is not manipulating consciousness or whatever you want to call it, the whole of life is a great big dream from the experiential point of view; not from this point of view here but from your point of view. You see, you give reality to things—not only to objects but also to feelings and experiences—and think that they are real. When you don't translate them in terms of your accumulated knowledge, they are not things. You really don't know what they are. To you, in relation to the reality you give to things, you would call this state of not knowing a dream.

★

Here there is no such thing as reality any more, let alone the ultimate reality. I function in the world as if I accept the reality of everything the way you accept it. It's like water flowing. When there is an obstacle to the water, there is an action there, either it overflows or it takes a diversion, but here and now when I begin to walk in that direction there is no question of an obstruction or anything there.

⊷⊜ ⊜⊶

There Are Only Answers, No Questions

Try and formulate a question which you can call your own. This you will discover: they are not your questions at all.

★

Questions are there because you already have a vague answer for the question.

★

Thought, as memory and knowledge, has created this mechanism. The only way it can perpetuate itself is to gather knowledge, to know more and more, to ask more and more questions. As long as you are seeking you will be asking questions, and the questioning mechanism only adds more momentum to the naming process…

⊷⊜ ⊜⊶

The Real Problem Is the Solution

The real problem is the solution. Your problems continue because of the false solutions you have invented. If the answers are not there, the questions cannot be there. They are interdependent; your problems and solutions go together. Because you want to use certain answers to end your problems, those problems continue. The numerous solutions offered by all these holy people, the psychologists, the politicians, are not really solutions at all. That is obvious. They can only exhort you to try harder, practise more meditations, cultivate humility, stand on your head, and more and more of the same. That is all they can do. If you brushed aside your hope, fear, and naiveté, and treated these fellows like businessmen, you would see that they do not deliver the goods, and never will. But you go on and on buying these bogus wares offered up by the experts.

★

Actually there are no problems, there are only solutions. But we don't even have the guts to say that they don't work. Even if you have discovered that they don't work, sentimentality comes into the picture. The feeling, 'That man in whom I have placed my confidence and belief cannot con himself and con everyone else' comes in the way of throwing the whole thing out of the window, down the drain. The solutions are still a problem. Actually there is no problem there. The only problem is to find out the inadequacy or uselessness of all the solutions that have been offered to us. The questions naturally are born out of the assumptions and answers that we have taken for granted as real answers. But we really don't want any answers to the questions, because an answer to the questions is the end of the answers. If one answer ends, all the other answers also go.

⊷⇒◉ ◉⇐⊷

Conditioning Is Intelligence...

It is not possible for you to be without conditioning. No matter what you do, you are conditioned. The unconditioning that the spiritual gurus are talking about in the marketplace is a bogus affair. You will find out. Anything you do is conditioning. What you have to be free from is the desire to be free from conditioning. Conditioning is intelligence. This conditioning I am talking about is happening in a different way—not [through] the ideations and mentations.

★

Why should you stop the past from interfering with the present? You have been brainwashed by all those holy men, gurus, teachers and the so-called enlightened people that the past should die, should come to an end. 'If you attain this, life would be hunky-dory—full of sweetness.' You have fallen for all that romantic stuff. If you try to suppress the past and try to be in the present, it will drive you crazy. You are trying to control something which is beyond your control.

★

It is not only your past. It's the entire past, entire existence of every human being and every form of life. It is not such an easy thing. It is like trying to stop this flow of the river through all those artificial means. It will inundate the whole thing. What is it that you can do? Anything you do in any direction, at any level, is perpetuating that.

⋇══◉   ◉══⋇

Health, Disease and Pain

I think what we are actually doing is trying to treat the symptoms of what we call a disease. But my question is, and I always throw this question at the people who are competent enough—the doctors—What is health? What is disease? Is there any such thing as disease for this body? The body does not know that it is healthy or unhealthy. You know, we translate the 'malfunctioning' (of the body) to mean that there is some imbalance in the natural rhythm of the body. Not that we know what actually is the rhythm of the body. But we are so frightened that we run to a doctor or to somebody who we think is in the know of things and can help us. We do not give a chance for the body to work out the problems created by the situation we find ourselves in. We do not give enough time for the body.

★

But what actually is health? Does the body know, or does it have any way of knowing, that it is healthy or unhealthy? And what is pain? I am not asking a metaphysical question. To me pain is a healing process. But we do not give enough chance or opportunity to the body to heal itself or help itself, to free itself from what we call pain.

We are frightened, you see. We are afraid that something terrible will happen to us and run to a doctor to get rid of pain.

★

That is what all these commercials are taking advantage of. They are exploiting the gullibility and credulity of people. It is not that I am saying that you should not go to a doctor or take the help of medicine. I am not one of those who believe that your prayers will help the body to recover from whatever disease it has, or that God is going to be the healer. Nothing like that. Pain is part of the biological functioning of the body, and that is all there is to it. And we have to rely or depend upon the chemistry of this body, and the body always gives us a warning. In the early stages we do not pay any attention, but when it becomes too much for the body to handle, there is panic and fear. Maybe it is necessary for us to go to a person who is in the know of affairs and get a helping hand from him. That's all we can do. The patient can be given a helping hand. All treatment, whether traditional or alternative, is based upon the account of the symptoms narrated by the patient.

⊷⟺ ⟺⊶

What Is Maya?

The Sanskrit word 'maya' does not mean illusion in the same sense in which the English word is used. 'Maya' means to measure. You cannot measure anything unless you have a point. So, if the centre is absent, there is no circumference at all. That is pure and simple basic arithmetic.... So, in that sense, anything you experience based on knowledge is an illusion.

★

You are not separate from that illusion. You are the illusion. If one illusion goes, it is always replaced with another illusion. Why? Because the ending of the illusion is the ending of 'you'. That is the death. The ending of belief is the ending of the 'you' that is there. So, that is not the poetic, romantic death—of 'dying to your yesterdays'. Physical death is the only way through which you flush out what your whole culture has put in there.

Every time a thought is born, you are born. When the thought is gone, you are gone. But the you does not let the thought go and what gives continuity to this you is the thinking. Actually, there is no permanent entity in you, no totality of all your thoughts and experiences. You think that there is somebody who is thinking your thoughts, somebody who is feeling your feelings. That's the illusion. I can say it is an illusion but it is not an illusion to you.

Whenever a thought takes its birth there, you have created an entity or a point, and in reference to that point you are experiencing things. So, when the thought is not there, is it possible for you to experience anything or relate anything to a non-existing thing here? Every time a thought is born, you are born. Thought, in its very nature, is shortlived, and once it is gone, that's the end of it. That is probably what the traditions meant by rebirth—death and birth and death and birth. It is not that this particular entity, which is non-existing even while you are living, takes a series of births. The ending of births and deaths is the state that they are talking about. But that state cannot be described in terms of bliss, beatitude, love, compassion and all that poetic nonsense and romantic stuff, because you have no way of experiencing what is there between these two thoughts.

★

The world you experience around you is from a point of view. There must be a point and it is this point that creates the space. If this point is not there, there is no space. So, anything you experience from this point is an illusion. Not that the world is an illusion. All the Vedanta philosophers in India, particularly the students of Sankara, indulge in such frivolous, absolute nonsense. The world is not an illusion, but anything you experience in relationship to this point, which itself is illusory, is bound to be an illusion, that's all.

★

This point has no continuity. It comes into being in response to the demands of the situation. The demands of the situation create this point. The subject does not exist there. It is the object that creates the subject. This runs counter to the whole philosophical thinking of India. The subject comes and goes and comes and goes in response to the things that are happening there. It is the object that creates the subject and not the subject that creates the object. This is a simple physiological phenomenon which can be tested. For example, if there is no object there, there is no subject here. What creates the subject is the object.

★

There is light. If the light is not there you have no way of looking at anything. The light falls on that object, and the reflection of that light activates the optic nerves, which in turn activate the memory cells. When the memory cells are activated, all the knowledge you have about that object comes into operation. It is that process which is happening there that has created the subject. And the subject is the knowledge you have about it. The word 'microphone' is the eye. There is nothing there other than the word microphone. When you reduce it to that you feel the absurdity of talking about the self. The lower self, the higher self, and self-knowing, self-knowledge, knowing from moment to moment, is absolute rubbish, balderdash! You can indulge in such absolute nonsense and build up philosophical theories, but there is no subject there at all at any time. There is no subject creating the object.

⭐︎═ ═⭐︎

There Is No Such Thing as Absolute

It is thought and thought alone that has created the absolute. Absolute zero, absolute power, absolute perfection, these have been invented by the holy men and experts. They kidded themselves and others. Down the centuries, the saints, saviours and prophets of mankind have kidded themselves and everybody else. Perfection and absolutes are false. You are trying to imitate and relate your behaviour according to these absolutes and it is falsifying you. You are actually functioning in an entirely different way. You are brutal. You feel you must be peaceful. It is contradictory. That's all I'm pointing out.

> When once you are freed from the pairs of opposites—right and wrong, good and bad—you will never be wrong. But until then the problem will be there.

Thought has also invented the opposite of time, the now, the eternal now. The present exists only as an idea. The moment you attempt to look at the present it has already been brought into the framework of the past. Thought will use any trick under the sun to give momentum to its own continuity. Its essential technique is to repeat the same thing over and over again. This gives it an illusion of permanency. This permanency is shattered the moment the falseness of the past–present–future continuum is seen. The future can be nothing but the modified continuity of the past.

⊶ ⊷

What is Morality?

What is morality? It is not the following of enjoined rules of conduct. It is not a question of standing above temptations, or of conquering hate, anger, greed, lust and violence. Questioning your actions before and after creates the moral problem. What is responsible for this situation is the faculty of distinguishing between right and wrong and influencing your actions accordingly.

Life is action. Unquestioned action is morality. Questioning your actions is destroying the expression of life. A person who lets life act in its own way without the protective movement of thought has no self to defend. What need will he have to lie or cheat or pretend or to commit any other act which his society considers immoral?

★

By morality I mean questioning your actions before and after. It is all social. For the smooth running of society these codes are necessary. These religious people have created a policeman inside you. Certain actions are termed good and certain other actions are termed bad either before or after you do them. That hasn't helped you in any way. It is thinking that has created the problem. Man's problem is basically the moral dilemma—questioning your actions before and after. It has become a neurological problem, not a religious problem. Even God is a neurological problem. God is the jumbled spelling of dog but the whole of your being is reacting to the word God.

★

All your beliefs, they are not just psychological, they are neurological. You don't know what is good. You know only what is good for you. That's all you are interested in. Everything centres around that; all your art and reason centres around that. I am not being cynical. That's a fact, nothing wrong with it. I'm not saying anything against it. The situations change but it is that which is guiding you through all situations. I'm not saying it is wrong, you see. If it is not so something must be wrong with you. As long as you are operating in the field of what they call the pair of opposites, good and bad, you will always be choosy in every situation. That is all, you cannot help that.

⤙⤜ ⤙⤜

Beauty Is Not in the Beholder's Eye

What is beauty? Where is beauty? Is it in the object or in the eye? You project your idea of beauty on the object you are looking at. That is all. There is a beautiful sunset there. The moment you even say to yourself that it is beautiful, you are not looking at it at all.

Beauty is not in the object. It is not in the beholder's eye either. It is in the total abandonment of yourself.

★

So, what is beauty? You really don't know. You wouldn't know what you are looking at. And in that state of not knowing what is there fills the whole of your being. That you may call beauty. But there is nobody who describes that beauty and says he is enjoying it. If you capture that in terms of your experiencing structure, it is lost.

★

You actually have no way of looking at the sunset because you are not separated from the sunset. The moment you separate your self from the sunset, the poet in you comes out. Out of that separation poets and painters have tried to express themselves, to share their experiences with others. All that is culture.

⊷⟺ ⟺⊷

Artists, Poets and Musicians

There is no such thing as an artist at all. He is just a technician. He or she has learned the technique of painting. They are just technicians, artisans, like the carpenters, masons, etc.

Why do you want to place art on a higher level than craft? If there is no market for an artist's creation, he will be out of business. It is the market that is responsible for all these so-called artistic beliefs. An artist is a craftsman like any other craftsman. He uses that tool to express himself. All human creation is born out of sensuality. I have nothing against sensuality. All art is a pleasure movement. Even that (the pleasure) has to be cultivated by you. Otherwise you have no way of appreciating the beauty and art that artists are talking about. If you question their creation, they feel superior, thinking that you don't have taste. Then they want you to go to a school to learn how to appreciate their art. If you don't enjoy a poem written by a so-called great poet, they forcibly educate you to appreciate poetry. That is all that they are doing in the educational institutions. They teach us how to appreciate beauty, how to appreciate music, how to appreciate painting and so on. Meanwhile they make a living off you. Artists find it comforting to think that they are creative: 'creative art', 'creative ideas', 'creative politics'. It's nonsense. There is nothing really creative in them in the sense of their doing anything original, new or free. Artists pick something here and something there, put it together and think they have created something marvellous. They are all imitating something that is already there. Imitation and style are the only 'creativity' we have. Each of us has our own style according to the school we attended, the language we were taught, the books we have read, the examinations we have taken. And within that framework again we have our own style. Perfecting style and technique is all that operates there. You will be surprised that one of these days computers will paint and create music much better than all the painters and musicians that the world has produced so far. It may not happen in our lifetime but it will happen. You are no different from a computer. We are not ready to accept that because we are made to believe that we are not just machines—that there is something more to us. You have to come to terms with this and accept that we are machines. The human intellect that we have developed through education, through all kinds of techniques is no match for nature. They (creative activities) assume importance because they have been recognized as expressions of spiritual, artistic and intellectual values. The drive for self-expression is born out of neurosis. This applies to the spiritual teachers of mankind too. There is no such thing as a direct

145

sense experience. All forms of art are nothing but an expression of sensuality.

→══◉   ◉══←

Mentally Different People

Some people who are in the All India Institute of Mental Health at Bangalore visited me. One of them is a top neurosurgeon. I asked him the same question, 'Who is normal? Who is sane and who is insane?'

He said, 'Statistically speaking, we are sane.'

That was quite satisfactory to me. And then I asked him, 'Why are you putting all of them there and treating them? How much help do you give them?'

He said, 'Not even two per cent of them are helped. We send them back to their homes but they keep returning.'

'Then why are you running this show?' I asked him.

He said, 'The government pays the money and the families don't want to keep those people in their homes.'

So, we now move on from there to the basic question, 'Who is sane and who is insane?' Sometimes such people come to see me. Even people who are hardcore cases come to me. But the line of demarcation between them and me is very thin. The difference seems to be that they have given up, whereas I am not in conflict with society. I take it. That's all the difference. There is nothing that prevents me from fitting into the framework of society. I am not in conflict with society. When once you are—I don't like to use the word 'freed' from—are not trapped in this duality of right and wrong, good and bad, you can never do anything bad. As long as you are caught up in wanting to do only good, you will always do bad. Because the 'good' you seek is only in the future. You will be good some other time and until then you remain a bad person. So, the so-called insane have given up and we are doing them the greatest harm and disservice by pushing them to fit themselves into this framework of ours which is rotten.

→══◉   ◉══←

The Roar of an Ocean Is Silence

What is the 'silence' that you are after? Do you hear those trucks passing by on the road and the flushing of the toilet? Do you want to escape from all this and go and sit in the caves? There is noise inside you wherever you go.

What is this silence you are talking about? The silence operates there in the city market. When I am talking, it is the expression of the silence. You think there is no silence, when I am talking? You think there is silence when you close your eyes, sit in one corner and try to stop the flow of thoughts? You are just choked—that is not silence. Go to the forest—that roar is the silence. Go to a sea—that is silence. Go right into the centre of the desert—that is silence. A volcano erupting— that is silence. Not the silent mind trying to experience 'silence'. Silence is energy bursting.

The peace there is not this inane dead silence you experience. It's like a volcano erupting all the time. That is the silence; that is peace. The blood is flowing through your veins like a river. If you tried to magnify the sound of the flow of your blood you will be surprised—it's like the roar of the ocean. If you put yourself in a soundproof room you will not survive even for five minutes. You will go crazy, because you can't bear the noises that are there in you. The sound of the beat of your heart is something which you cannot take. You love to surround yourself with all these sounds and then you create some funny experience called the 'experience of the silent mind', which is ridiculous. Absurd. That is the silence that is there—the roar—the roar of an ocean. Like the roaring of the flow of blood.

How can you understand that silence—chaotic or otherwise? Is it possible for you to capture that silence? When that silence starts operating through you, it is something extraordinary, something vital and living. This structure which is trying to understand the nature of it, capture it, contain it or give expression to it, cannot co-exist with it.

The difficulty is you seem to know a lot about this state—you have imagination. You imagine it to be what is described as 'Silence is

Brahman' and begin to think about it. This imagination must go. That [silence] is something living and the structure which is trying to capture it is a dead structure. You are all dead. You are not living human beings at all. You have never known one living moment in your life. You are living the lives of your thoughts. All thoughts are dead—it doesn't matter whose thoughts—whether those of Sankara, of Ramanuja or of the hundreds of sages, saints and saviours we have had and perhaps have still. It is useless to try to understand that. How can you capture it?

If there is any such thing as silence, chaotic or otherwise, living or dead, it will begin to express itself. When it expresses itself you are not there. So, you will never know the nature of that silence at all. What you call silence is not silence at all.

⊷═◉ ◉═⊷

The Body Is Immortal

It is the body which is immortal. It only changes its form after clinical death, remaining within the flow of life in new shapes. The body is not concerned with 'the afterlife' or any kind of permanency. It struggles to survive and multiply *now*. The fictitious 'beyond', created by thought out of fear, is really the demand for more of the same, in modified form. This demand for repetition of the same thing over and over again is the demand for permanence. Such permanence is foreign to the body. Thought's demand for permanence is choking the body and distorting perception. Thought sees itself as not just the protector of its own continuity, but also of the body's continuity. Both are utterly false.

The moment you die, the body begins to decay, returning back to other, differently organized forms of life, putting an end to nothing. Life has no beginning and no end. A dead and dying body feeds the hungry ants there in the grave, and rotting corpses give off soil-enriching chemicals, which in turn nourish other life forms. You cannot put an end to your life, it is impossible. The body is immortal and never asks silly questions like, 'Is there immortality?' It knows that it will come to an end in that particular form, only to continue on in others. Questions about life after death are always asked out of fear.

> This body has not fundamentally changed for hundreds of thousands of years. Its propensity to follow leaders, to avoid solitude, to wage war, to join groups—all such traits are in the genetic make-up of mankind, part of his biological inheritance.

The human body, when broken into its constituent elements, is no different from the tree out there or the mosquito that is sucking your blood. Basically, it is exactly the same. The proportions of the elements may be higher in one case and lesser in the case of the others. You have eighty per cent of water in the body, and there is eighty per cent of water in the trees and eighty per cent on this planet. So that is the reason why I maintain that we are nothing but a fortuitous concourse of atoms. If and when death takes place, the body is reshuffled, and then these atoms are used to maintain the energy levels in the universe. Other than that, there is no such thing as death to this body.

★

Thought is only a response to stimuli. The brain is not really a creator; it is just a container. The function of the brain in this body is only to take care of the needs of the physical organism and to maintain its sensitivity, whereas thought, through its constant interference with sensory activity, is destroying the sensitivity of the body. That is where the conflict is. The conflict is between the need of the body to maintain its sensitivity and the demand of thought to translate every sensation within the framework of the sensual activity. I am not condemning sensual activity. Mind, or whatever you want to call it, is born out of this sensuality. So, all activities of the mind are sensual in their nature, whereas the activity of the body is to respond to the stimuli around it. That is really the basic conflict between what you call the mind and the body.

⊷⊜ ⊜⊷

Hinduism Is Not a Religion

Hinduism is not a religion. It is a combination and confusion of many things. The actual word 'Hindu' comes from a lost non-Sanskrit word no longer in use. You wouldn't know anything about it. The invading Aryans who set up the Brahmanic social structure found the native Indians to have a dark complexion and called their religion the religion of the blacks—the 'hindus'. The scholars and pundits may not like my interpretation, but it is correct and historical. Again, I repeat, Hinduism is not a religion in the usual sense; it is like a street with hundreds of shops.

★

I am not for a moment expounding Hinduism here or in India. In fact, they think that I am not a Hindu. Yet the Hindus are ready to accept (to some degree) what I am saying. They say, 'What you are saying seems to be true, but the way you are putting things is not acceptable.' They brush me aside. But at the same time they cannot totally brush me aside. They always try to fit me into their framework or reference point. If they cannot do that, the whole tradition in which they have a tremendous investment is at stake. So they necessarily have to try to fit me into that framework. So far nobody has succeeded.

★

Many philosophers in India have been asked about my statements, and they know that they can very well deal with any philosophy, any thinker, past and present, but they have some difficulty in fitting me into any particular frame that they know of. What they say is, and I quote,

'There is no way we can fit this man into any known cage. So what we have to do is to let the bird fly.'

→══◉   ◉══←

Material And Spiritual Goals—Are They Different?

There is no such thing as spirituality at all. If you superimpose what you call spirituality on what is called material life, you create problems for yourself. Because you see growth and development in the material world around you, you are applying that to this so-called spiritual life also. There is only one life…. This is a material life, and that other has no relevance. Wanting to change your material life into that so-called religious pattern given to you, placed before you by these religious people, is destroying the possibility of your living in harmony and accepting the reality of this material world exactly the way it is. That is responsible for your pain, for your suffering, for your sorrow.

★

All civilizations, all cultures, place before you a goal, whether material or spiritual. There are ways and means of achieving your material goals but even in this respect there is a lot of pain, there is a lot of suffering. And you have superimposed on that what is called a spiritual goal. Christianity, for example, is built on the foundation of suffering as a means to reach your goal. What you are left with is only the suffering and you make a great big thing out of suffering. And yet, you are not anywhere near the goal, whatever is the nature of your goal, whereas in the material world the goal is something tangible.

The instrument which you are using to achieve your material goal does produce certain results. By using that more and more you can achieve the desired results but there is no guarantee. The instrument which you are using is limited in its scope. It is applicable only in this area. So the instrument which you are using to achieve your so-called spiritual goals is the same instrument. You do not realize that all the spiritual goals that are superimposed on your so-called material goals are born out of your fantasy because you have divided life into material and spiritual. It doesn't matter what instrument you use to achieve your goal. Whether it is material or spiritual it is exactly the same.

★

The spiritual people are the most dishonest people. I am emphasizing that foundation upon which the whole of spirituality is built. If there is no spirit, the whole talk of spirituality is bosh and nonsense. You can't come into your own being until you are free from the whole thing surrounding the concept of self. To be really on your own, the whole basis of spiritual life, which is erroneous, has to be destroyed. It does not mean that you become fanatical or violent, burning down temples, tearing down the idols, destroying the holy books like a bunch of drunks. It is not that at all. It is a bonfire inside of you. Everything that mankind has thought and experienced must go.

⊸═◉ ◉═⊷

The Fundamental Mistake

The fundamental mistake that humanity made somewhere along the line was to experience this separateness from the totality of life. At that time there occurred in man, which includes woman also, this self-consciousness which separated him from the life around. He was so isolated that it frightened him. The demand to be part of the totality of life around him created this tremendous demand for the ultimate. He thought that the spiritual goals of God, truth, or reality, would help him to become part of the 'whole' again. But the very attempt on his part to become one with or become integrated with the totality of life has kept him only more separate. Isolated functioning is not part of nature. But this isolation has created a demand for finding out ways and means of becoming a part of nature. But thought in its very nature can only create problems and cannot help us solve them.

★

We don't seem to realize that it is thought that is separating us from the totality of things. The belief that this is the one that can help us to keep in tune with the totality is not going to materialize. So, it has come up with all kinds of ingenuous, if I may use that word, ideas of insight and intuition.

★

When man first experienced the division in his consciousness, when he experienced his self-consciousness, he felt superior to other animals, which he is not, and therein sowed the seeds of his own destruction.

⊷═▣ ▣═⊶

The Psychiatrist Is the Enemy of this Culture

The brain is not a creator. This is a statement which many people may not accept, but this is what I have found out. Thoughts come from outside. There are no individuals at all. It is culture, society, or whatever you want to call it, that has created all of us for the sole purpose of maintaining its status quo.

At the same time, it has also created the idea that you must become something different from what you are. That is why you try to better yourself, improve yourself. You want to become something other than what you are. That creates this neurotic situation.

The neurosis in the human species is absolutely essential. We have to maintain this neurosis in order to function in this society. There is no other way that we can function in this society except to live in hope and die in hope. There are some people who have given up. But we force them to become functional in this value system which we have created. We even push them to commit suicide lest they become manic-depressive individuals. We are solely responsible for driving all these people into a situation where they have to put an end to themselves. They don't want to be functional here. They have given up. That is the reason why I say that the psychiatrist is the enemy of this culture, because he is forcing all those people who have given up fitting into this value system. One of the tragic things that human culture has done to us is that it has placed before us the model of a perfect being. That perfect being is modelled after the great spiritual teachers. The human being modelled after the great spiritual teachers has totally failed. The model has not touched anything there. Your value system is the one that is responsible for the human malady, the human tragedy, forcing everybody to fit into that model.

⊷═ ═⊷

What is Keeping You from Being in Your Natural State?

What is keeping you from being in your natural state? You are constantly moving away from yourself. You want to be happy, either permanently or at least for this moment. You are dissatisfied with your everyday experiences, and so you want some new ones. You want to perfect yourself, to change yourself. You are reaching out, trying to be something other than what you are. It is this that is taking you away from yourself.

Society has put before you the ideal of a 'perfect man'. No matter in which culture you were born, you have scriptural doctrines and traditions handed down to you to tell you how to behave. You are told that through due practice you can even eventually come into the state attained by the sages, saints and saviours of mankind. And so you try to control your behaviour, to control your thoughts, to be something unnatural.

We are all living in a 'thought sphere'. Your thoughts are not your own; they belong to everybody. There are only thoughts, but you create a counter-thought, the thinker, with which you read every thought.

Your effort to control life has created a secondary movement of thought within you, which you call the 'I'. This movement of thought within you is parallel to the movement of life, but isolated from it; it can never touch life. You are a living creature, yet you lead your entire life within the realm of this isolated, parallel movement of thought. You cut yourself off from life—that is something very unnatural.

> The natural state is not a 'thoughtless state'—that is one of the greatest hoaxes perpetrated for thousands of years on poor, helpless Hindus. You will never be without thought until the body is a corpse, a very dead corpse. Being able to think is necessary to survive. But in this state thought stops choking you; it falls into its natural rhythm. There is no longer a 'you' who reads the thoughts and thinks that they are 'his'.

Have you ever looked at that parallel movement of thought? The books on English grammar will tell you that 'I' is a first person singular pronoun, subjective case; but that is not what you want to know. Can you look at that thing you call 'I'? It is very elusive. Look at it now, feel it, touch it, and tell me. How do you look at it? And what is the thing that is looking at what you call 'I'? This is the crux of the whole problem: the one that is looking at what you call 'I' is the 'I'. It is creating an illusory division of itself into subject and object, and through this division it is continuing. This is the divisive nature that is operating in you, in your consciousness. Continuity of its existence is all that interests it. As long as you want to understand that 'you' or to change that 'you' into something spiritual, into something holy, beautiful or marvellous, that 'you' will continue. If you do not want to do anything about it, it is not there, it's gone.

How do you understand this? I have for all practical purposes made a statement: 'What you are looking at is not different from the one who is looking.' What do you do with a statement like this? What instrument do you have at your disposal for understanding a meaningless, illogical, irrational statement? You begin to think. Through thinking, you cannot understand a thing. You are translating what I am saying, in terms of the knowledge you already have, just as you translate everything else, because you want to get something out of it. When you stop doing that, what is there is what I am describing. The absence of what you are doing—trying to understand, or trying to change yourself—*is* the state of being that I am describing.

⊶⊜ ⊜⊷

Speaking to Yourself Constantly Is Your Problem

You must always recognize what you are looking at, otherwise you are not there. The moment you translate, the 'you' is there. You look at something and recognize that it is a bag, a red bag. Thought interferes with the sensation by translating. Why does thought interfere? And can you do anything about it? The moment you look at a thing, what comes inside of you is the word 'bag', if not 'bag', then 'bench' or 'bannister', 'step', 'that man sitting there, he has white hair.' It goes on and on—you are repeating to yourself all the time. If you don't do that, you are preoccupied with something else: 'I'm getting late for the office.' You are either thinking about something which is totally unrelated to the way the senses are functioning at this moment, or else you are looking and saying to yourself 'That's a bag, that's a red bag,' and so on and so on—that is all that is there. The word 'bag' separates you from what you are looking at, thereby creating the 'you'; otherwise there is no space between the two.

Every time a thought is born, you are born. When the thought is gone, you are gone. But the 'you' does not let the thought go, and what gives continuity to this 'you' is the thinking. Actually there is no permanent entity in you, no totality of all your thoughts and experiences. You think that there is 'somebody' who is thinking your thoughts, 'somebody' who is feeling your feelings—that's the illusion. I can say it is an illusion; but it is not an illusion to you.

Your emotions are more complex, but it is the same process. Why do you have to tell yourself that you are angry, that you are envious of someone else, or that sex is bothering you? I am not saying anything about fulfilling or not fulfilling. There is a sensation in you, and you say that you are depressed or unhappy or blissful, jealous, greedy, envious. This labelling brings into existence the one who is translating this sensation. What you call 'I' is nothing but this word 'red bag', 'bench', 'steps', 'banister', 'light bulb', 'angry', 'blissful', 'jealous', or whatever. You are putting your brain cells to unnecessary activity making the memory cells operate all the time, destroying the energy that is there. This is only wearing you out.

This labelling is necessary when you must communicate with someone else or with yourself. But you communicate with yourself all the time. Why do you do this? The only difference between you and the person who talks aloud to himself is that you don't talk aloud. The moment you do begin to talk aloud, along comes the psychiatrist. That chap, of course, is doing the same thing that you are doing, communicating to himself all the time—'bag', 'red bag', 'obsessive', 'compulsive', 'Oedipus complex,' 'greedy', 'bench', 'banister', 'martini'. Then he says something is wrong with you and puts you on the couch and wants to change you, to help you.

Why can't you leave the sensations alone? Why do you translate? You do this because if you do not communicate to yourself, you are not there. The prospect of that is frightening to the 'you'.

⊷⊜ ⊜⊷

You Stand On Your Own

You are lost in a jungle and you have no way of finding your way out. Night is fast approaching. The wild animals are there including the cobras and still you are lost. What do you do in such a situation? You just stop. You don't move. As long as there is that hope that you can somehow or the other get out of the jungle, so long will you continue what you are doing, searching, and so long you feel lost. You are lost only because you are searching. You have no way of finding your way out of the jungle.

★

You can stop it in you. Free yourself from that social structure that is operating in you without becoming antisocial, without becoming a reformer, without becoming anti-this, anti-that. You can throw the whole thing out of your system and free yourself from the burden of this culture, for yourself and by yourself. Whether it has any usefulness for society or not is not your concern. If there is one individual who walks free, you don't have any more the choking feeling of what this horrible culture has done to you. It's neither East nor West, it's all the same. Human nature is exactly the same—there's no difference.

★

I am telling you to stand on your own. You can walk. You can swim. You are not going to sink. That's all that I can say. As long as there is fear, the danger of your sinking is almost certain. Otherwise, there is a buoyancy there in the water that keeps you afloat. The fear of sinking is the very thing that makes it impossible for you to let the movement happen in its own way. You see, it has no direction. It is just a movement with no direction. You are trying to manipulate and channel that movement along a particular direction so that you can have some benefits. You are just a movement without a direction.

⋆⇌ ⇌⋆

You Are Unique

By using the models of Jesus, Buddha, or Krishna we have destroyed the possibility of nature throwing up unique individuals. Those who recommend that you forget your own natural uniqueness and be like someone else, no matter how saintly that person may be, is putting you on the wrong track. It is like the blind leading the blind.

★

When dealing with these yogins and holy men the first wrong turn you take is in trying to relate the way they are functioning with the way you are functioning. What they are describing may not be related to the way you are functioning at all. Uniqueness is not something which can be turned out in a factory. Society is interested only in the status quo and has provided all these so-called special individuals so that you'll have models to follow. You want to be like that fellow—the saint, the saviour, or the revolutionary—but it is an impossibility. Your society, which is only interested in turning out copies of acceptable models, is threatened by real individuality because it [individuality] threatens its continuity. A truly unique person, having no cultural reference point, would never know that he is unique.

★

What nature has created in the form of human species is something extraordinary. It is an unparalleled creation. But culture is interested in fitting the actions of all human beings into a common mould. That is because it is interested in maintaining the status quo, its value system. That is where the real conflict is.

★

Man cannot become man so long as he follows somebody. What is responsible for man remaining an animal is that culture—the top dog, following somebody—that has not helped you at all. You want to be a cheap imitation of Sankara or Buddha; you don't want to be yourself. What for? I tell you, you are far more unique and extraordinary than all those saints and saviours of mankind put together. Why do you want to be a cheap imitation of that fellow? That is one of the myths. Forget it.

⋯⇒◉ ◉⇐⋯

Discover Your Own Path Rejecting All Others...

The path has to be yours. I don't want to use the term 'path', because it has mystical overtones.... 'My' path, Ramakrishna's path, Jesus's path, or the Buddha's path—they are all worthless. Nobody can come into this unless or until all the other paths are rejected by him. Then it becomes his own path. So, only if you reject all the other paths can you discover your own path.

★

Just look at yourself and find out what the hell you are doing with yourself, how you are kidding yourself all the time—how you follow the path of this man, that man and the other man. You are not interested in my path. The path is not going to lead you anywhere. And the path is going to give you what that man has experienced.

★

What makes you unhappy is the search for a thing that does not exist. This is the unfortunate situation. You are not getting anywhere. That is not the way at all. Then what is the way? There is no way. Anything I say you turn into a way and add to the momentum. That is not the way. That is not the path. It has to be yours.

All paths must go. As long as you follow somebody else's path, the path is the product of thought. So it is actually not a new path, it's the same old path, and you are playing the same old game in a new way. It is not a new game. It is the same old game that you are playing all the time, but you think you are playing a new game. You have to come to a point where you can't do anything at all.

⊷⊜ ⊜⊶

No Power Outside of You

Psychic powers, clairvoyance, clairaudience—they are all human instincts. And they are necessary because there are two things that the human organism is interested in. One: its survival at any cost. Why should it survive? I don't know; it is a foolish question to ask. That is one of the most important things: it has a survival mechanism of its own, which is quite different from the survival mechanism of the movement of thought. The second thing is to reproduce itself. It has to reproduce. These are the two fundamental characteristics of the human organism, the living organism.

★

I can tell you that there is no power outside of you—no power. This does not mean that you have all the attributes that you read about of the super-duper gods; but there is no power outside of you. If there is any power in this universe, it is in you.

★

It's there in you. That's what I mean by saying there's no power outside of man. It is the same power, the same life, that is functioning there in you. Something is trying to express itself and the culture is pushing it down. When once it throws the culture out, it expresses itself in its own way…. That is the fragrance of this flower. Such an individual cannot retire into a cave or hide himself. He has to live in the midst of the world. He has no place to go to. That is the fragrance of this flower.

⊷═◑ ◐═⊶

Courage to Stand Alone

Man has to be saved from the saviours of mankind! The religious people—they kidded themselves and fooled the whole of mankind. Throw them out! That is courage itself, because of the courage there; not the courage you practise.

★

Fearlessness is not freedom from all the phobias. The phobias are essential for the survival of the organism. You must have the fear of heights and the fear of depths—if that is not there, there is a danger of your falling. But you want to teach courage to man to fight on the battlefield. Why do you want to teach him courage? To kill others and get killed himself— that is your culture. Crossing the Atlantic in a balloon or the Pacific on a raft—anybody can do that—that is not courage. Fearlessness is not a silly thing like that.

Courage is to brush aside everything that man has experienced and felt before you. You are the only one, greater than all those things. Everything is finished, the whole tradition is finished, however sacred and holy it may be—then only can you be yourself—that is individuality. For the first time you become an individual.

◦══ ══◦

J. Krishnamurti Is Playing the Same Guru Game

To me there is no such thing as mind; mind is a myth. Since there is no such thing as mind, the 'mutation of mind' that J. Krishnamurti is talking about has no meaning. There is nothing there to be transformed, radically or otherwise. There is no self to be realized. The whole religious structure that has been built on this foundation collapses because there is nothing there to realize. To me, Krishnamurti is playing exactly the same game as all those ugly saints in the market whom we have in the world today. Krishnamurti's teaching is phoney baloney. There is nothing to his teaching at all, and he cannot produce anything at all. A person may listen to him for sixty, seventy or a hundred years, but nothing will ever happen to that man, because the whole thing is phony. If the number of followers is the criterion of a successful spiritual teacher, JK is a pygmy. He's a mere wordsmith. He has created a new trap.

You want to smoke cigarettes, and there are always peddlers selling their own brands of cigarettes. Each one says that his is the one and only one, the best cigarette; and Krishnamurti comes around and says that his is nicotine-free. So the problem is not the gurus, but you. If you don't want to smoke, all these brands will disappear. These *gurus* are the worst egotists the world has ever seen. All gurus are welfare organizations providing petty experiences to their followers. The guru *game* is a profitable industry: try and make two million dollars a year any other way. Even JK, who claims he has no possessions, is the president of an eighty-million-dollar empire.

Yes, I am using 80 per cent of his words and phrases, the very phrases he has used over the years to condemn gurus, saints, and saviours like himself. He has it coming. If he sees the mess he has created in his false role as world messiah and dissolves the whole thing, I will be the first to salute him. But he is too old and senile to do it. His followers are appalled that I am giving him a dose of his own medicine. Do not compare what I am saying with what he or other religious authorities have said. If you give what I am saying any spiritual overtones, any religious flavour at all, you are missing the point.

Choiceless awareness is poppycock. Who is the one being choicelessly aware? You must test this for yourself. J. Krishnamurti has gathered about him the spiritual dead wood of a twenty-, thirty- and forty-year club. What good is that? I lived with him for years, and I can tell you he is a great actor. 'Gentlemen, we are taking a journey together'—but you can never go on that journey with him. Whatever you do, it is always the same. What you experience with him is the clarification of thought. You are that thought. He is a do-gooder who should have given up long ago.

As long as you think that you can see more and more clearly, I say you have seen nothing. J. Krishnamurti says, 'Seeing is the end.' If you say you have seen, you have not seen, because seeing is the end of the structure that says that. There is no seeing you can know. In other words, there is no seeing. As long as you think you can understand or see the world around you more clearly, I say you will see nothing and understand nothing.

J. Krishnamurti has subtly enticed people into believing in a spiritual goal, a goal which moreover can be reached through specific techniques—'passive awareness', 'free inquiry', 'direct perception', 'skepticism', etc. I reject the idea of transformation altogether. There is nothing to be transformed, no psyche to revolutionize, and no awareness you can use to improve or change yourself.

He is a showman par excellence and master of words. Krishnamurti's teachings may have sounded very revolutionary a century ago. But with the emergence of new revelations in the fields of microbiology and genetics, the ideas taken for granted in the field of psychology will be challenged. The 'mind' (which Krishnamurti's teaching assumes), the exclusive franchise of psychologists and religious teachers and all the assumptions connected with it will also be undermined.

No. What I'm saying has nothing to do with the same negative approach that J. Krishnamurti uses. The problem is that what you call a 'negative approach' is a positive approach; you just call it a 'negative approach', but you have turned the whole thing into a positive approach. If it is a negative approach, it has to negate itself somewhere along the line. It is very essential to use the negative approach, but you have unfortunately turned the whole negative approach into a positive approach. That man is not responsible for that; anything this structure touches, it *must* turn into a positive thing, because it is a product of positive thinking. So anything you listen to is turned into a method, a system—you want to *get* something through this. For example, somebody says there is a mind and you must uncondition your mind. How are you going to uncondition your mind? You are conditioning your mind through this lingo—that is all that it is necessary for you to see. Don't blame the other chap. Leave him alone.... I'll sing this song the rest of my life until I drop dead; whether anybody listens to it or not is of no importance to me. So then you leave this chap alone: you never establish any relationship with this man. The moment you use this to get whatever you want to get, or to arrive at some kind of a destination, you are tricking yourself into the same old game—this you have to see. Seeing is the end—*finished,* you see. But you haven't understood a thing; you go there again and again. And you have only clarified your thoughts, and through this so-called clarification you have given strength to the continuity of thought—this is all that has happened. So, it is the hope that keeps you going. You have gotten into a habit, a routine: instead of going to church, you go there—that's all you are doing. If you see the *absurdity* of what you are doing, then there is a possibility of your saying to yourself 'What the hell am I doing? What am I doing? How am I different? Why am I listening to this?'

⊷⭑═◉ ◉═⭑⊶

Who Is a Genuine Guru?

I am blocking every escape. Each outlet has to be blocked to put you in a corner. You must be choked to death, as it were. Only a real teacher can find that out and tell you, nobody else. Not those people who interpret the texts; all that is totally unrelated. Only such a man can talk. And such a man never encourages you because he knows that if this kind of a thing has to happen to somebody, that person will not need the help of anybody.

★

A guru is one who tells you to throw away all the crutches that we have been made to believe are essential for our survival. The true guru tells you, 'Throw them away and don't replace them. You can walk and if you fall you will rise and walk again.' Such is the man whom we consider or even tradition considers to be the real guru and not those who are selling those shoddy pieces of goods in the marketplace today. It is a business It has become a holy business to people.

★

I am not condemning anything but as long as you depend upon somebody for solving your problems, you remain helpless. And this helplessness is exploited by the people who actually do not have the answers to your problems but they give you some sort of a comforting. People are satisfied with and fall for this kind of thing instead of dealing with the problems by themselves and for themselves. There is no need for me to free you or enlighten you because to do that I must have an image of myself and in relationship to that an image of you.

★

To be an individual and to be yourself you don't have to do a thing. Culture demands that you should be something other than what you are. What a tremendous amount of energy we waste trying to become that! If that energy is released what is it that we can't do? How simple it would be for every one of us to live in this world! It is so simple.

⊷⟹ ⟸⊶

Saints and Mystics

The saint or mystic is a second-hand man who experiences what the sages have talked about, so he is still in the field of duality, whereas the sages or seers are functioning in the undivided state of consciousness. The mystic experience is an extraordinary one because it is not an intellectual experience; it helps them to look at things differently, to feel differently, to experience things differently and to interpret the statements of the sages and seers for others.

★

The world should be grateful to the saints rather than to the sages. Had it not been for the saints, the sages would have been clean forgotten long ago. The sages don't depend upon any authority; what they say is the authority. This the sages talked about, and the saints—some of them—

had experiences, and this became a part of their experience. They tried to share that (experience) through music and all kinds of things. But this is not an experience which can be shared with somebody else; this is not an experience at all.

→═● ●═←

Can Jesus, Buddha and Such Persons Be Our Models?

Culture, society, or whatever you want to call it, has placed before us the model of a perfect being, which is the model of the great spiritual teachers of mankind. But it is not possible for every one of us to be like that. You are unique in your own way. There is no way you can copy those men. That is where we have created the tremendous problem for the whole of mankind.

We have been brainwashed for centuries that the end product of human evolution is the creation of perfect models such as the great spiritual teachers of mankind with their special behavioural patterns. But nature is not interested in creating a perfect being, only a perfect species. It is only interested in making a species more adaptable to changing environment. Nature does not use any models. The creation of the human species is an unparalleled event. But culture is interested in fitting all into a common mould, and that is the cause of our tragedy.

By using the models of Jesus, Buddha, or Krishna we have destroyed the possibility of nature throwing up unique individuals. The one who recommends that—to be like someone else and forget your own natural uniqueness—no matter how saintly that person may be, is putting you on the wrong track. It is like the blind leading the blind.

It's not the avatars that can help; it's the individual that can help. It is an individual problem, so it is not the avatar who can help. There is a saviour in every individual, and if that saviour is brought out, blossoms, then perhaps there is a hope.

167

The human being modelled after the perfect being has totally failed. The model has not touched anything there. Your value system is the one that is responsible for the human malady, the human tragedy, forcing everybody to fit into that model. So, what do we do? You cannot do anything by destroying the value system, because you replace one value system with another. Even those who rebelled against religion, like those in the communist countries, have themselves created another kind of value system.

⊷═◉ ◉═⊶

Sages Are Different

The sage, or seer, or whatever you want to call him, is in the state of undivided consciousness. He does not know that he is a free man, so for him there is no question of trying to free others. He is just there. He talks about it and then he goes.

Gaudapada had no disciples. He refused to teach anybody. Great teachers never use any authority and they do not interpret anyone. The mystics help you to look at things differently, to interpret things differently. You cannot become a sage through any effort. It is not in your hands. A sage cannot have a disciple. A sage cannot have a follower because it is not an experience that can be shared. Even an ordinary experience you can't share with others. Can you tell somebody who has never experienced sex what the sex experience is like?

★

You cannot become a sage through any sadhana (spiritual practice); it is not in your hands. A sage cannot have a disciple, a sage cannot have a follower, because it is not an experience that can be shared. The sages and seers are original and unique because they have freed themselves from the entire past. Even the mystic experience is part of the past. Not that the past goes for such a man but for him the past has no emotional content. It is not continually operative, colouring the actions. This is the ultimate. You have to surrender yourself totally. It is not surrender in the ordinary sense of the word. It means there isn't anything you can do. That is total surrender, total helplessness. It can't be brought about through any effort or volition of yours. If you want to surrender to something it's only to get something. That's why I call it a state of total surrender. It's a state of surrender where all effort has come to an end, where all movement in the direction of getting something has come to an end.

★

It seems to have happened to some people during the course of history. Each one has given expression to that uniqueness in their own way according to their background. It is an expression of that background. Nature, in its own way, throws out from time to time some flower, but this end product of human evolution cannot be used by this evolutionary process as a model to create another one. If it throws out one flower, that is it, you see. You can't preserve it. You can't preserve the perfume of that because if you preserve it, it will stink. The evolutionary process or movement is not interested in using the one that it has perfected as a model for further creation. It has a creation of its own.

Telling It Like It Is

We are no more purposeful or meaningful than any other thing on this planet.... We are not created for any grander purpose than the ants that are there or the flies that are hovering around us or the mosquitoes that are sucking our blood.

★

The plain fact is that if you don't have a problem, you create one. If you don't have a problem you don't feel that you are living.

★

When you are no longer caught up in the dichotomy of right and wrong or good and bad, you can never do anything wrong. As long as you are caught up in this duality, the danger is that you will always do wrong.

★

In nature there is no death or destruction at all. What occurs is the reshuffling of atoms. If there is a need or necessity to maintain the balance of 'energy' in this universe, death occurs.

★

An artist is a craftsman like any other craftsmen. He uses that tool to express himself. All art is a pleasure movement.

★

There is more life in the chorus of the barking dogs than in the music or singing of your famous musicians and singers.

★

A messiah is the one who leaves a mess behind him in this world.

★

Religions have promised roses but you end up with only thorns.

★

It is terror, not love, not brotherhood, that will help us to live together.

★

Meditation itself is evil. That is why you get evil thoughts when you start meditating.

★

Anything you want to be free from for whatever reason is the very thing that can free you.

★

Atmospheric pollution is most harmless when compared to the spiritual and religious pollution that have plagued the world.

★

Going to the pub or the temple is exactly the same; it is a quick fix.

★

The body has no independent existence. You are a squatter there.

★

God and sex go together. If God goes, sex goes too.

★

When you know nothing, you say a lot. When you know something, there is nothing to say.

★

You have to touch life at a point where nobody has touched it before. Nobody can teach you that.

★

All I can guarantee you is that as long as you are searching for happiness, you will remain unhappy.

★

Understanding yourself is one of the greatest jokes perpetrated not only by the purveyors of ancient wisdom– the holy men– but also the modern scientists. The psychologists love to talk about self-knowledge, self-actualization, living from moment to moment, and such rot.

★

The more you know about yourself the more impossible it becomes to be humble and sensitive. How can there be humility as long as you know something?

★

It is mortality that creates immortality. It is the known that creates the unknown. It is time that has created the timeless. It is thought that has created the thoughtless.

★

You actually have no way of looking at the sunset because you are not separated from the sunset. The moment you separate your self from the sunset, the poet in you comes out. Out of that separation poets and painters have tried to express themselves, to share their experiences with others. All that is culture.

★

All experiences, however extraordinary they may be, are in the area of sensuality.

★

Humility is an art that one practises. There is no such thing as humility. As long as you know, there is no humility. The known and humility cannot coexist.

★

Man cannot be anything other than what he is. Whatever he is, he will create a society that mirrors him.

★

Inspiration is a meaningless thing. Lost, desperate people create a market for inspiration. All inspired action will eventually destroy you and your kind.

★

Love and hate are not opposite ends of the same spectrum; they are one and the same thing. They are much closer than kissing cousins.

★

It is a terrible thing to use somebody to get pleasure. Whatever you use, an idea, a concept, a drug, or a person, or anything else, you cannot have pleasure without using something.

★

Hinduism is not a religion in the usual sense. It is a combination and confusion of many things. It is like a street with hundreds of shops.

★

Gurus play a social role, so do prostitutes.

★

Society, which has created all these sociopaths, has invented morality to protect itself from them. Society has created the 'saints' and 'sinners'. I don't accept them as such.

★

By using the models of Jesus, Buddha, or Krishna we have destroyed the possibility of nature throwing up unique individuals.

★

As long as you are doing something to be selfless, you will be a self-centred individual.

★

The subject does not exist there. It is the object that creates the subject. This runs counter to the whole philosophical thinking of India.

★

When thought is not there all the time, what is there is living from moment to moment. It's all in frames, millions and millions and millions of frames, to put it in the language of film.

★

The man who spoke of 'love thy neighbour as thyself' is responsible for this horror in the world today. Don't exonerate those teachers.

*

Life has to be described in pure and simple physical and physiological terms. It must be demystified and depsychologized.

*

Society is built on a foundation of conflict, and you are society. Therefore you must always be in conflict with society.

*

You know the story of 'Alice in Wonderland'. The red queen has to run faster and faster to keep still where she is. That is exactly what you are all doing. Running faster and faster. But you are not moving anywhere.

*

The appreciation of music, poetry and language is all culturally determined and is the product of thought. It is acquired taste that tells you that Beethoven's *Ninth Symphony* is more beautiful than a chorus of cats screaming; both produce equally valid sensations.

*

The peak of sex experience is the one thing in life you have that comes close to being a first-hand experience; all the rest of your experiences are second-hand, somebody else's.

*

The problem with language is, no matter how we try to express ourselves, we are caught up in the structure of words. There is no point in creating new language, a new lingo, to express anything. There is nothing there to be expressed except to free yourself from the stranglehold of thought.

★

What you call 'yourself' is fear. The 'you' is born out of fear; it lives in fear, functions in fear and dies in fear.

★

It would be more interesting to learn from children, than try to teach them how to behave, how to live and how to function.

★

Food, clothing and shelter—these are the basic needs. Beyond that, if you want anything, it is the beginning of self-deception.

★

You must accept yourself and others as you and they are because they cannot and will not change, nor can you.

★

There is no difference between any aspects of human experience, they are all the same.

★

We are no more purposeful or meaningful than any other thing on this planet.

★

The plain fact is that if you don't have a problem, you create one. If you don't have a problem you don't feel that you are living.

★

You are what you do, not what you say you want to do. You think when you don't want to do anything. Thinking is a poor alternative to acting. Your thinking is consuming all your energy. Act, don't think.

★

Nature is interested in only two things—to survive and to reproduce one like itself. Anything you superimpose on that, all the cultural input, is responsible for the boredom of man.

★

The body here is so peaceful. It is only interested in pumping blood, secreting pancreatic juices, moving its bowels. It is so blissful in and of itself that it is not at all interested in your so-called 'spiritual bliss', your yoga, your divine peace, your moksha, etc.

★

Boredom is a bottomless pit. As long as you think that there is something more interesting, more purposeful, more meaningful to do than what you are actually doing, you have no way of freeing yourself from boredom.

★

Man eats for pleasure. Your food orgies are not different from your sex orgies. Everything that man does is for pleasure.

★

It is fear that makes you believe that you are living and that you will be dead. What we do not want is the fear to come to an end. That is why we have invented all these new minds, new sciences, new talks, therapies, choiceless awareness and various other gimmicks.

⋆

A 'moral man' is a frightened man, a chicken-hearted man; that is why he practises morality and sits in judgement over others.

⋆

The so called self-realization is the discovery for yourself and by yourself that there is no self to discover. That will be a very shocking thing because it's going to blast every nerve, every cell, even the cells in the marrow of your bones.

⋆

Thought is something dead and can never touch anything living. It cannot capture life, contain it, and give expression to it. The moment it tries to touch life it is destroyed by the quality of life.

⋆

Cabbages are more alive than human beings.

⋆

Anything you experience based on knowledge is an illusion.

⋆

The body has no independent existence. You are a squatter there.

*

The day man experienced the consciousness that made him feel separate and superior to the other forms of life, he began sowing the seeds of his own destruction.

*

All I can guarantee you is that as long as you are searching for happiness, you will remain unhappy.

*

These memories have a great deal of emotional content for you, but not for me. I am only interested in what is actually happening now, not tomorrow or yesterday.

*

When the movement in the direction of becoming something other than what you are isn't there any more, you are not in conflict with yourself.

*

While you are living, the knowledge that is there does not belong to you. So, why are you concerned as to what will happen after what you call 'you' is gone?

*

Thought can never capture the movement of life, it is much too slow. It is like lightning and thunder. They occur simultaneously, but sound, travelling slower than light, reaches you later, creating the illusion of two separate events.

*

The questioner is nothing but the answers. That is really the problem. We are not ready to accept this answer because it will put an end to the answers which we have accepted for ages as the real answers.

*

You eat not food but ideas. What you wear are not clothes, but labels and names.

*

If you do not know what happiness is, you will never be unhappy.

*

QUESTIONING UG

Questioning UG – I

Q: *We want to know on what grounds you make the uncompromising statement that there is no soul.*

UG: There is no self, there is no I, there is no spirit, there is no soul, and there is no mind. That knocks off the whole list, and you have no way of finding out what you are left with. You may very well ask me the question, 'Why do you go on telling people about the way you are functioning?' It is only to emphasize that we have been for centuries using some instrument, that is, thinking or mind, or whatever you want to call it, to free ourselves from the whole of what you call the 'I' or the 'self', and all kinds of things. That is what the whole quest of spirit is all about. But once it dawns on you that there is nothing to be free from, these questions don't arise at all. How that dawned on me, I have no way of finding out for myself.

The answers I give are only to emphasize that what we are left with is the functioning of the living organism. How it is functioning is all that I am trying to put across, emphasize, and overemphasize all the time. My interest is to make you see somehow that the whole attempt on your part to understand what you are left with is a lost battle.

Q: *Are you saying that there is only the physical body and nothing else?*

UG: Even that statement cannot be experienced by what is left there. When once the whole thing is flushed out of your system, the statement, 'We are left with only the physical body and the universe—' that statement also cannot stand any more.

Q: *Let's probe around this...*

UG: The more the questions you throw at me the more there is a need to emphasize the physical aspect of our existence, namely, that there is nothing to what we have been made to believe. All our problems have arisen because of our acceptance that it is possible for us to understand the reality of the world, or the reality of our existence. What I am saying is that you have no way of experiencing anything that you do not know. So anything that you experience through the help of your knowledge is fruitless. It is a lost battle.

Q: *Are you saying that there is only the actual physical body and the world as it is…?*

UG: That is the reason why I say that the instrument which we are using to understand the reality of our existence and the reality of the world around us is not part of this mechanism [the body] that is there. That is the reason why I say thoughts are not self-generated and are not spontaneous. There are no thoughts there even now. If you want to find out whether there is any such thing as thought, the very question which we are posing to ourselves, namely, 'Is there a thought?' is born out of the assumption that there is a thought there. But what you will find there is all about thought and not thought. All about thought is what is put in there by the culture. That is put in by the people who are telling us that it is very essential for you to free yourself from whatever you are trying to free yourself from through that instrument. My interest is to emphasize that that is not the instrument, and there is no other instrument. And when once this hits you, dawns upon you that thought is not the instrument, and that there is no other instrument, then there is no need for you to find out if any other instrument is necessary. No need for any other instrument. This very same structure that we are using, the instrument which we are using, has in a very ingenious way invented all kinds of things like intuition, right insight, right this, that, and the other. And to say that through this very insight we have come to understand something is the stumbling block. All insights, however extraordinary they may be, are worthless, because it is thought that has created what we call insight, and through that it is maintaining its continuity and status quo.

Q: *How does one observe the human organism there and its interrelated functions....*

UG: As a matter of fact even that is not possible to experience and understand except through the knowledge that is given to us by the physiologists.

Q: *You mean our own observation...?*

UG: There is no such thing as your own observation. Your own observation is born out of the knowledge that you have. This knowledge comes from the physiologists. This knowledge comes from those who have been involved in medical technology. They are trying to find out how this body is functioning, how the heart is functioning, and the whole lot of things that we have become familiar with, though what they have discovered is something which cannot be experienced by us.

Q: *What you are saying then is that there is really no such thing as direct or immediate experience....*

UG: There is no experience at all without the help of knowledge. That is all that I am saying. There is no way you can experience the reality of anything except through the help of this knowledge. So what I am saying is that you cannot experience what you do not know. Therefore, you project that there is something beyond the mechanism of the experiencing structure. There is no 'beyond'. But that 'beyond' is again affirmed or rejected by this experiencing structure to maintain its continuity. It is a game.

Q: *But then, isn't there an experience of touch?*

UG: No. The only way you can even experience the sense of touch is through this contact; that is what you call the sense of touch. So you are bringing your fingers here and touching it here. [*UG touches the arm of the chair.*] The eye is looking at it. But it does not translate the movement of that as somebody putting his finger here to know what exactly happens when you touch this. The eye cannot say that, and the sense of touch does not translate that for any reason. Unless you ask the question...

Q: But one can feel...

UG: It is born out of your imagination and translation of this particular tactile sensing within the framework of your past experience. At this moment if that is not translated as a soft touch or a hard touch, or even as a touch of your hand, you have no way of separating the two and experiencing that.

Q: No more separating the two...

UG: Supposing you ask me a question for whatever reason that you want to know, the sole knowledge you have is here in the computer [*pointing to his head*], and it comes out and tells me and tells you that you are touching this, and that the sense of touch is translating that as the soft touch of the friend who is sitting next to me.

Q: I might be walking alone, and I feel a breeze coming. I am not doing anything, but it is blowing in my way.

UG: If you do not translate the breeze touching your body...

Q: I am feeling the breeze.

UG: The feeling is also a thought. The moment you separate yourself from the breeze, that sensory activity is translated within the framework of the knowledge you already have. I am not for a moment saying that you are the breeze. What I am saying is that all that you are saying is part of the knowledge you have. Otherwise, there is no way you can separate the breeze and the body.

Q: So you are saying that there is no such thing as a new experience.

UG: There is no new experience at all. But the demand to experience the same thing over and over again is the one that is wearing off the whole mechanism of memory for purposes for which it is not intended.

Q: Is it possible for us to see that memory should not be the operative factor in consciousness?

UG: I question consciousness because what we call consciousness is memory. You become conscious of something through the help of the knowledge you have, and that knowledge is locked up in the memory. So the whole talk of the subconscious, unconscious, levels of consciousness, and all that, is the ingenious invention of the thinking mechanism. Through this cleverness, inventiveness, it maintains its continuity.

Q: Do you make any distinction between awareness and consciousness?

UG: Awareness has no meaning to me because awareness is not an instrument to be used to understand anything, much less to bring about a change there. First of all, there is nothing there to be changed. Since there is nothing there to be changed, whether you use awareness or any other instrument to bring about a change is irrelevant.

Awareness can never be separated from the activity of the brain. That is the reason why I always describe what is happening here [*pointing to himself*] in physical terms. The reflection of that, [*pointing to a cushion*] whatever it is, on the retina, and to experience that 'without naming it,' is only a clever game we are playing with ourselves. You think that recognition is separate from naming. This is not true. Recognition and naming are one and the same. Whether I name it or not, the very recognition of you as a man or that as a pillow, itself means that the naming is already there, whether I use the word or not. That is the reason why I point out to the people who say that the word is *not* the thing, the word *is* the thing. If the word is not the thing, what the hell is it? It is all right for the philosophers to sit and discuss everlastingly that the word is not the thing. That implies that there is something there other than the word. So you cannot accept the fact that the word *is* the object. That is, even if you say that there is an object without using the word, it means that there is a separation there. What I am trying to tell you is how this division, separation, is occurring.

Q: Separation is really the beginning of duality.

UG: I never tell myself and tell you that I am the table. That is too absurd. So what I am saying is that there is no way you can separate yourself with your own free will and volition except when there is a demand from outside. You ask the question, 'What is that?' You and I have the same information in our memories. Whether you use a French word, an English word, a German word, or a Latin word, it doesn't matter. The reference point is the table you are asking me about. So, I say it is a table, and that it is a white table. You and I have the same information. When that question is not there, I would at no time look at it and tell myself that it is a table. It does not mean that I am 'choicelessly aware' of that. What is there is only the reflection of this object on the retina. Even this statement cannot be experienced by me, because the stimulus and response are one unitary movement. The moment you say there is awareness, there is already a division.

Q: Why do we maintain this position, this duality, this separation?

UG: That is the only way you can continue. Otherwise you are coming to an end. The 'you' as you know yourself, the 'you' as you experience yourself, that 'you' is the identity there. Through the constant demand for using memory it maintains its continuity. If that 'you' is not there, you don't know what will happen. That is why the phrase, 'freedom from the known' is very attractive up to a point. Once you are free from the known, there is no way you can say anything about it. So, if I am listening to somebody like you who is talking about the need to have the freedom from the known, your emphasis that there is a need to free yourself from the known has already become part of the known. Thought has survived for millions and millions of years, and it knows every trick in the world. It will do anything to maintain its continuity.

Q: *So thinking has really no place in understanding?*

UG: There is no thinking at all. If there is no thinker, there are no thoughts at all. You cannot say there is only thought and there is no thinker. The thoughts do not come from here [*pointing to his head*], they are coming from outside. The translation of a sensory perception within the framework of your experiencing structure is thought. And you are using those thoughts to achieve a goal.

Q: *What really is this thinking?*

UG: No, you can try that. I am not your teacher. What is happening here is a mechanical thing like in a computer. It is mechanically operating, trying to find out if there is any information stored in the computer [*pointing to his head*] related to what we are talking about. 'Let me see,' ' Let me think,' these are statements you are just making, but there is no further activity and no thinking taking place there. You have an illusion that there is somebody who is thinking and bringing out the information.

Look, this is no different from the extraordinary instrument we have, the word-finder. You press a button and 'Ready,' it says. Then you ask for a word; 'Searching,' it says. That searching is thinking. But it is a mechanical process. In that word-finder or computer there is no thinker. There is no thinker thinking there at all. If there is any information or anything that is referred to, the computer puts it together and throws it out. That is all that is happening. It is a very mechanical thing that is happening. We are not ready to accept that thought is mechanical because that knocks off the whole image that we are not just machines. It is an extraordinary machine. It is not different from the computers we use. But this [*pointing to his body*] is something living, it has got a living quality to it. It has a vitality. It is not just mechanically repeating; it carries with it the life energy like that current energy.

Q: One of the things that human beings use most often is imagination . . .

UG: The idea that you experience the totality of your body is born out of your imagination. Actually, there is no way you can experience the totality of it. Your experience of the heaviness of your body is due to the gravitational force. Sometimes you experience the heaviness of your body when thoughts are not in operation. Sometimes thoughts slow down in everybody. That is the time when you feel heavier than the heaviest object. You feel as if you weigh 640 kilos, or suddenly you feel as if you are walking on air. These are the actual functionings of the body which they have described in some spiritual terms and given so much importance to.

Q: So, people in this area of imagination think that unfettered thinking can sometimes come up with new possibilities, of ways in which you can live more fruitfully, more easily or more pleasurably?

UG: That is something that is not valid and true.

Q: This is what people assume. If one has an opportunity to do that, one can do so. What is wrong with that?

UG: See, it works in certain areas. You know, we have a mathematical problem. We are thinking about it. You come out with an answer and say that this is the product of your thinking. But sometimes you exhaust all the possibilities, the variations and and combinations of finding out the solution of a particular mathematical problem or a scientific problem. You are so tired that you go to sleep. But when you wake up the answer is there. This is possible only in the area of mechanical problems. Thinking cannot help us to solve living problems. There is no way we can use that to solve human problems. That is why it has failed to solve our problems. It has not touched anything there [pointing to his body].

All our beliefs have not touched anything there. We don't know what we would do in a given situation. You can say that you are going to be a non-violent man. But what you would do in a given situation you would never know. The demand to be prepared for all future actions and situations is the cause of our problems. Every situation is so different, and our preparedness to meet that situation with this knowledge we have of answering and dealing with such situations cannot help us.

Q: *Then what does the phrase 'living challenge' mean?*

UG: I don't know, the way you are putting questions…

Q: *You meet a new situation…*

UG: It is not a challenge. The inadequacy of using what you have, preparing yourself, and the question of how to deal with the situation are absent here. It ceases to be a challenge then. That is why I say there are no problems there. We create the problems. If the solutions we are offered by those people are really not the solutions, you really don't have a problem. But the fact of the matter is, if you do not have a problem, you create a problem. You cannot live without problems.

Q: *That is right. What you are saying in one sense is that the human being is not really different from animals.*

UG: I must admit that we are probably far more evolved than the other animals. That is an advantage to us in functioning in a much better way. I don't like to use the word 'better', but rather 'in a more natural way'. We are free from some dangers. All these problems can be handled with the highly evolved structure which we have been endowed with. That is why what we call psychic powers—clairvoyance, clairaudience, etc.—are already there in the animals. We also have them in us. In the case of some, through techniques of meditation and such gimmicks, thought slows down. Then they experience these so-called powers, temporarily, and they think that they are all spiritual experiences.

Probably in our case the mechanism is more sensitive than in the case of animals. I don't know; I cannot make any definitive statement. There is no way you can really understand how animals are functioning. All these gimmicks, all these ideas of experiencing your birth again, rebirthing, this, that, and other things—they are absolute rubbish, because you are trying to go back to the time of your birth and experience your own birth from this point. What you are experiencing is not the experience of your own birth, but something from where you are. You use all these experiences, colour them, and imagine that you are experiencing your own birth. This is good for marketing their 'rebirth', but there is nothing to it.

Q: Why is it that human beings have developed some traits which have made them masterful destroyers of the earth, the air, the water, and everything around them?

UG: As I said the last time, this separateness from the totality of things around us, and the idea that the whole thing is created for our benefit and that we are created for a grander and nobler purpose than all the other species on this planet, are the causes of this destruction. This powerful use of thought is what is destructive. Thought is a self-protective mechanism. So anything that is born out of thought is destructive— whether it is religious thought or scientific thought or political thought— all of them are destructive. But we are not ready to accept that it is thought that is our enemy. We don't know how to function in this world without the use of thought. You can invent all kinds of things and try to free yourself from this stranglehold of thought, but there is no way we can accept the fact that that is not the instrument to help us to function sanely and intelligently in this world. Thought is a self-perpetuating mechanism. It controls, moulds, shapes our ideas and actions. Idea and action—they are one and the same. All our actions are born out of ideas. Our ideas are thoughts passed on to us from generation to generation. Thought is not the instrument to help us to live in harmony with the life around us. That is why you create all these ecological problems, problems of pollution, and the problem of possibly destroying ourselves with the most destructive weapons that we have invented. So, there is no way out. You may say that I am a pessimist, that I am a cynic, or that I am this, that, and the other. But I hope one day we shall realize that the mistakes we have made will destroy everything. The planet is not in danger. We are in danger.

Q: If we are, we can go to another planet. The desire to survive—whence comes this desire to survive beyond the death of the body and its inevitable demise?

UG: Because you know in a way that what you know of yourself is coming to an end there. You have lived sixty, seventy, or a hundred years of your life; you have been through so many experiences; you have achieved so many things; you have attained and accomplished so many things. 'Is all that coming to an end—leaving behind nothing?' So, naturally we create something 'beyond'.

Q: Why do you think that we have allowed an illusion and unreality to persist in consciousness or human thought?

UG: You are not separate from that illusion. You are the illusion. If one illusion goes, it is always replaced with another illusion. Why? Because the ending of the illusion is the ending of 'you'. That is the death. The ending of belief is the ending of the 'you' that is there. So, that is not the poetic, romantic death—of 'dying to your yesterdays'. Physical death is the only way through which you flush out what your whole culture has put in there.

Q: In a smaller and minor way, one can see through an illusion...

UG: That is another illusion. The illusion is that 'the seeing is the ending.' There is no way you can separate yourself and the seeing. Seeing is the illusion; the seer is the illusion. The seer tells himself that 'seeing is ending,' but it does not end. So the seer does not want to come to an end. The seer is the illusion. I don't know; it is better not to discuss these things. The seer is the illusion. Through the invention of what is called 'the seeing of the illusion is the ending', the seer is gathering momentum and continuing. The moment you want to 'see' something you have separated yourself from that and the seer has come into being, and through that seeing he is maintaining his continuity. That is why seeing has not helped us; it has ended nothing there.

Q: This dialogue, our talking together now—what would you like to call it? Is it just a physical exchange … this interplay that is going on now?

UG: [*Laughs*] I don't really want to repeat it again and again. This is just a puppet sitting here. And, two puppets, two computers, two tape recorders playing, that is all.

Q: Whatever you are saying—listening to you, will it not bring about a change in us?

UG: Not at all. You are not even listening. There is no such thing as the art of listening. You are not listening at all. Listening is not in your interest. You are interpreting.

Q: Surely there is some kind of listening…

UG: We don't have to use all those phrases such as, 'I am aware of this, that, and the other.' If you put into practice what they call 'awareness', you will go the way of Alzheimer's disease which is hitting everybody. I read it in some magazine that it is hitting everybody. It has hit already the famous musician, what is his name, Frank Sinatra. It is there in one of your papers. He is very young. They mention him as an example of how a person suffering from Alzheimer's disease functions. You have the 'key' there in your hand. But you don't know how to use the key and open the door.

Q: Then really what you are saying is that the body has an enormous intelligence because all its functions go on interplaying beautifully in their own way.

UG: Our interest to teach that body something which it is not interested in is causing, creating problems for it.

Q: Is there anything else that you would like to say? For instance, about physical pain—whether...

UG: Leave it alone. If there is pain you take some pain killer. I am not saying you should do nothing, and let the body suffer and go through the pain. You are actually adding more to the pain. See, as long as the pain is there, I might as well take a pill and free myself from the pain temporarily, because there is no special charm, spiritual or otherwise, to prove to ourselves and to others that we can endure pain. That is not what we are talking about. But what we can do is to leave that pain alone without interfering all the time. We think we know a lot more than this body. We think that we know what is good for that body, and that is why we are creating problems for it. It knows what it wants to know. It doesn't want to learn anything from us. If we understand this simple relationship that thought and the body have, probably we will allow the body to function and use thought for functional purposes only. Thought is functional in value, and it cannot help us to achieve any of the goals we have placed before us, or what the culture has placed before us.

Q: Is there no such thing as a physical purpose for pain?

UG: It is a healer. Pain is a healing process. But we are paranoid. We are overanxious to see that we don't suffer. I am not saying that you should not get any help that is available to you. There is no point in suffering, like the Christian saints who suffer and don't go to a doctor. That is not what I am saying. In fact, anything we say now is of no use. What we would do in any given situation is anybody's guess.

Let us stop and leave it at that. If you make some sense out of that, you make it. If you don't, you simply don't. I wish that nobody remembers anything of what we have discussed so far. If you remember anything, it is lost. Nor am I trying to say that what I say is in a mysterious way affecting the whole of human consciousness.

Q: *All right, pain is really a healer. But pain is inborn…*

UG: It is there. It is trying to heal us because of some disequilibrium. But what I am suggesting is that there is no charm in suffering; some helping hand can be given to make it a little bit bearable. I don't see any point in any kind of suffering.

Q: *If the pain is in your knee, in your back, or in your head, it is already there…*

UG: May I say something? Anything that we discuss about pain at this moment has no meaning, because we are not having any pain now. If some pain is really there then we wouldn't discuss it; some action would be there.

Q: *Yes, that is right.*

UG: Your value system is the one that is responsible for the human malady, human tragedy, forcing everybody to fit into that model.

⊷⟞⟝⊙   ⊙⟞⟝⊶

Questioning UG – II

Q: *Brain science tells us that the brain records every experience in our life. Is it all there somewhere in the basement of the brain? How would you explain that?*

UG: There is no such thing as the totality of experiences. Memory is in frames. In order to explain what I mean when I say that it is all in frames and that the whole human body is functioning from moment to moment, I must point to one basic thing, that is, how the senses are operating. What is there is only a response to a stimulus. The response is not translated by anything that is there, except that it registers the stimuli in the same way as information is registered when transferring images from one floppy disc to another. There is no linking up of all these responses. Each one is an independent frame. A lot of imagination is involved in our trying to understand what is actually happening there. I give you the example of what a friend wanted me to do when I was in a hill resort in India. He said that when he reached the top of a particular mountain he would have a 360-degree view of the whole place. So he dragged me up to the top. Unwillingly, hesitantly, I pushed myself to the top of that hill and tried to experience what he called a 360-degree view of the whole place. I said to myself, 'That fellow is kidding himself and imagining things. How is it possible to experience the 360-degree view of this place? I can see only 180 degrees. So what he thinks he is experiencing is born out of his own imagination.' This [*pointing to himself*] is singularly incapable of creating images. Translating the sensory perceptions into images is the cultural input there. When my eyes are not looking at you, there is no way that this organism [*pointing to himself*] can create the image of what you look like. The problem is the creation of images which is born out of our imagination and mostly out of what is put in there by our culture.

Q: I am listening…

UG: So what I am trying to say is that what the brain does is to translate these sensory perceptions into the framework of memory. Memory is not a constant factor. What happens is that when the light falls on the object and activates your optic nerve, it throws an image on the retina. This is what we have learnt from the study of our biology, and that is what the physiologists have taught us in our schools. But actually if you want to experience the fact, that is, the image of what you are looking at, it is something which cannot be experienced by you. Why I give this example is to free us from many of the ideas we have of what memory is. When once the optic nerves are activated, they in their turn activate the neurons in the brain, bring the memory into operation, and tell us that the object is this or that. So the next frame is quite different from the previous frame.

Let me give the example of a movie camera. The movie camera captures whatever is happening in frames. You take, for example, the movement of my hand from here to there—it has ten different frames to show that the hand has moved from here to there. And in order to see the movement on the screen you have to use an artificial thing called the projector. And only then do you see the movement of hand artificially created through the help of the projector. The sound is something like what they do in the movie industry. The sound is nineteen-and-a-half frames behind the corresponding picture frame. There is a gap between the picture you take and the sound—nineteen-and-a-half frames. In exactly the same way, thought is very slow. By the time it comes and captures this 'whatever is there' within its framework, your eyes have moved somewhere else, and that other thing is completely wiped out.

Q: I am thinking of television. It might be a good example too. There the picture is never really there. It is just a collection of dots. It required the brain to put the picture together.

UG: The brain is operating in exactly the same way. The whole thing is registered as dots and the pictures are taken in frames. There is an illusion that there is somebody who is looking at the things. Actually there is nobody who is looking at the things. It may sound very strange to you when I say that there is nobody who is talking. You are the one that is making me talk; there is nobody here [*pointing to himself*] who is talking. There is nobody. It may sound very strange to you but that is the way it is. It is so mechanical, yet we are not ready to accept the mechanical functioning of this living organism.

Q: So, you have no sense of identity, personal identity, of yourself?

UG: No way, because there is no centre there; there is no psyche there; there is no 'I' there. The only 'I' that I can find there is the first person singular pronoun. I have to use that first person singular pronoun to differentiate it from the second person singular pronoun. That is all. But there is nothing there which you can say is 'me'. That is the reason why I cannot tell myself that I am a free man, that I am an enlightened man. Also I have no way of knowing that you are not an enlightened man, that you are not a free man. There is no need for me to free you or enlighten you because to do that I must have an image of myself and in relationship to that I can have an image of you. So the images we have there are related to what we would like to be, what we ought to be, what we should be, and what we must be.

Q: As you travel around the world there are people that gather around you. Why do people gather around you, why do they come to see you?

UG: They still think that I can help them. I will relate to you some conversation that took place recently in Bangalore. They are all my friends. I don't have any devotees or disciples or followers. I tell them that they are my followers because they are repeating whatever I am saying. They are memorizing my statements and repeating them. And there is no use kidding themselves that they are not following me. The moment they repeat something which is not theirs, they have become the followers of somebody.

On one occasion, when I asserted with great vehemence that whatever happened to me had happened despite everything, despite my visit to Ramana Maharshi, despite my contacts with J. Krishnamurti and my personal conversations with him, and despite all the things that were expected of somebody who wanted to be an enlightened man, one friend in the audience said, 'We cannot accept your statement of "despite" ....' He said that my statements were irrelevant. 'The problem is very simple,' he said. 'If we accept what you are saying, namely, that whatever has happened to you has happened regardless of what you did, and that everything you did was irrelevant, we lose the only hope that we have in you. We still feel that although we have lost faith in them all, we cannot lose faith in you.' I told him that that is the one thing that is standing there in him which makes it impossible for him to free himself from whatever he is trying to free himself from, because he has replaced one thing with another. That is all that we can do. One illusion is replaced by another illusion and one teacher is replaced by another teacher. There is no way you can function without replacing one thing with another.

Q: *J. Krishnamurti maintained that there is no authority, no teacher, and that there is no path. Everyone has a life path that has taken him to wherever he ought to be. You also have a life path that has gotten you to where you are.*

UG: But I cannot suggest anything that did not play a part in my life. That would be something false, falsifying the thing you see.

Q: *Why should you not say that each of us has an individual and unique life path and out of that comes whatever that is?*

UG: The uniqueness of every individual cannot express itself because of the stranglehold of the experiences of others. After all, you don't exist, and I don't exist. You and I have been created by the totality of those experiences, and we have to use them in order to function sanely and intelligently in this world.

Q: *So you are creating me now?*

UG: You are creating me.

Q: *You are creating me now?*

UG: No. I am not creating you because I don't have an image of myself here. So, whatever you see here [*pointing to himself*] is your own creation and the projection of the knowledge you have of me. I don't know if you get what I am trying to say. I am not involved in what is going on there in you. What is involved here is only a reflection of whatever is there in front of me on the retina. But the translation of it is absent because it is part of that movement that is going on there.

Q: So, what I get from what you say is that it is a matter of living each moment as it comes.

UG: Such statements are very misleading. We place ourselves in a situation where we think that it is possible for us to live from moment to moment. But it is the body that is functioning from moment to moment.

Q: All right, the body is functioning from moment to moment.

UG: The one that is interested in living from moment to moment, which is the mind (quote and unquote), cannot live that way because its survival depends upon repeated experiences. The continuity of the knowledge that it is 'me' is not something else. You have to maintain that centre all the time, and the only way you can maintain that centre is through the repetitive process, repeating the same old experiences over and over again, and yet imagining that one day you are going to function from moment to moment. It is this hope that gives you the feeling and also some sort of experience that you are living from moment to moment. But the possibility of actually living from moment to moment is never there because the mind's interest is only to continue. Therefore, it has invented the ideal of living from moment to moment, no-mind, and all that kind of stuff. Through these gimmicks it knows it can maintain its own continuity.

Q: Sometimes we are so involved with our activity that we lose ourselves in it, and in that sense we are living in the moment.

UG: It is not correct to say that, because your involvement in whatever you are doing is a sort of 'high'. It is an experience which you want to place on a higher level and then think that you are absorbed in it.

Q: But you are not thinking about it, for there is no interval.

UG: No. Thought is very much there. But you have made that into an extraordinary experience, and your wanting to be like that always is

201

one thing that is not possible. A musician thinks that he is absorbed in what he is doing. It is demanding your total attention to express whatever you are doing, and when two things are not there it is a lot easier for you to express it effectively than when you are thinking about it.

Q: I really think about experiences after they happen. Then I reflect on them. When I look up in the sky and see a hawk flying across, I see the hawk and afterwards I reflect on it, 'Oh, I saw a hawk!' But at the moment when I see it I am not thinking about it.

UG: You see, that is not correct, because we have been made to believe, and you probably accept that statement, that while you are experiencing a thing you are not aware of it. The fact that you recall, whether you name that as a hawk or not, implies that you were very much there. I know a lot of people who tell me that they were in a thoughtless state, that there were moments when the 'I' was not there. But when once such a thing really happens, it is finished once and for all, and there is no way you can link those moments up together and create a continuity there. So, the statements that when you are experiencing a thing you are not aware of the experience and that you become aware or conscious of it only after the experience is gone are highly questionable. If that were so, it would have shattered the whole experiencing structure once and for all. It would be something of an earthquake hitting this place, and what happens then nobody knows. A shifting of things would have taken place, and thereafter the organism functions in a very normal and natural way. It would have found a new sort of equilibrium.

Q: Why are we here as human beings?

UG: Why do we ask that question, 'Why are we here?' What is it that tells you that you are here? Are you there now? It is the knowledge that tells you that you are here, that I am here.

Q: I have some awareness of being here, a feeling of being here.

UG: Feeling is also thought. We want to feel that feelings are more important than thoughts, but there is no way you can experience a feeling without translating that within the framework of the knowledge that you have. Take for example that you tell yourself that you are happy. You don't even know that the sensation that is there is happiness. But you capture that sensation within the framework of the knowledge you have of what you call a state of happiness, and the other state, that of unhappiness. What I am trying to say is that it is the knowledge that you have about yourself which has created the self there and helps you to experience yourself as an entity there.

I am not particularly fond of the word 'awareness'. It is misused. It is a rubbed coin, and everybody uses it to justify some of his actions, instead of admitting that he did something wrong. Sometimes you say, 'I was not aware of what was going on there.' But awareness is an integral part of the activity of this human organism. This activity is not only specifically in the human organism but in all forms of life—the pig and the dog. The cat just looks at you, and is in a state of choiceless awareness. To turn that awareness into an instrument which you can use to bring about a change is to falsify that. Awareness is an integral part of the activity of the living organism. And so, 'awareness' is not just the right kind of word to use.

It is impossible for us to separate ourselves from the rest of the things that are out there. You are not different from the chair that you are sitting on. But what separates you from the chair is the knowledge you have of that—'This is a chair.' You are sitting on the chair. But the fact is that the sensation that is involved in this relationship between you and the chair is the sense of touch. The sense of touch does not, however, tell you that you are separate from this chair on which you are sitting. I am not trying to say that you are the chair. That is too absurd.

Actually what makes you feel that the body is there is the gravitational pull of the body, the heaviness of the body. You feel the existence of the body because of the gravitational pull. I said somewhere in the beginning that you are affecting everything there and everything that is there is affecting you. The fact of this statement is something which cannot be experienced by you because it is one unitary movement.

The moment you separate the two and say that this is the response to that, you have already brought the knowledge you have of the things into operation and told yourself that this is the response to that stimulus.

Q: *The quantum physicists tell us that it is all connected and we are all part of the universe.*

UG: But they have arrived at that as a concept. So did the metaphysicians in India. They arrived at that fact and said that there is no such thing as space. Space is a very essential thing for you to survive in this world. But the fact that there is such a thing as space can never be experienced by you. A scientist came to see me and made this statement that there is no such thing as space, there is no such thing as time, and there is no such thing as matter. I said, 'You are repeating a memorized statement. Probably you will give me an equation to prove that there is no such thing as space. But supposing it is a fact in your life that there is no space, (I always give crude examples,) what happens to your relationship with your wife?' When people throw these kinds of phrases at me— that there is no observer, or that the observer is the observed—I give them a hard time and try to make them realize the implications of what they are saying. It is very interesting for the theologians, the metaphysicians, and the scientists to discuss these things. But when it percolates to the level of our day-to-day existence, and of our relationship with the people around us, it is very different. If you tell yourself that the observer is the observed, and apply that to a situation where you are about to make love to your wife, what will happen?

Q: *Is there a situation where the observer is really the observed?*

UG: That is the end of all relationship. It's finished. To say the observer is the observed is a meaningless statement, repeated ad nauseam. They actually do not know what will happen when that is the case. All relationships will be finished.

Q: *So we are just automata....*

UG: Automatically repeating words and phrases which are memorized. They have no relevance to the way we are functioning.

Q: *Are you just an automaton?*

UG: Oh, I am an automaton. There is not one thought which I can call my own. If this computer [*pointing to his head*] has no information on a particular subject, it is silent. So you are operating the computer [*pointing to himself*]. It is your interest to find out what there is in this computer. And whatever comes out of me is yours. What you call the printout is yours and you are reading something in it.

Q: *So I am the dreamer and you are the dream.*

UG: You have created me. You have all the answers and you are asking the questions.

Q: *I think I already have answers.*

UG: Otherwise how can there be questions? You are not sure that they are the answers.

Q: *Well, I am like everyone here, asking questions that any person might ask.*

UG: For which they already have the answers. But they are not sure that they are the answers. And they don't have the guts to brush aside the persons that have given those answers. Sentiments come into picture there, and you lose the guts to throw away the answers, and the ones who have given the answers, out the window.

Q: *What I get from this is that you have to be an individual.*

UG: To be an individual and to be yourself you don't have to do a thing. Culture demands that you should be something other than what you are. What a tremendous amount of energy—the will, the effort—

we waste trying to become that! If that energy is released, what is it that we can't do? How simple it would be for every one of us to live in this world! It is so simple.

⊷⊜⊸ ⊷⊜⊸

Questioning UG – III

Q: Are you in conflict with society?

UG: No, not in conflict with the society. This is the only reality I have, the world as it is today. The ultimate reality that man has invented has absolutely no relationship whatsoever with the reality of this world. As long as you are seeking, searching, and wanting to understand that reality (which you call 'ultimate reality', or call it by whatever name you like), it will not be possible for you to come to terms with the reality of the world exactly the way it is. So, anything you do to escape from the reality of this world will make it difficult for you to live in harmony with the things around you.

We have an idea of harmony. How to live at peace with yourself—that's an idea. There is an extraordinary peace that is there already. What makes it difficult for you to live at peace with yourself is the creation (of the idea) of what you call 'peace', which is totally unrelated to the harmonious functioning of this body. When you free yourself from the burden of reaching out there to grasp, to experience, and to be in that reality, you will find that it is difficult to understand the reality of anything. You will find that you have no way of experiencing the reality of anything, but at least you will not be living in a world of illusions. You will accept that there is nothing, nothing that you can do to experience the reality of anything, except the reality that is imposed on us by the society. We have to accept the reality as it is imposed on us by the society because it is very essential for us to function in this world intelligently and sanely. If we don't accept that reality, we are lost. We will end up in the loony bin.

So we have to accept the reality as it is imposed on us by the culture, by society or whatever you want to call it, and at the same time understand that there is nothing that we can do to experience the reality of anything. Then you will not be in conflict with the society, and the demand to be something other than what you are will also come to an end.

The goal that you have placed before yourself, the goal which you have accepted as the ideal goal to be reached, and the demand to be something other than what you are, are no longer there. It is not a question of accepting something, but the pursuit of those goals which the culture has placed before us, and which we have accepted as desirable, is not there any more. The demand to reach that goal also is not there any more. So, you are what you are. When the movement in the direction of becoming something other than what you are isn't there any more, you are not in conflict with yourself. If you are not in conflict with yourself, you cannot be in conflict with the society around you. As long as you are not at peace with yourself, it is not possible for you to be at peace with others. Even then there is no guarantee that your neighbours will be peaceful. But, you see, you will not be concerned with that. When you are at peace with yourself, you are a threat to the society as it functions today. You will be a threat to your neighbours because they have accepted the reality of the world as real, and because they are also pursuing some funny thing called 'peace'. You will become a threat to their existence as they know it and as they experience it. So you are all alone—not the aloneness that people want to avoid—you are all alone.

It's not ultimate reality that one is really interested in, not the teachings of the gurus, not the teachings of the holy men, not the umpteen number of techniques you have, which will give you the energy which you are seeking. Once that movement (of thought) is not there, that will set in motion and release the energy that is there. It doesn't have to be the holy man's teaching. It doesn't have to be any techniques that man has invented—because there is no friction there. You really don't know what it is.

The movement there [*pointing to the listeners*] and the movement here [*pointing to himself*] are one and the same. The human machine is no different from the machine out there. Both of them are in unison.

Whatever energy is there, the same energy is in operation here. So, any energy you experience through the practice of any techniques is a frictional energy. That energy is created by the friction of thought—the demand to experience that energy is responsible for the energy you experience. But this energy is something which cannot be experienced at all. This is just an expression of life, a manifestation of life.

You don't have to do a thing. Anything you do to experience that [energy] is preventing the energy which is already there, which is the expression of life, which is the manifestation of life, from functioning. It has no value in terms of the values we give to whatever we are doing—the techniques, meditation, yoga, and all that. I am not against any one of those things. Please don't get me wrong. But they are not the means to achieve the goal that you have placed before yourself—the goal itself is false. If the suppleness of the body is the goal you have before you, probably the techniques of yoga will help you to keep the body supple. But that is not the instrument to reach the goal of enlightenment or transformation or whatever you want to call it. Even the techniques of meditation are self-centred activities. They are all self-perpetuating mechanisms which you use. So the object of your search for ultimate reality is defeated by all these techniques because these techniques are self-perpetuating instruments. You will suddenly realize, or it will dawn on you, that the very search for ultimate reality is also a self-perpetuating mechanism. There is nothing to reach, nothing to gain, nothing to attain.

As long as you are doing something to attain your goal, it is a self-perpetuating mechanism. I use the word self-perpetuating mechanism, but I don't mean that there is a self or an entity. I have to use the word 'self' because there is no other word. It's like the self-starter you have in the car. It perpetuates itself. That is all that it is interested in. Anything you want to achieve is a self-centred activity. When I use the term 'self-centred activity,' you always translate it in terms of something that should be avoided, because selflessness is your goal. As long as you are doing something to be selfless, you will be a self-centred individual. When this movement in the direction of wanting to be a selfless man is not there, there is no self and there is no self-centred activity. So it is the very techniques, the systems and methods which you are using to reach your goal of selflessness, which are self-centred activities.

Unfortunately, society has placed that goal before us as the ideal goal, because a selfless man will be a great asset to the society, and the society is interested only in continuity—the status quo. So all those values, which we have accepted as values that one should cultivate, are invented by the human mind to keep itself going. The goal is what is making it possible for you to continue in this way, but you are not getting anywhere. The hope is that one day, through some miracle or through the help of somebody, you will be able to reach the goal. It is the hope that keeps you going, but, actually and factually, you are not getting anywhere. You will realize somewhere along the line that whatever you are doing to reach your goal is not leading you anywhere. Then you will want to try this, that, and the other. But if you try one and you see that it doesn't work, you will see that all the other systems are exactly the same. This has to be very, very clear, you see.

Q: Don't you think we need to change human consciousness if we have to create a better world? But you seem to completely disagree.

UG: What exactly do people mean when they talk of consciousness? There is no such thing as unconsciousness. Medical technology can find out the reason why a particular individual is unconscious, but the individual who is unconscious has no way of knowing that he is unconscious. When he comes out of that unconscious state, he becomes conscious. So do you think you are conscious now? Do you think you are awake? Do you think you are alive? It is your thinking that makes you feel that you are alive, that you are conscious. That is possible only when the knowledge you have about things is in operation. You have no way of knowing or finding out whether you are alive or dead. In that sense, there is no death at all, because you are not alive. You become conscious of things only when the knowledge is in operation. When the knowledge is absent, whether the person is dead or alive is of no importance to this movement of thought which comes to an end before what we call 'death' takes place. So, it really doesn't matter whether one is alive or dead. Of course, it does matter to one who considers that it [being alive] is very important and those who are involved with that individual, but you have no way of finding out whether you are alive or dead, or whether you are conscious or not. You become conscious only through the help of thought. But unfortunately it is there all the time. So, the suggestion that it is not possible to experience anything makes no sense to you at all, because you have no reference point there when this movement is absent. When this movement is absent, all those questions about consciousness are not there. That is what I mean when I say that the questions are absent.

How can you bring about a change in consciousness which has no limits, which has no boundaries, which has no frontiers? They can spend millions and millions and millions of dollars and do every kind of research to find the seat of human consciousness, but there is no such thing as the seat of human consciousness at all. They can try—and they are going to spend billions of dollars to try to find out—but the chances of their succeeding in that are slim. There is no such thing as a seat, located in any particular individual. What there is, is thought.

Q: Is it possible to free oneself from the quagmire of thought or say, knowledge, and come face to face with reality?

UG: If you are lucky enough (it's only luck), to get out of this trap of knowledge, the question of reality is not there any more (for you). The question arises from this knowledge, which is still interested in finding out the reality of things, and to experience directly what that reality is all about. When this [knowledge] is not there, the question is also not there. Then there is no need for finding any answer. This question which you are posing to yourself, and also to me, is born out of the assumption that there is a reality, and that assumption is born out of this knowledge you have of and about the reality. The knowledge is the answer you already have. That is why you are asking the question. The question automatically arises.

What is necessary is not to find out the answer to the question, but to understand that the question which you are asking, posing to yourself, and putting to somebody else, is born out of the answer you already have, which is the knowledge. So, the question and answer format, if we indulge in it for long, becomes a meaningless ritual.... If you are really interested in finding reality, what has to dawn on you is that your very questioning mechanism is born out of the answers that you already have. Otherwise there can't be any question.

First of all, there is an assumption on your part that there is a reality, and then, that there is something that you can do to experience that reality. Without the knowledge [about reality], you have no experience of reality, that is for sure. 'If this knowledge is not there, is there any other way of experiencing the reality?' You are asking the question. The question goes with the answer. So there is no need to ask questions and there is no need to answer. I am not trying to be clever. I am just spotlighting what is involved in the question and answer business. I am not actually answering any of your questions. I am just pointing out that you cannot have any questions when you have no answers.

Q: You say I cannot have thoughts of my own, but I do believe my thoughts are unique and purely my own.

UG: We are always talking about thought and thinking. What is thought? Have you ever looked at thought, let alone controlling thought; let alone manipulating thought; let alone using that thought for achieving something material or otherwise? You cannot look at your thought, because you cannot separate yourself from thought and look at it. There is no thought apart from the knowledge you have about those thoughts— the definitions you have. So if somebody asks you the question, 'what is thought?' any answer you have is the answer that is put in there—the answers that others have already given.

You have, through combinations and permutations of ideation and mentation about thoughts, created your own thoughts which you call your own. Just as when you mix different colours, you can create thousands of pastel colours, but basically all of them can be reduced to only seven colours that you find in nature. What you think is yours is the combination and permutation of all those thoughts, just the way you have created hundreds and hundreds of pastel colours. You have created your own ideas. That is what you call thinking. When you want to look at thought, what there is is only whatever you know about thought. Otherwise you can't look at thought. There is no thought other than what there is in what you know about thought. That's all that I am saying. So when that is understood the meaninglessness of the whole business of wanting to look at thought comes to an end. What there is is only what you know, the definitions given by others. And out of those definitions, if you are very intelligent and clever enough, you create your own definitions. That's all.

Q: You keep rejecting the importance of knowledge except in the technical field, but isn't there some knowledge which helps us to solve the problems of life?

UG: No. Not at all. That knowledge cannot help you to understand or solve living problems. Because there are no problems at all in that sense. We have only solutions. You are interested only in solutions, and those solutions have not solved your problems. So you are trying to find different kinds of solutions. But the situation will remain exactly the same. There is somehow the hope that maybe you will find the solution for solving your problems.

So your problem is not the problem but the solution. If the solution is gone, there is no problem there. If there is a solution, the problem shouldn't be there anymore. If the answers given by others (the 'wise men') are the answers, the questions shouldn't be there at all. So they are obviously not the answers. If they were the answers, the questions would not be there. So why don't you question the answers? If you question the answers, you must question those who have given the answers. But you take it for granted that they are all wise men; that they are spiritually superior to us all; and that they know what they are talking about. They don't know a damn thing!

But why are you asking these questions?—if I may ask you that counter-question. Where do these questions come from, first of all? Where do they originate in you? I want you to see very clearly the absurdity of asking these questions. It is essential to ask questions to learn the technical know-how of certain things. Somebody can help you, if something is wrong with the television, with the help of his technical know-how. That is understood. I am not talking about that at all. But the questions which you are asking, you see, are of a different kind. Where do you think these questions take their birth? How do they formulate themselves in you? They are all mechanical questions. What I am trying to emphasize all the time is that it is essential for you to understand how mechanical the whole thing is. There is nobody who is asking the questions there. There is no questioner who is asking the questions there. There is an illusion that there is a questioner who is formulating these questions and throwing them at somebody and expecting somebody to answer them. The answers that you get really are not the answers, because the questions persist in spite of the answers you think the other chap is giving you. The question is still there. This answer, which you think is the answer (satisfactory or otherwise), is really not the answer. If it were, the question should go once and for all. All questions are variations of the same question. You already have the answer, and all these questions are the questions that are not interested in getting any answers. The answer, if there is any to that question, should destroy the answer you already have. There is no questioner there. If the answer goes, along with the question, the questioner—the non-existent questioner—also has to go. I don't know if I make myself clear.

Do you have any question which you can call your own? If you can come out with a question which you can call your own, a question that has never, never been asked before, there is a meaning in talking things over. Then you don't have to sit and ask anybody those questions, because such questions don't exist at all. A question which you can call your own, has never been asked before. All the answers are there for those questions. You probably do not realize that the questions which you are asking are born out of the answers you already have, and that they are not your answers at all. The answers have been put in there. So, why are you asking these questions, why are you not satisfied with the answers that are already there? That is my question. Why? If you are satisfied, yes, it's alright, you see. [Then you would say:] 'I don't want any answers.' Still, the question is there inside of you. Whether you go and ask

213

somebody or expect an answer from some wise man, it is still there. Why is it there? What happens if the question comes to an end? You come to an end. You are nothing but the answers. That's all that I am saying. If you understand that there is no questioner who is asking the questions, the answer that is there is in great jeopardy. That is why it does not want any answer. The answer is the end of that answer you have, which is not yours.

So, what the hell if it is gone. The answers you have are already dead, they have been given by dead persons. Anybody who repeats those answers is a dead person. A living person cannot give any answer to those questions, because any answer that you get from anybody is a dead answer, because the question is a dead question. That's the reason why I am not giving any answer to you at all. You are living in a world of dead ideas. All thoughts are dead, they are not living. You cannot invest them with life. That's what you are trying to do all the time: you invest them with emotions. But they are not living things. They can never touch anything living. The spiritual and psychological problems you think you have are really living problems. So, the solutions that you have are not adequate enough to handle the living problems. They are good enough to discuss in a classroom or in some sort of question-and-answer ritual—repeating the same old dead ideas—but those things can never, never touch anything living, because the living thing will burn out the whole thing completely and totally. So, you are not going to touch anything living at any time. You are not looking at anything; you are not in contact with anything living, as long as you use your thoughts to understand and experience anything. When that is not there, there is no need for you to understand and experience anything. So anything you experience only gathers momentum—adds to that—that's all. There is nothing that you can call your own.

Q: You pooh-pooh goals, especially spiritual goals. It is depressing...

UG: All civilizations, all cultures place before you a goal, whether it is a material goal or a spiritual goal. There are ways and means of achieving your material goals, but even in this respect there is a lot of pain, there is a lot of suffering. And you have superimposed on that what is called a spiritual goal.

Christianity, for example, is built on the foundation of suffering as a means to reach your goal. What you are left with is only the suffering, and you make a great big thing out of suffering, and yet you are not anywhere near the goal, whatever is the nature of your goal. Whereas in the material world the goal is something tangible. The instrument which you are using to achieve your material goal does produce certain results. By using that more and more you can achieve the desired results. But there is no guarantee. The instrument which you are using is limited in its scope. It is applicable only in this (material) area. So, the instrument which you are using to achieve your so-called spiritual goals is the same instrument. You do not realize that all the spiritual goals that are superimposed on your so-called material goals are born out of your fantasy, because you have divided life into material and spiritual. It doesn't matter what instrument you use to achieve your goal, whether it is material or spiritual, it is exactly the same.

What you are interested in doesn't exist. It's your own imagination, based upon the knowledge you have about those things. And so, there is nothing that you can do about it. You are chasing something that does not exist at all. I can say that until the cows return home—I don't know when they return home here—or till the kingdom come—but that kingdom will never come. So, you keep on going, hopingthat somehow you will find some way of achieving your goals. Your interest in attaining that for the purpose of solving your day-to-day problems is a far-fetched idea because that cannot be of any help to you to solve your problems. 'If I had that enlightenment I would be able to solve all my problems.' You cannot have all that *and* enlightenment. When that comes, it wipes out everything. You want all this and heaven too. Not a chance! That is something which cannot be made to happen through your effort or through the grace of anybody, through the help of even a god walking on the face of this earth claiming that he has specially descended from wherever (from whatever heavens) for your sake and for the sake of mankind— that is just absolute gibberish. Nobody can help you. Help you to achieve what? That is the question, you see.

As long as your goal is there, these persons, their promises and their techniques will look very, very attractive to you. They go together. There is not anything you must do. Anyway, you are already doing [many things]. Can you be without doing anything? You can't be without doing anything. Unfortunately you are doing something, and that doing has got to come to an end. In order to bring that doing to an end, you are doing something else. That is really the crux of the problem. That's the situation in which you find yourself. That's all that I can say. I point out the absurdity of what you are doing. As I said yesterday, what brings you here will certainly take you somewhere else. You have nothing to get here, you will not get anything here. Not that I want to keep anything for myself; you can take anything you want. I have nothing to give you. I am not anything that you are not. You think that I am something different. The thought that I am different from others never enters my head. Never. Whenever they ask questions I feel, 'Why are these people asking these questions? How can I make them see?' I still have some trace of illusion. Maybe I can try. [But] even that 'try' has no meaning to me. There's nothing that I can do about it. There is nothing to get. Nothing to give and nothing to get. That is the situation. In the material world, yes. We have a lot of things. There is always somebody who can help you with the knowledge, with the money, with so many things in the world. But here in this field there is nothing to give and nothing to get. As long as you want, you can be certain you ain't got a chance. You see, wanting implies that you are going to set your thinking in motion to achieve your goal. It is not a question of achieving your goal, but it is a question of this movement coming to an end here. The only thing that you can do is to set in motion this movement of thought in the direction of achieving that. How are you going to achieve this impossible task?

Wanting and thinking—they always go together. I am not for a moment suggesting that you should suppress all your wants, or free yourself from all your wants, and control all your wants. Not at all. That's the religious game. If you want anything, the one thing that you will do is to set in motion the movement of thought to achieve your goal. Material goals, yes, but even there it's not so easy. It is such a competitive world. Not much is left for us to share. Not enough to go around. The talk of sharing with somebody is poppycock to me. There is nothing to be shared here. This is not an experience. Even assuming for a moment that this is an experience, even then it is so difficult to share with somebody else unless the other individual has some reference point within the framework of his experiencing structure. So, then you see the whole business becomes a sort of meaningless ritual—sitting and discussing these matters. That's all. It's not so easy for you to give up. Not at all.

Don't you see the absurdity of what you are doing? All this search is like trying to chase something that does not exist at all. I always give my pet simile. We all take it for granted that there is such a thing as a horizon there. So, if you look at that and you say that it is a horizon, it sounds very simple to you. But you forget that the physical limitation, the limitation of your physical eye fixes that point there and it calls it 'horizon'. If you move in the direction of the horizon, the faster you move in the direction, even in a supersonic plane, the farther it moves away. What you are stuck with is only the limitation. I also give the example of trying to overtake your shadow. As children we played this game of trying to overtake our shadows—all the other boys running with you, everybody trying to overtake his own shadow. It never occurred to us then that it is this body that is casting this shadow there, and that your wanting to overtake that shadow is an absurd game that you are playing. You can run for miles and miles and miles. You know the story of *Alice In Wonderland*. The red queen has to run faster and faster and faster in order to keep still where she is. You see that's exactly what you are all doing. Running faster and faster and faster. But you are not moving anywhere. All that you are doing to find exactly where you are is not moving at all. That gives you the feeling that you are working on something, you are doing something to achieve your goal, not knowing that what you are doing is totally unrelated to the natural functioning of this body. You are not acting in a natural way, because the ideal that has been placed before you by the culture has falsified the natural actions here. You are frightened of acting in a natural way because you have been told the way you should act.

Q: *All the saints, saviours and religions of all times have encouraged us to be unselfish, to be self-effacing, to be meek. It must therefore be possible. How can you be so certain of such a thing?*

UG: Because it is crystal clear to me that you have invented this idea of selflessness to protect yourself from the actual—your selfishness. In any case, whether you believe in selflessness or not, you remain at all times selfish. Your so-called selflessness exists only in the future, tomorrow. And when tomorrow comes, it is put off until the next day, or perhaps next life.

Look at it this way; it is like the horizon. Actually, there is no horizon. The more you move towards the horizon, the more it moves away. It is only the limitations of the eyes that creates the horizon. But there is no such thing as the horizon. Likewise, there is no such thing as selflessness at all. Man has tortured himself for generations with this idea of selflessness, and it has only afforded a living for those who sell the idea of selflessness for a living, like the priests and moralists.

I am not condemning you or anyone else, just pointing out the absurdity of what you are doing. When the energy that is spent in the pursuit of something that does not exist, like selflessness, is released, your problem becomes very simple, no matter what it is. You will cease to create problems on the material plane, and that's the only plane there is.

Q: *Yes, but what about those who are not searching for some illusory abstraction, but simply happiness?*

UG: Their search for happiness is no different from the spiritual pursuit. It is the pursuit of pleasure, spirituality being the greatest, ultimate pleasure.

Q: *So this pursuit has to go?*

UG: Don't say it should go. Wanting selfishness to go is part and parcel of the selfish pursuit of a more pleasurable state—selflessness. Both do not exist. That is why you are eternally unhappy. Your search for happiness is making you unhappy. Both the spiritual goal and the search for happiness are the same. Both are essentially selfish, pleasurable pursuits. If that understanding is somehow there in you, you will not use the energy in that direction at all. You know, I've been everywhere in the world, and have found that people are exactly the same. There is no difference at all. Becoming is the most important thing in the world for everybody—to become something. They all want to become rich, whether materially or spiritually, it is exactly the same. Don't divide it; the so-called spiritual is the materialistic. You may think you are superior because you go to temple and do puja, but the woman there is doing puja in the hope of having a child. She wants something, so she goes to the temple. So do you; it is exactly the same. For sentimental reasons you go, but in time it will become routine and become abhorrent to you. What I am trying to point out is simply this: your spiritual and religious activities are basically selfish. That is all I am pointing out. You go to the temple for the same reason you go to other places—you want some result. If you don't want anything there is no reason to go to the temple.

Q: *Many philosophies, including Marxism, say that war and struggle are inevitable.*

UG: True, they are inevitable. The Marxists and others posit a thesis which, through struggle, becomes an antithesis, and so on. These are philosophical inventions devised to give life some coherence and direction. I, on the other hand, maintain that life may have started arbitrarily, it may have been put together by accident. Man's efforts to give life direction can only meet with frustration, for life has no direction at all. But this does not imply that the missiles are on their way, that doomsday is just around the corner. Man's instinct for survival is very deep-rooted. What I am saying is that all this sweet talk of peace, compassion, and love has not touched man at all. It's rubbish. What keeps people together is terror. The terror of mutual extinction has had a strong and ancient influence upon man. This is, of course, no guarantee. I don't know.

Q: Now the problem is greatly increased by the fact that our technologies guarantee the extinction of all life forms, not just man, in the event war breaks out at the higher levels.

UG: The day man felt this self-consciousness in him, which made him feel superior to every other species on the planet, is the day he set out on the road to complete and total self-destruction. If man is destroyed, probably nothing is lost. Unfortunately, the instruments of destruction he has been able to stockpile over the ages are getting worse and worse, more and more dangerous. He will take everything with him when he goes.

Q: From where does this basic urge to assume mastery over himself and the world arise?

UG: Its genesis was in the religious idea that man is at the centre of the universe. For example, the Jews and Christians believe that everything is created for the benefit of man. That is why man is no longer a part of nature. He has polluted, destroyed, and killed off everything, all on account of his wanting to be at the centre of the universe, of all creation.

Q: But man has to belong somewhere, surely, even if it is not at the centre of creation. The Fall represents the beginning, not the end of man.

UG: The doctrine of the Fall comes in very handy for Christians, that's all; it doesn't mean a thing. The whole Christian tradition exploits this idea of Original Sin to the hilt, resulting in massacre, bloodshed, and such incredible violence.

Q: Well, Eastern philosophies talk of a 'still centre' that can be found through meditation …

UG: I question the very existence, the very idea of the self, the mind, or the psyche. If you accept the concept of the self (and it is a concept), you are free to pursue and gain self-knowledge. But we never question the idea of the self, do we?

Q: *What is this self you are talking of?*

UG: You are interested in the self, not I. Whatever it is, it is the most important thing for man as long as he is alive.

Q: *I exist, therefore, I am. Is that it? Descartes?*

UG: You have never questioned the basic thing assumed here. That is: I think, therefore, I am. If you don't think it never occurs to you that you are alive or dead. Since we think all the time, the very birth of thought creates fear, and it is out of fear that all experience springs. Both 'inner' and 'outer' worlds proceed from a point of thought. Everything you experience is born out of thought. So, everything you experience, or can experience, is an illusion. The self-absorption in thought creates a self-centredness in man; that is all that is there. All relationships based upon that will inevitably create misery for man. These are bogus relationships. As far as you are concerned, there is no such thing as a relationship. And yet society demands not just relationships, but permanent relationships.

Q: *Would you consider yourself an Existentialist?*

UG: No, don't think you can put a label on me. The Existentialists talk of despair and absurdity. But they have never really come to grips with despair or absurdity. Despair is an abstraction for them.

Q: *But what about angst? Naufrage? Nausea? What was Raskolnikov's [one of the major characters in Fyodor Dostoyevsky's novel* Crime and Punishment] *feeling if not despair?*

UG: These are abstract concepts on which they have built a tremendous philosophical structure. That's all there is to it. What I refer to when

I talk of self-centred activity is an autonomous, automatic self-perpetuating mechanism, entirely different from what they are theorizing about.

Q: You mean that the self survives mortality?

UG: No. There is no question of a self there, so how can the question of immortality, the beyond, arise?

Q: What beyond? Is there a beyond?

UG: It is mortality that creates immortality. It is the known that creates the unknown. It is time that has created the timeless. It is thought that created the thoughtless...

Q: Why?

UG: Because thought in its very nature is short-lived. So every time a thought is born, you are born. But you have added to that the constant demand to experience the same things over and over again, thus giving a false continuity to thought. To experience anything you need knowledge. Knowledge is the entire heritage of man's thoughts, feelings, and experiences, handed on from generation to generation.

Just as we all breathe from a common fund of air, we appropriate and use thoughts from the surrounding thought-sphere to function in this world. That's all there is to it. Man's insistence that thought must be continuous denies the nature of thought, which is short-lived. Thought has created for itself a separate destiny. It has been very successful in creating for itself a separate parallel existence. By positing the unknown, the Beyond, the immortal, it has created for itself a way to continue on. There is no timeless, only time. When thought creates time, a space is created there; so thought is also space as well. Thought also creates matter; no thought, no matter. Thought is a manifestation or expression of life, and to make of it a separate thing, impute to it a life of its own, and then allow it to create a future for its own unobstructed continuity, is man's tragedy.

Q: *No peace. No religion. No compassion. No hope. What does that leave us with, UG?*

UG: Nothing. I am questioning the whole spiritual experience. That's what I am trying to rip apart.

Q: *What about the kind of love associated with Mother Teresa's work? Isn't it an act of compassion?*

UG: They are all born out of the divisive consciousness in man. Ultimately they will end up defeating the very cause they are working and dying for. The people around Mother Teresa are capitalizing on her fame. All they are interested in now is money, you know, to carry on her work. Why should all these things be institutionalized? You see someone in pain, hungry. You respond to him. That's all there is to it. So, why should that be institutionalized? You corrupt that feeling, the immediate response, which is not just a thought or petty emotion, when you attempt to institutionalize generosity and empathy. It is the immediate response to the situation that counts.

Q: *Rajneesh's Sex Shop, J. Krishnamurti's Awareness Shop, Maharshi's Self-Enquiry or Meditation Shop, Sai Baba's Magic Shop. What's yours: Nothing Shop?*

UG: Basically they are all the same, exactly the same. Each claims that his wares are the best to be found in the market. Some products, like Pears Soap, have been in the market so long that people have come to know, depend upon them, and consider them superior to others. The durability of a particular product doesn't mean very much.

I am not a saviour of mankind, or any such thing. People come here. Why they come is not my concern. They come out of their own free will and volition because they have heard of me or out of sheer

223

curiosity. It doesn't matter. A person may come here out of any one of a number of reasons. He finds me somehow different, a rare bird, and cannot figure me out or fit me into any framework he knows. He tells his friends, and soon they arrive at the door. I can't tell them to get lost. I invite them in, knowing very well that there is nothing I can do for them. What can I do for *you*? 'Come in, sit down, make yourself comfortable,' is all I can say. Some people make tape recordings of our conversations together. It is their concern, not mine. It is their property first of all, not mine.

I have no interest in asking the questions you are interested in. I have no questions of any kind, except those which help me to function in daily living: 'What time is it?' 'Where is the bus stop?' That is all. These are the simple questions that are necessary to function in an organized society. Otherwise, I never ask any questions.

Q: You are ruthlessly condemning whatever people have said so far. You may, in time, also be condemned and blasted for what you are saying.

UG: If you have the guts, I will be the very first to salute you. But you must not rely on your holy books—the Bhagavad Gita or Upanishads. You must challenge what I am saying without the help of your so-called authorities. You just don't have the guts to do that because you are relying upon the Gita, not upon yourself. That is why you will never be able to do it. If you have that courage, you are the only person who can falsify what I am saying. A great sage like Gaudapada can do it, but he is not here.

You are merely repeating what Gaudapada and others have said. It is a worthless statement as far as you are concerned. If there were a living Gaudapada sitting here, he would be able to blast what I am saying, but not you. So don't escape into meaningless generalizations. You must have the guts to disprove what I am saying on your own. What I am saying must be false for you. You can only agree or disagree with what I am saying according to what some joker has told you. That is not the way to go about it.

I am just pointing out that there are no solutions at all, only problems.

If others have said the same thing I am saying, why are you asking questions and searching for solutions here? Forget about the masses; I am talking about you. You are merely looking for new, better methods. I am not going to help you. I am saying, 'Don't bother about solutions; try to find out what the problem is.' The problem is the solution; solutions just don't solve your problem. Why in the hell are you looking for another solution? Don't come to me for solutions. That is all I am saying. You will make out of what I am saying another solution, to be added to your list of solutions, which are all useless when it comes to actually solving your problems. What I am saying is valid and true for me, that is all. If I suggest *anything,* directly or indirectly, you will turn it into another method or technique. I would be falsifying myself if I were to make any such suggestion.

If *anyone* says there is a way out, he is not an honest fellow. He is doing it for his own self-aggrandizement, you may be sure. He simply wants to market a product and hopes to convince you that it is superior to other products on the market. If another man comes along and says that there is no way out, you make that another method. It is all a fruitless attempt to overtake your own shadow. And yet you can't remain where you are. *That* is the problem. From all this you inevitably draw the conclusion that the situation is hopeless. In reality you are creating that hopelessness because you don't really want to be free from fear, envy, jealousy, and selfishness. That is why you feel your situation to be hopeless. The only hope lies in selfishness, greed, and anger, not in its fictitious opposite, i.e. the practice of selflessness, generosity, and kindness. The problem, say selfishness, is only strengthened by the cultivation of its fictitious opposite, the so-called selflessness.

Sitting here discussing these things is meaningless, useless. That is why I am always saying to my listeners, 'Get lost, please!' What you want you can get elsewhere, but not here. Go to the temple, do puja, repeat mantras, put on ashes. Eventually some joker comes along and says, 'Give me a week's wages and I will give you a better mantra to repeat.' Then another fellow comes along and tells you not to do any of that, that it is useless, and that what he is saying is much more revolutionary. He prescribes 'choiceless awareness', takes your money and builds schools, organizations and Tantric centres.

Q: Why shouldn't we brush aside what you are saying, just as you brush aside the teachings and efforts of others?

UG: You will never blast me; the attachment you have to religious authority prohibits you from questioning anything, much less a man like me. I am certain you will never challenge me. For that reason what I am saying will inevitably create an unstable, neurotic situation for you. You cannot accept what I am saying, and neither are you in any position to reject it. If it wasn't for your very thick skin, you would certainly end up in the loony bin. You simply cannot and will not question what I am saying; it is too much of a threat. Absolutely nothing is going to penetrate your defences; Gaudapada provides the gloves, the Bhagavad Gita a snug coat jacket, and the Brahmasutra a bullet-proof vest. So you are safe, and that is all you are really interested in. You can't blast what I am saying as long as you are relying upon what someone has said before. Please don't say that there are thousands of seers and sages; there are only a very few. You can count them all on your fingers. The rest are merely technocrats. The saint is a technocrat. That is what most people are. But now with the development of drugs and other techniques, the saint is dispensable. You don't any longer need a priest or saint to instruct you in meditation. If you want to control your thoughts, simply take a drug and forget them, if that is what you want. If you can't sleep, take a sleeping pill. Sleep for a while, then wake up. It is the same.

Don't listen to me. It will create an unnecessary disturbance in you. It will only intensify the neurotic situation you are already caught in. Having taken for granted the validity of all this holy stuff, having never questioned, much less broken away from it, you not only have learned how to live with it, but also how to capitalize on it. It is a matter of profiteering, nothing more.

Q: If all this is so, then why do you go on talking?

UG: There is no use asking me why I talk. Am I selling or promising you anything? I am not offering you peace of mind, am I? You counter by saying that I am taking away your precious peace of mind. On the contrary, I am singing my own song, just going my own way, and you come along and attempt to disturb my peace.

Q: *If all you say is true, we are in a bad way indeed. We are not in a position to accept or reject what you are saying. I ask you again why, then, do you go on talking to us? What meaning can it have?*

UG: This dialogue with you has no meaning at all. You may very well ask why the hell I am talking. I emphatically assure you that, in my case, it is not at all in the nature of self-fulfilment. My motive for talking is quite different from what you think it is. It is not that I am eager to help you understand, or that I feel that I must help you. Not at all. My motive is direct and temporary: you arrive seeking understanding, while I am only interested in making it crystal clear that there is nothing to understand.

As long as you want to understand, so long there will be this awkward relationship between two individuals. I am always emphasizing that somehow the truth has to dawn upon you that there is nothing to understand. As long as you think, accept, and believe that there is something to understand, and make that understanding a goal to be placed before you, demanding search and struggle, you are lost and will live in misery. I have only a few things to say and I go on repeating them again and again and again. There are no questions for me, other than the practical questions for everyday functioning in this world. You, however, have many, many questions. These questions all have the same source: your knowledge. It is simply not in the nature of things that you can have a question without knowing the answer already. So meaningful dialogue is simply not possible when you are asking questions to yourself and to me, because you have already made up your mind, you already possess the answers. So communication between us is impossible; what is the point of carrying on any dialogue? There is the actual need to be free from answers themselves. The search is invalid because it is based upon questions which in turn are based upon false knowledge. Your knowledge has not freed you from your problems. Your dilemma is that you are searching for answers to questions you already know the answer to. This is making you neurotic. If the questions you have were actually solvable, it, the question, would blow itself up. Because all questions are merely variations on the same question, the annihilation of one means the annihilation of all. So freedom exists not in finding answers, but in the dissolution of all questions. This sort of problem-solving you are not, unfortunately, the least interested in.

What others and you yourself think are the answers cannot help you at all. It is really very simple: if the answer is correct, the question disappears. I have no questions of any kind. They never enter my head. All my questions, which resolved themselves into one great question, have disappeared entirely. The questioner simply realized that it was meaningless to go on asking questions, the answers to which I already knew. You have foolishly created this search as an answer to your questions, which in turn have been invented out of the knowledge you have gathered. The questions you are formulating are born out of answers you already have. So what is your goal? You must be very clear about it; otherwise there is no point in proceeding. It becomes a game, a meaningless ritual.

What do you want to get? There is always somebody to help you get what you want, for a price. You have foolishly divided life into higher and lower goals, into material and spiritual paths. In either case great struggle, pain, and effort is involved. I say, on the other hand, that there are no spiritual goals at all; they are simply the extension of material goals into what you imagine to be a higher, loftier plane. You mistakenly believe that by pursuing the spiritual goal you will somehow miraculously make your material goals simple and manageable. Such pursuits are in actuality not possible. You may think that only inferior persons pursue material goals, that material achievements are boring. But in fact the so-called spiritual goals you have put before yourself are exactly the same. You are your search, and it will not help to think that you have understood and are free of this. If you don't come here, you will go elsewhere in search of answers.

Q: So all the religions, all the avatars have failed?

UG: All of them have totally failed. Otherwise we wouldn't be where we are today. If there is anything to their claims, we would have created a better and happier world. But we are not ready to accept the fact that it is they who are responsible for creating the sorry mess that we are all facing today.

We are partly responsible for this situation because we want to be victimized by them. What is the point in blaming those people? There is no point in blaming ourselves either because it is a two-way game: we play the game and they play the game. And playing games is all that we are doing. We are used to patting our own backs and telling ourselves, 'God is in the far heavens and all is right with the world.' It is very comforting to believe that we are going to do something extraordinary in the future. What we are left with is the hope; and we live in hope and die in hope. What I say doesn't sound promising, but it's a fact.

Q: But we still have hope that...

UG: That's a very comforting thing—to hope that the future is going to be a marvellous thing and tremendously different from what it has been all these years.

It is just a rehash of the past, the dead past. We only give new names and put new labels. But basically and essentially it (the religious teaching) has not helped us and it is not going to help us. It is not a question of replacing our ideas with new ideas, our thoughts with new thoughts, our beliefs with new beliefs, for the whole belief structure is very important to us. We do not want to free ourselves from this illusion. If we free ourselves from one illusion, we always replace it with another. If we brush aside or drop one belief, we will always replace that belief with another belief.

Q: If we have created the problems, we are also fighting them.

UG: Yes. But we are not ready to accept the fact that what has created the problems cannot itself solve them. What we are using to solve our problems is what we call 'thought'. But thought is a protective mechanism. Thought is only interested in maintaining the status quo. We may talk of change, but when actually the time comes for us to change things, we are not ready for it. We insist that change must always be for the better and not for the worse. We have a tremendous faith in the mechanism that has created the problems for us. After all, that is the only instrument that we have at our disposal, and we don't have any other instrument. But actually it cannot help us at all. It can only create problems, but cannot solve them. We are not ready to accept this fact because accepting it will knock out the whole foundation of human culture. We want to replace one system with another. But the whole structure of culture is pushing us in the direction of completely annihilating all that we have built with tremendous care.

We don't want to be free from fear. Anything you do to free yourself from fear is what is perpetuating the fear. Is there any way we can be freed from fear? Fear is something that cannot be handled by thought; it is something living. So we want to put on our gloves and try to touch it, play with it. All that we want to do is to play games with it and talk about freeing ourselves from fear. Or go to this therapist or that, or follow this technique or that. But in that process, what we are actually doing is strengthening and fortifying the very thing that we are trying to be free from, that is, fear.

Q: So what do you suggest? We are struck with problems, all kinds…what does one do?

UG: You cannot but create the problems. You are creating the problems, number one. But actually you are not looking at the problems at all. You are not dealing with the problems. You are more interested in solutions than the problems. That makes it difficult for you to look at the problem. I am suggesting, 'Look here, you don't have any problems.' You assert with all the emphasis at your command, with tremendous animation, 'Look, I have a problem here.' All right, you have a problem. That problem you are talking about is something which you can pinpoint and say, 'This is the problem.' Physical pain is a reality. So, you go to a doctor, whether it (the medicine) is good for the body or not, whether it is a poison or not, it produces the required relief, however short it may be. But the therapies that those people are dishing out are intensifying the problem which is non-existent.

...You are only searching for the solutions. If there is anything to those solutions that they are offering, the problems should go, should disappear. Actually the problem is still there, but you never question the solutions that those people are offering you as a relief or as something that can free you from the problems. If you question the solutions that have been offered to us by all those people who are marketing these goodies in the name of holiness, enlightenment, transformation, you will find they are really not the solutions. If they were the solutions, they should produce the results and free you from the problem. They do not.

You don't question the solutions because the sentiment creeps in there. 'That fellow who is selling this in the marketplace cannot be a fraud, cannot be a fake.' You take him to be an enlightened man or a god walking on the face the earth. That god may be fooling and killing himself, may be indulging in self-deception all the time and then selling that stuff, that shoddy piece of goods, to you. You don't question the solutions because then you will be questioning the man who is selling this. He cannot be dishonest, a holy man cannot be dishonest. Yet you have to question the solutions because those solutions are not solving your problems. Why don't you question those solutions and put them to test—test the validity of those solutions? When you realize that they don't work, you have to throw them out, down the drain, out of the window. But you don't do it because of the hope that somehow those solutions will give you the relief that you are after. The instrument (thought) which you are using is the one that has created this problem. So that instrument will never, never accept the possibility that those solutions are fake solutions. They are not the solutions at all.

The hope keeps you going. That makes it difficult for you to look at the problems. If one solution fails, you go somewhere else and pick up another solution. If that solution fails you go find another. You are shopping around for all these solutions but never once will you ask yourself, 'What is the problem?' I don't see any problem. I see only that you are interested in solutions and that you come here and ask the same question. 'I want another solution.' I say, 'Those solutions have not helped you at all, so why do you want another solution?' You will add one more to your list of solutions, but you will end up in exactly the same situation. If you find the uselessness of one, if you see one of them, you have seen them all. You don't have to try one after the other.

What I am suggesting is if that is the solution you should be free from the problem. If that is not the solution, there is nothing that you can do about it; and then the problem is not even there. So, you are not interested in solving the problem, because that will put an end to you. You want the problems to remain. You want the hunger to remain because if you are not hungry you will not seek this food from all these holy men. What they are giving you are some scraps, bits of food, and you are satisfied. Even assuming for a moment that he (the spiritual leader or therapist) can give you the whole loaf of bread, which he cannot do, he will only promise to keep it here, hidden somewhere— promises. Bit by bit, bit by bit—he gives you. And thereby you are not dealing with the problem of hunger, but you are more interested in getting a bit more from that fellow who is promising you a solution rather than dealing with your problem of hunger. You are not dealing with the problem of hunger, but you are more interested in getting more crumbs from that fellow, than dealing with your problem of hunger.

Q: So no solution…

UG: Solutions are really worthless. Those solutions don't solve your problem, whatever is the problem. Those solutions keep the problems going. They don't solve them. If there is something wrong with your tape recorder, or television, that can be remedied. There is a technician who can help you. But this is an endless process going on and on and on and on, all your life. More and more of something and less and less of the other.

So, you never question the solutions. If you really question the solutions, you will have to question the ones who have offered you those solutions. But sentimentality stands in the way of your rejecting not only the solutions, but those who have offered you the solutions. Questioning that requires a tremendous courage on your part. You can have the courage to climb the mountain, swim the lakes, go on a raft to the other side of the Atlantic or Pacific. That any fool can do, but the courage to be on your own, to stand on your two solid feet, is something which cannot be given by somebody. You cannot free yourself of that burden by trying to develop that courage. If you are freed from the burden of the entire past of mankind, then what is left there is the courage.

Q: *All that you have been saying conflict with what we have been taught, our experience, our belief!*

UG: What I am saying conflicts with your logical framework. You are using logic to continue that separative structure, that is all. Your questions are again thoughts and therefore reactive. All thought is reactive. You are desperately protecting this armour, this shield of thought, and are frightened that the movement of life might smash your frontiers. Life is like a river in spate, lashing at the banks, threatening the limits that have been placed around it. Your thought structure and your actual physiological framework are limited, but life itself is not.

Q: *Surely you have a message?*

UG: Not at all. There is nobody here talking, giving advice, feeling pain, or experiencing anything at all. Like a ball thrown against the wall, it bounces back, that is all. My talking is the direct result of your question, I have nothing here of my own, no obvious or hidden agenda, no product to sell, no axe to grind, nothing to prove.

Q: *You are not helping us. Why?*

UG: Your problems continue because of the false solutions you have invented. If the answers are not there, the questions cannot be there.

They are interdependent; your problems and solutions go together. Because you want to use certain answers to end your problems, those problems continue. The numerous solutions offered by all these holy people, the psychologists, the politicians, are not really solutions at all. That is obvious. If there were legitimate answers, there would be no problems. They can only exhort you to try harder, practise more meditations, cultivate humility, stand on your head, and more and more of the same. That is all they can do. The teacher, guru, or leader who offers solutions is also false, along with his so-called answers. He is not doing any honest work, only selling a cheap, shoddy commodity in the marketplace. If you brushed aside your hope, fear, and naiveté, and treated these fellows like businessmen, you would see that they do not deliver the goods, and never will. But you go on and on buying these bogus wares offered up by the experts.

Q: *But the whole field is so complicated that it seems necessary for us to rely on those who have studied carefully and devoted their lives to self-realization and wisdom.*

UG:All their philosophies cannot compare to the native wisdom of the body itself. What they are calling mental activity, spiritual activity, emotional activity, and feelings are really all one unitary process. This body is highly intelligent and does not need these scientific or theological teachings to survive and procreate. Take away all your fancies about life, death, and freedom, and the body remains unscathed, functioning harmoniously. It does not need your or my help. You don't have to do a thing. You will never again ask stupid, idiotic questions about immortality, afterlives, or death. The body is immortal.

Q:*You have mercilessly cut off every possibility of rehabilitation, obliterating even the faint hope of escaping this unhappiness. There seems to be nothing left but self-destruction. Why not suicide?*

UG: If you commit suicide, it does not help the situation in any way. The moment after suicide the body begins to decay, returning back to other, differently organized forms of life, putting an end to nothing.

Life has no beginning and no end. A dead and dying body feeds the hungry ants there in the grave, and rotting corpses give off soil-enriching chemicals, which in turn nourish other life forms. You cannot put an end to your life, it is impossible. The body is immortal and never asks silly questions like, 'Is there immortality?' It knows that it will come to an end in that particular form, only to continue on in others. Questions about life after death are always asked out of fear.

Those leaders who would direct your 'spiritual life' cannot be honest about these things, for they make a living out of fear, speculations about future life, and the 'mystery' of death. And as for you, the followers, you are not really interested in the future of man, only your own petty little destinies. It is just a ritual you go through, talking for hours and hours about mankind, compassion, and the rest. It is *you* that you are interested in, otherwise there would not be this childish interest in your future lives, and your imminent demise.

Q: But for many of us life is a sacred thing. We struggle to protect our children, the environment, to avert another war...

UG: You are all neurotic people. You talk against birth control, drone on and on about the preciousness of life, then bomb and massacre. It is too absurd. You are concerned with an unborn life while you are killing thousands and thousands of people by bombing, starvation, poverty and terrorism. Your 'concern' about life is only to make a political issue out of it. It is just an academic discussion. I am not interested in that.

Q: Yes, but many of us see all this and nevertheless are interested in changing things. It is not just egoism on our parts.

UG: Are you really interested? Are you interested in the future of mankind? Your expressions of anger, righteousness, and caring have no meaning to me. It is just a ritual. You sit and talk, that's all. You are not at all angry. If you were angry at this moment, you would not ask this question, even to yourself. You sit everlastingly talking of anger. The angry wouldn't talk about it. The body has already acted with regard to that anger by absorbing it. The anger is burnt, finished then and there. You don't do anything; the body just absorbs it. That is all. If all this is too much for you, if it depresses you, don't ever go to the holy men. Take pills, do anything, but don't expect the holy business to help you. It is a waste of time.

Q: You make me want to just drop the whole thing, to renounce …

UG: As long as you think you have something to renounce, you are lost. Not to think of money and the necessities of life is an illness. It is a perversion to deny yourself the basic needs of life. You think that through a self-imposed asceticism you will increase your awareness and then be able to use that awareness to be happy. No chance. You will be peaceful when all your ideas about awareness are dropped and you begin to function like a computer. You must be a machine, function automatically in this world, never questioning your actions before, during, or after they occur.

Q: Are you denying the importance of yogic practices, religious renunciation, or the value of a moral upbringing? Man is more than a machine, surely.

UG: All moral, spiritual, ethical values are false. The psychologists, searching for a pragmatic way out, are now at the end of their tethers, even turning to the spiritual people for answers. They are lost, and yet the answers must come from them, not from the encrusted, useless traditions of the holy business.

Q: This makes us all so helpless. No wonder people have relied upon messiahs, mahatmas and prophets.

UG: The so-called messiahs have left nothing but misery in this world. If a modern messiah came before you, he would be unable to help you at all. And if he can't help, no one can.

Q: *If an anointed person, a saviour or sage for example, can't be of help, then perhaps it is as the scriptures say, we must 'know the truth and the truth shall make us free.'*

UG: Truth is a movement. You can't capture it, contain it, give expression to it, or use it to advance your interests. The moment you capture it, it ceases to be the truth. What is the truth for me is something that cannot, under any circumstances, be communicated to you. The certainty here cannot be transmitted to another. For this reason the whole guru business is absolute nonsense. This has always been the case, not just now. Your self-denial is to enrich the priests. You deny yourself your basic needs while that man travels in a Rolls Royce car, eating like a king, and being treated like a potentate. He, and the others in the holy business, thrive on the stupidity and credulity of others. The politicians, similarly, thrive on the gullibility of man. It is the same everywhere.

Q: *Your emphasis is always on the negative side, the classic 'neti neti' approach. Are you not pointing out the necessity of dropping all excess baggage, including the scriptures, gurus, and authorities, if one is to find that state you indicate is our natural birthright?*

UG: No. Doing away with the gurus, temples, and holy books as a prescription for freedom is ridiculous. You search for answers only as remedies for your problems, to avoid pain. Everything that is born is painful. There is no use asking why it is so. It is so. You think that by renouncing gurus and authorities you will suffer some divine endurance; endurance of pain is not going to help you spiritually. There is no way.

Q: *But we know you to be more than a fatalist, a cynic. You are pointing out a different destiny for man, not just critiquing his present predicament, are you not?*

UG: There is a solution for your problems—death. That freedom you are interested in can come about only at the point of death. Everybody

237

attains moksha eventually, for moksha always foreshadows death, and everyone dies.

Q: So then the only refuge is God!

UG: No. God is the ultimate pleasure, uninterrupted happiness. No such thing exists. Your wanting something that does not exist is the root of your problem. Transformation, moksha, liberation, and all that stuff are just variations on the same theme: permanent happiness. The body cannot take that. The pleasure of sex, for instance, is by nature temporary. The body can't take uninterrupted pleasure for long, it would be destroyed. Wanting to impose a fictitious, permanent state of happiness on the body is a serious neurological problem.

Q: But the religions warn against pleasure-seeking. Through prayer, meditation, and various practices one is encouraged to transcend mere pleasure ...

UG: They sell you spiritual pathedrins, spiritual morphine. You take that drug and go to sleep. Now the scientists have perfected pleasure drugs, it is much easier to take. It never strikes you that the enlightenment and God you are after is just the ultimate pleasure, a pleasure moreover, which you have invented to be free from the painful state you are always in. Your painful, neurotic state is caused by wanting two contradictory things at the same time.

Q: But we are not interested in any petty experiences, we want freedom ...

UG: What is the difference whether or not you find this freedom, this enlightenment or not. You will not be there to benefit from it. What possible good can this state do you? This state takes away *everything* you have. That is why they call it 'jivanmukti'—living in liberation. While living, the body has died. Somehow the body, having gone through death, is kept alive. It is neither happiness nor unhappiness. There is no such thing as happiness. This you do not, cannot, want. What you want is everything, here you lose everything. You want everything, and that is not possible. The religions have promised you so much—roses, gardens—and you end up with only thorns.

Q: *At least JK talked of transformation…*

UG: There is no transformation, radical or otherwise. It is a bogus charter flight. There is no such journey. The Vedic stuff is no more helpful. It was invented by some acid-heads after drinking some soma juice. JK is more neurotic than the people who go to listen to him.

Q: *If you put no credence in the ancient religious teachings, do you take modern psychology any the more seriously?*

UG: The whole field of psychology has misled the whole thinking of man for a hundred years and more. Freud is the stupendous fraud of the twentieth century. J. Krishnamurti talks of a revolution in the psyche. There is no psyche there. Where is this mind which is to be magically transformed? JK's disciples have come to the point where all they can do is to repeat meaningless phrases. They are shallow, empty people. The fact that JK can draw large crowds means nothing; snake charmers also draw big crowds. Anybody can draw crowds.

Q: *But you are using a similar approach as …*

UG: Yes, I am using 80 per cent of his words and phrases, the very phrases he has used over the years to condemn gurus, saints, and saviours like himself. He has it coming. One thing I have never said: he is not a man of character. He has great character, but I am not in the least interested in men of character. If he sees the mess he has created in his false role as world messiah and dissolves the whole thing, I will be the first to salute him. But he is too old and senile to do it. His followers are appalled that I am giving him a dose of his own medicine. Do not compare what I am saying with what he, or other religious authorities, have said. If you give what I am saying any spiritual overtones, any religious flavour at all, you are missing the point. All this has to be dropped.

Q: But still it seem to us that J. Krishnamurti, and perhaps a few others in history, have something to say. J. Krishnamurti appears to be what he claims he is, a free man.

UG: He has something. I am fond of saying that he has *seen* the sugar cube, but has not *tasted* the sugar cube. Whether that man, myself, or any other person is free or not is not your problem; it is the shibboleth of escapist minds, an amusement invented to avoid the real issue, which is your unfreedom.

You may be sure of one thing; he who says he is a free man is a phoney. Of this you may be sure. The thing you have to be free of is the 'freedom' discussed by that man and other teachers. You must be free from 'the first and last freedom', and all the freedoms that come in between.

Q: If the notion of a life of grace, peace, and freedom are just fictions invented to escape our universal shallowness, why proceed at all? If there is no abiding, transcendent reality to which man may turn, then why should we carry on our existence? Is there only eating, sleeping, and breathing?

UG: That is all that is there. Go. Look, I am only saying that you must go find out for yourself if there is anything behind these meaningless abstractions being thrown at you. They talk of sacred hearts, universal minds, oversouls, you know, all the abstract, mystical terms used to seduce gullible people. Life has to be described in pure and simple physical and physiological terms. It must be demystified and de-psychologized. Don't talk of 'higher centres' and chakras. It is not these but glands that control the human body. It is the glands that give the instructions for the functioning of this organism. In your case you have introduced an interloper—thought. In your natural state thought ceases to control anything; it comes into temporary function when a challenge is put before it, immediately falling into the background when it is no longer needed.

Q: *So then no matter what we do, we are functioning in an unnatural way, is that it?*

UG: That is why I am pointing these things out. Forget about the ideal society and the ideal human being. Just look at the way you are functioning. That is the important thing. What has prevented the organism from fully flowering into its own uniqueness is culture. It has placed the wrong thing—the ideal person—before man. The whole thing is born out of the divisive consciousness of mankind. It has brought us nothing but violence. That is why no two gurus or saviours ever agree. Each is intent upon preaching his own nonsense.

Q: *Is there any difference between going to a church and coming here?*

UG: Basically the motivation is the same: you are looking for a new teacher, a new Bible, a new order, a new church—that is all you can do. Basically it's still the same thing: you have not moved one step from the Catholic Church. If religiousness is all you are interested in, there is no need to look anywhere other than in Christianity. The profound statements of the great teachers are not any different in the different religions. All I am saying is that looking to alien lands and religions does not mean anything. You learn new techniques, new systems, new phrases, and then you begin to think and speak in terms of this new language, and probably you feel just great, but basically it does not mean anything at all.

Q: *Your statements seem to resemble what the quantum physicists are telling us today.*

UG: We are creating the universe ourselves. We have no way of looking at the universe at all. The model that we see is created by our thought. Even the scientists who say that they are observing certain things have actually no way of observing anything except through the mirror of their own thinking. The scientist is influencing what you are looking at. Whatever theories he comes up with are only theories; they are not

241

facts to him. Even if you are looking at an object physically, without the interference of thought and without translating what you are looking at, the physical looking is affecting the object that you are looking at. Actually there is no way you can capture, contain and give expression to what you are looking at. You dare not look at anything. Scientists can come up with all kinds of theories, hundreds and hundreds of them. You can only reward them with Nobel prizes or give them some prestigious awards, and that is all that they are interested in. But, are we ready to accept the fact that there is no way that you can look at anything? You are not looking at anything at all. Even the physical looking is influenced by your thoughts. There is no way you can look at anything without the use of the knowledge that you have of what you are looking at. In fact, it is that (the knowledge) that is creating the object. It is your thinking that is creating the observer. So this whole talk of the observer and the observed is balderdash. There is neither the 'observer' nor the 'observed'. [The talk of] the 'perceiver' and the 'perceived', the 'seer' and the 'seen' is all bosh and nonsense. These themes are good for endless metaphysical discussions. There is no end to such discussions. And to believe that there is an observation without the observer is a lot of baloney.

Q: Do you think that the discovery of the laws of nature and the enormous money that is invested in it will ultimately help mankind?

UG: Even if we discover the laws of nature, for whatever reason we are interested in doing so, ultimately they are used to destroy everything that nature has created. This propaganda that the planet is in danger is a media hype. Everybody has in fact forgotten about it. Actually it is not the planet that is in danger, but we are in danger. We are not ready to face this situation squarely. We must not look for answers in the past or in the great heritage of this or that nation. And we must not look to the religious thinkers. They don't have any answers. If the scientists look to the religious leaders for their solutions, they are committing the biggest blunder. The religious people put us all on the wrong track, and there is no way you can reverse the process.

Q: *What do you think we should do then?*

UG: I am not here to save mankind or prophesy that we are all heading towards a disaster. I am not talking of an Armageddon, nor am I prophesying that there is going to be a paradise on this planet. Nothing of the sort; there is not going to be any paradise. It is the idea of a paradise, the idea of creating a heaven on this earth, that has turned this beautiful paradise that we already have on this planet into a hell. We are solely responsible for what is happening. And the answers for our problems cannot come from the past and its glory, or from the great religious teachers of mankind. Those teachers will naturally claim that you all have failed and that they have the answers for the problems that we are confronted with today. I don't think that they have any answers. We have to find out the answers, if there are any, for ourselves and by ourselves.

Q: *Intellectually you make sense, but…*

UG: Isn't it a joke to tell me that you understand what I am telling you? You say that you at least understand me intellectually, as if there were some other way of understanding. Your intellectual understanding, in which you have a tremendous investment, has not done one damn thing for you so far. You persist in the cultivation of this intellectual understanding, knowing all the while that it has never helped you at all. *This is amazing.* When hoping and attempting to understand is not there, then life becomes meaningful. Life, your existence, has a tremendous living quality about it. All your notions about love, beatitude, infinite bliss, and peace only block this natural energy of existence. How can I make you understand that what I am describing has absolutely nothing to do with all that religious stuff? You see hundreds of bodies carried off in the van after death, and yet you can't possibly imagine your own death. It is impossible, for your own death cannot be experienced by you. It is really something. It is no good throwing all this junk at me. Whatever hits this is immediately burnt—that is the nature of the energy here.

The spiritual people are the most dishonest people. I am emphasizing that foundation upon which the whole of spirituality is built. I am emphasizing that. If *there is no spirit*, the whole talk of spirituality is bosh and nonsense. You can't come into your own being until you are free from the whole thing surrounding the concept of 'self'. To be really on your own, the whole basis of spiritual life, which is erroneous, has to be destroyed. It does not mean that you become fanatical or violent, burning down temples, tearing down the idols, destroying the holy books, like a bunch of drunks. It is not that at all. It is a bonfire inside of you. Everything that mankind has thought and experienced must go. The incredible violence in the world today has been created by the Jesuses and Buddhas.

Q: You seem to be keen on demolishing everything, everything that the sacred scriptures and the masters have taught...

UG: My interest is not to knock off what others have said (that is too easy), but to knock off what I am saying. More precisely, I am trying to stop what you are making out of what I am saying. This is why my talking sounds contradictory to others. I am forced by the nature of your listening to always negate the first statement with another statement. Then the second statement is negated by a third, and so on. My aim is not some comfy dialectical thesis, but the total negation of everything that can be expressed. Anything you try to make out of my statements is not it.

You may sense a freshness, a living quality to what is being said here. That is so, but this cannot be used for anything. It cannot be repeated. It is worthless. All you can do with it is to try to organize it; create organizations, open schools, publish holy books, celebrate birthdays, sanctify holy temples, and the like, thus destroying any life it may have had in it. No individual can be helped by such things. They only help those who would live by the gullibility of others.

Q: My God, what a mess! How can I save myself from all this? It is a sad destiny to contemplate.

UG: You have to be saved from the very idea that you have to be saved. You must be saved from the saviours, redeemed from the redeemers. If it is to happen, it must happen now. My words cannot penetrate the lunacy there. It is the madness of the spiritual search that makes you unmoved and impervious to my words. The line between the madman and the mystic is a very, very thin one. The madman is regarded as a clinical case, while the other, the mystic, is equally pathological.

Forget the rosaries, the scriptures, the ashes on your forehead. When you see for yourself the absurdity of your search, the whole culture is reduced to ashes inside you. Then you are out of that. Tradition is finished for you. No more games. Vedanta means the end of knowledge. So why write more holy books, open more schools, preserve more teachings? The burning up inside you of everything you want is the meaning of ashes. When you know nothing, you say a lot. When you know something, there is nothing to say.

Q: *What are you? Where do you fit yourself?*

UG: I don't know. I won't say I am a misfit. I am part of the mainstream of life everywhere. At the same time I have no roots anywhere. If I may put it that way, I am a rootless man of sorts. I have lived everywhere in the world, and I don't feel at home anywhere. It's very strange. I am one of the most travelled persons in this world. I have been travelling ever since I was fourteen, and since then I have never lived in any place for more than six months at a time. My travelling is not born out of my compulsive need to travel. When people ask me, 'Why do you travel?' I answer them, 'Why do some birds travel from Siberia to a small bird sanctuary in Mysore state and then go back all the way?' I am like those migratory birds. It's very strange. I have travelled everywhere except in China. I have gone to all the communist countries. And in America I have spent several years. Nowadays I divide my time between Bangalore, Switzerland and the US.

Q: *If the world can't find a label for you, what kind of label do you find for the world?*

UG: I am quite satisfied with the world! [*Laughter*] Quite satisfied. The world cannot be any different. Travelling destroys many illusions and creates new illusions for us. I have discovered, to my dismay, if I may put it that way, that human nature is exactly the same whether a person is a Russian, or an American or someone from somewhere else. It is as though we all speak the same language, but the accent is different. I probably speak [English] with an Andhra accent, you with a Kannada accent, and someone else with a French accent. But basically human beings are exactly the same. There is absolutely no difference. I don't see any difference at all. Culture is probably responsible for the differences. We being what we are, the world cannot be any different. As long as there is a demand in you to bring about a change in yourself, you want to bring about a change in the world. Because you can't fit into the framework of culture and its value system, you want to change the world so that you can have a comfortable place in the world.

Q: You say that you are satisfied with the world. Why do you say that?

UG: What makes you think that the world can be any different? Why do you want to change the world? All these utopias, all these ideas of creating a heaven on this earth are born out of the assumption that there is a heaven somewhere there and that we have to create that heaven on this planet. And that's the reason why we have turned this into a hell. You see, I don't call this a hell. I'd like to say it cannot be any different.

Nature has provided us with tremendous wealth on this planet. If what they say is correct, twelve billion people can be fed with the resources that we already have on this planet. If 80 per cent of the people are underfed, there is something wrong—something is wrong because we have cornered at one place all the resources of this world. I don't know, I am not competent enough to say, but they say that 80 per cent of this world's resources are consumed by the Americans alone. What is it that is responsible for that? The problem is this: nature has assembled all these species on this planet. The human species is no more important than any other species on this planet. For some reason, man accorded himself a superior place in this scheme of things. He thinks that he is created for some grander purpose than, if I could give a crude example, the mosquito that is sucking his blood. What is responsible for this is the value system that we have created. And the value system has come out of the religious thinking of man. Man has created religion because it gives him a cover. This demand to fulfil himself, to seek something out there was made imperative because of this self-consciousness in you which occurred somewhere along the line of the evolutionary process. Man separated himself from the totality of nature. The religious thinking of man originated from the idols, gods, and spiritual teachers that we have created.

Q: *How would you like to be remembered?*

UG: After I am dead and gone, nothing of me must remain inside of you or outside of you. I can certainly do a lot to see that no establishment or institution of any kind mushrooms around me whilst I am alive. But how do I stop all you guys from enshrining me in your brains?

⊷⊜ ⊜⊷

LAUGHING WITH UG

If Not Liberation at Least a Transistor

Once, a harikatha dasa, a traditional teller of stories of Gods, famously called Bhagavatar throughout south India, visited UG. He came dressed in a white dhoti, a white shirt, a Kashmir shawl on his shoulders, and prayer beads around his neck. He wore marks of vibhuti (ashes) on his forehead. In the middle of those marks, he wore a round red vermillion mark. He was over seventy-five years old, yet looked healthy and strong. He believed UG was an enlightened man and addressed him as 'Appa' although UG was twenty years younger than he. UG never condemned the Bhagavatar's faith or beliefs. But, whenever UG started his tirade on human culture and civilization, Bhagavatar would immediately get up and run out saying, 'Father, it's time for me to go. But I'll come again.'

One day, apparently overcome with emotion, the Bhagavatar held UG's feet begging, 'Appa, no one else cares for me. Only you can show me the way to moksha.'

UG instantly held him up trying to prevent him from holding his feet. And then he asked, 'You spent so many years with Ramana Maharshi. Why didn't you ask him?'

'At that time, I didn't have either that interest or yearning. Now, I feel I don't want anything else,' he answered.

UG said, 'That's the only thing I cannot give. It's not something that someone can give and someone else can receive. Ask for anything else. I will give that.'

As soon as he said that, the Bhagavatar, a shy smile creasing his lips, asked UG to get him a small 'foreign' transistor.

No Prior Appointments

There is no need to wait for a fixed appointment or time to see UG, people come at different times. On Sundays, from morning until night various people continuously come and go. One day (in 1986) he was talking incessantly without a respite. The visitors came and left one after another. Even after it was past the time for lunch, the hall did not become vacant. When there was hardly any space and many stood outside waiting to get in, UG stood up, and smiling, said, 'This has turned into a barber shop. One after another, people come and get their hair cut. They have been coming since morning without a break.' Peals of laughter broke out from the crowd, but still nobody showed any sign of leaving. And UG sat back, saying, 'Anyway, this is how it should be. There should be no special duration, prior appointment, and such.'

⊷⊜ ⊜⊷

I Like Madhvacharya the Most Because...

In 1972, along with Valentine, UG visited Udupi, a place famous for temples and monastries. A senior swamiji of a famous Math who had heard about UG, invited him to accept his hospitality.

'If I come to your Math, would I have to wear clothing appropriate to your ritual rules? I wouldn't be allowed with my pyjama and *lalchi*. Besides, Valentine also will have to come with me. She is a foreigner,' said UG, trying to discourage the swami from inviting him.

The swami reassured UG that he could come dressed just the way he was and of course bring Valentine as well. 'But, please don't force me to sit with you to eat. That's all I ask,' he said, repeating his invitation.

UG, Valentine and friends were treated to a tasty meal with twenty-five delicious items. The swamiji sat in front of them while they ate their lunch. Later there was a discussion on many things. At one point, after listening to UG for a while, the swami said to his disciples, 'That Krishna and this Krishna say the same thing.'

Then UG remarked, 'Among the three Acharyas, I like Madhvacharya the most.'

The swamiji was flattered by this remark, believing that UG was admiring his guru and their tradition. 'Why, UG, why?' he asked with excitement.

'It is because of him that Udupi restaurants have sprung up all over the world. Whether we go to New York or London or some other place, thanks to those restaurants, I can find the idlis I need.'

⊷≡⊙ ⊙≡⊶

A Parliament of Dacoits

Once, a noted journalist brought along a VIP who was responsible for the surrender of six hundred dacoits. The VIP spoke about his good work and his great struggle to get the dacoits to surrender to the government. When he had finished there was profound silence and then quiet murmurs of appreciation from the little crowd. But UG looked at the man and asked simply, 'Yes, but what about the six hundred dacoits you have put there in the Parliament?'

The man rose in a hurry, saying, 'I will return when you are in a better mood.'

⊷≡⊙ ⊙≡⊶

No Need to Touch Anybody's Feet, Not Even Your Own

Once, a pious old man, after listening to UG, with tears in his eyes, went down on his knees to touch UG's feet. Quickly UG withdrew his legs preventing the man from touching his feet. But the old man, not willing to give up, kept persisting. It was quite a funny tussle: one old man trying to touch the feet of another and the other doing his best to stop him. At last, UG said, 'No, don't do that, sir. Not only to me but to anyone else either. No one is worth that, believe me. How can I convince you that there is no power outside of you? I never touched anybody's feet, not even my own.'

Therapy is the Disease

One morning, Dr Modi, a renowned eye surgeon who had performed many eye operations free by setting up camps all over India, came to see UG. After a long chat over spiritual matters, the good doctor said, 'Sir, I am fully blind. Please help me see.'

UG humbly replied, 'I am not competent enough to do the operation. I can only tell you that there is nothing wrong with your eyes and no operation is necessary.'

But when the doctor persisted that UG should suggest some therapy for his spiritual malady, UG said, 'Sir, the therapy is the disease.'

★

A long-time admirer and friend of UG once declared grandly that he thought UG was the only reliable and dependable friend he had in the whole world, and that he trusted UG so much that if at that minute UG asked him to jump from the window he would obey him blindly. UG immediately said, 'Really? Let's go on the terrace. That's high enough for you to jump from.'

★

One day, while having a meal, UG poured some ghee in his rasam, looked at Shanta and said, 'See how the ghee floats on this rasam! This reminds me of how your Shirdi Baba performed the miracle of lighting lamps on water. Obviously this is how the layer of oil must have floated in the tin pot.'

★

Once, an old friend and schoolmate of UG, recalling his days with UG, recounted the night they both went to see the film *Raja Harishchandra*, and how he was quite surprised to see tears rolling down UG's cheeks at the plight of the honest king Harishchandra. This surprised many in the crowd and they stared at UG as if to ask if it was true that he shed tears. UG smiled and replied, 'I was crying because of the poor Indians who have to live up to Harishchandra's lofty ideal.'

★

A childless couple once came to UG asking for his blessings for a child, and UG as usual replied, 'You don't need my blessings. All you need is to go to the doctor, to find out which of you needs medical help.'

★

One evening, surprising everyone sitting around him in the room, UG got into a playful mood. Louis, an American, was sitting by his side. He was a tall, broad-shouldered, muscular man, who looked more a WWF wrestler than a spiritual seeker. That day, he became the target of UG's mischief. One had never seen UG so childishly mischievous. Without his dentures, he looked like a grandma playing pranks with her overgrown grandchild. He kept nudging, poking and hitting Louis all over his bulky frame. At one point, he suddenly stretched out his hand and ordered Louis to read his palm. Sometimes UG played this game with palmists, asking, 'Tell me, where will I get my money from and how much?' We were all familiar with this game of UG and so was Louis. Promptly now, Louis held UG's palm and then screwing up his mischievous eyes, said, 'Look here, the lines here are in the shape of MW. Ah, M for money and W for wealth. You are lucky!' 'No,' bellowed UG, 'M means murder, and W means whacking.' And he started whacking Louis hard on his tonsured head and bulky frame.

★

Once, a religious man, who believed in miracles as the sign of the existence of God, asked seriously, 'UG, what do you think of Jesus Christ walking on water?'

Smiling, UG replied, 'Jesus walked on water probably because he did not know how to swim. Fortunately for him and unfortunately for others the water was only knee-deep. And in the story of the multiplication of the loaves of bread and fishes, he probably cut the bread into many smaller pieces.'

★

'Are there any boots to walk on thorns.'

UG's reply came back crisp and direct, 'There are no thorns.'

Not satsified, the woman pursued, 'The thorns are very much there for me!'

With quiet patience he answered, 'Stop looking for roses and there will be no thorns.'

★

A very famous man from USA was very curious to meet with UG to find out why so many of his friends were gaga about him. One evening he did finally meet him in a friend's house. He asked UG directly, 'I have heard quite a lot about you. I'm really curious. What do you do?'

UG replied simply, 'I'm retired, sir.'

'I'm retired too. What did you retire as?'

'I was born retired.'

★

A Sweater for the Spider

Once, an American friend had to leave for India with UG and was caught in a dilemma over the safety of her spider friend who had been keeping her company over the past few weeks. She didn't want the spider hanging in her bathroom, with one of his legs missing, to be killed by the cleaning woman the next day. So, carefully, delicately she picked up the spider and put him outside near the steps. It was quite cold and suddenly the spider seemed frozen out there. Worried she asked UG his opinion. UG scoffed at her insensitivity about American boys (soldiers) dying in the Middle East deserts and fussing over the safety of one spider in the bathroom.

The American friend said, 'But I don't condone sending soldiers anywhere, don't condone anything my government does. It's just that I have grown attached to my spider.'

UG said, 'Why don't you knit a sweater for the spider?'

★

Hoping to be commended for his brave act, a friend told UG that he had taken down all the guru pictures in his room, all his ex-teachers, Zen masters, including a photo of UG.

UG laughed and said there would now be less lizards on the walls.

★

An American who was visiting India for the first time and quite worried about the living conditions there, asked UG whether she would need to get shots for India.

'Oh no,' he replied. 'We're not worried about your germs there!'

★

At the end of an interview, quite fascinated by UG's message, the interviewer burst out, 'I just have to tell you that you're so incredibly handsome!'

UG laughed and said it was because he ate foods with preservatives, no health foods, no vegetables, didn't exercise and rarely slept.

★

SOURCES

The Mystique of Enlightenment: The Unrational Ideas Of a Man Called UG, edited by Rodney Arms, Dinesh Vaghela, 1982.

Mind is a Myth: Disquieting Conversations With the Man Called UG, edited by Terry Newland, Dinesh Publications, 1988.

The Sage and the Housewife by Shanta Kelker, Sowmya Publishers, Bangalore, 1990.

No Way Out: Conversations with U.G. Krishnamurti, edited by JSRL Narayana Moorty, Antony Paul Frank Noronha and Sunita Pant Bansal, Smriti Books, New Delhi, 2002.

Thought Is Your Enemy: Conversations with U.G. Krishnamurti, edited by JSRL Narayana Moorty, Antony Paul and Frank Noronha, Smriti Books, New Delhi, 2002.

The Courage to Stand Alone: Conversations with U.G. Krishnamurti transcribed and edited by Ellen J. Chrystal, Smriti Books, New Delhi, 2002.

Stopped In Our Tracks : Stories of UG in India, from the notebooks of K. Chandrasekhar, Smriti Books, New Delhi, 2005.

U.G. Krishnamurti: A Life by Mahesh Bhatt, Penguin Books India, New Delhi, 1992.